DEMOCRACY
IN THE
DEVELOPING
WORLD

Consolidate
" firm"

consolidate "strengthen

DEMOCRACY IN THE DEVELOPING WORLD

Africa, Asia, Latin America and the Middle East

Jeff Haynes

Polity

First published in 2001 by Polity Press in association with Blackwell
Publishers Ltd

Editorial office:
Polity Press
65 Bridge Street
Cambridge CB2 1UR, UK

Marketing and production:
Blackwell Publishers Ltd
108 Cowley Road
Oxford OX4 1JF, UK

Published in the USA by
Blackwell Publishers Inc.
350 Main Street
Malden, MA 02148, USA

ISBN 0-7456-2141-4
ISBN 0-7456-2142-2 (pbk)

A catalogue record for this book is available from the British Library and
has been applied for from the Library of Congress.

Typeset in $10\frac{1}{2}$ on 12 pt Sabon
by Best-set Typesetter Ltd., Hong Kong
Printed in Great Britain by MPG Books Ltd, Bodmin, Cornwall

This book is printed on acid-free paper.

Contents

1

The Third Wave of Democracy

1.1 Introduction

Until recently there were very few democratically elected governments in Latin America, Asia or Africa. Instead, political terrains were filled with various kinds of unelected regimes, including military, one-party or no-party systems and personalist dictatorships. The 'third wave of democracy' is said to have started in Southern Europe in the mid-1970s, before spreading to Latin America, Eastern Europe, Asia and Africa (Huntington 1991). Eventually the result was that, whereas in the early 1970s only a quarter of countries had democratically elected governments, two decades later more than 50 per cent had them. By the end of the 1990s, about 75 per cent of governments around the world had come to power via the ballot box. Such was the shift to elected governments during this time that a new area of concern in political science was born: 'transitology', that is, the study of *democratization*, 'the process of becoming democratic' (Bealey 1999: 100). As time went on, studies of democratic transition were augmented by investigations of the difficulties of *consolidating democracy*, known as 'consolidology'.

By the 1990s, all 23 Latin American countries, with the exception of Cuba, had elected governments, as did several formerly authoritarian countries in Asia – including Bangladesh, Nepal, the Philippines, Taiwan, South Korea and Mongolia. Africa showed a similar picture, with over 20 democratically elected governments. The only region that seemed apart from the democratic trend was the Middle East. With the exception of Turkey and the partial exceptions of

Jordan, Morocco, and Kuwait, *authoritarian* – that is, democratically unaccountable – regimes remained the norm.

By 1999, as table 1.1 indicates, there were 48 new democracies in Latin America, Asia (counting in Turkey) and Africa: 16 in Latin America, 10 in Asia and 22 in Africa. Of the 10 in Asia, 4 (40 per cent) – Mongolia, South Korea, Taiwan and the Philippines –

Table 1.1 New democracies in Latin America, Africa and Asia, 1999: ratings by Freedom House

	Political rights	Civil liberties	Freedom rating
Latin America (16 countries)			
Uruguay	1	2	Free
Bolivia	1	3	Free
Chile	3	2	Free
Ecuador	2	3	Free
Panama	2	3	Free
Honduras	2	3	Free
Argentina	3	3	Partly free
Dominican Rep	3	3	Partly free
El Salvador	3	3	Partly free
Nicaragua	3	3	Partly free
Brazil	3	4	Partly free
Colombia	3	4	Partly free
Paraguay	4	3	Partly free
Guatemala	3	4	Partly free
Peru	5	4	Partly free
Haiti	5	5	Partly free
Africa (22 countries)			
Cape Verde	1	2	Free
Sao Tomé e Principe	1	2	Free
South Africa	1	2	Free
Benin	2	2	Free
Namibia	2	3	Free
Malawi	2	3	Free
Mali	3	3	Partly free
Madagascar	2	4	Partly free
Seychelles	3	3	Partly free

Table 1.1 *continued*

	Political rights	Civil liberties	Freedom rating
Ghana	3	3	Partly free
Mozambique	3	4	Partly free
Central African Rep.	3	4	Partly free
Guinea-Bissau	3	5	Partly free
Lesotho	4	4	Partly free
Uganda	4	4	Partly free
Ethiopia	4	4	Partly free
Burkina Faso	5	4	Partly free
Comoros	5	4	Partly free
Gabon	5	4	Partly free
Zambia	5	4	Partly free
Tanzania	5	4	Partly free
Zimbabwe	5	5	Partly free

South East/East Asia (4 countries)

	Political rights	Civil liberties	Freedom rating
South Korea	2	2	Free
Taiwan	2	2	Free
Philippines	2	3	Free
Thailand	3	3	Partly free

South Asia (3 countries)

	Political rights	Civil liberties	Freedom rating
Bangladesh	2	4	Partly free
Nepal	3	4	Partly free
Pakistan	4	5	Partly free

Central Asia (2 countries)

	Political rights	Civil liberties	Freedom rating
Mongolia	2	3	Free
Kyrgyzstan	5	5	Partly free

West Asia [Middle East] (1 country)

	Political rights	Civil liberties	Freedom rating
Turkey	4	5	Partly free

The Freedom House scale runs from 1 = most free, to 7 = least free; see the appendix to this book for Freedom House criteria and methodology. All data from 'Annual survey of Freedom country scores, 1972–3 to 1998–9', http://www.freedomhouse.org/survey99/method/

were classified as 'free' by Freedom House (see below); the other 6 (60 per cent) – Bangladesh, Kyrgyzstan, Nepal, Pakistan, Thailand and Turkey – were judged 'partly free'. Of the 16 in Latin America, Freedom House perceived 6 (37.5 per cent) as 'free', while the remaining 10 (62.5 per cent) were 'partly free'. Africa had 6 (27.3 per cent) new democracies rated 'free' and 16 (72.7 per cent) 'partly free'.

As table 1.2 shows, there was relatively little difference in the percentages of 'free' states – that is, where democracy might be said to be consolidated – among the new democracies in the three regions. In other words, democracy appeared to be consolidated, with democratic institutions developed to a considerable degree, in about one-third of the new democracies. Why was the average consolidation rate as it was? Was it simply that insufficient time had elapsed since the initial democratic transitions? A comparison can be made with three Southern European third wave democracies: Greece, Portugal and Spain. All are said to have completed democratic transitions – and to have been well on the way to democratic consolidation – within a decade following the collapse of authoritarian governments in the mid-1970s. But such a fast rate of democratic progress is historically most unusual. Even under broadly favourable conditions, it normally takes much time and effort to develop democracy and democratic institutions to the point of consolidation. For example, democratic consolidation in Britain and the United States gradually evolved over a long period of time – decades or longer. Consequently, judged in such a historical context, 'only' limited signs of democratic consolidation a few years after authoritarian rule ends do not necessarily signify that democratic progress is not being made. On the other hand, while democratic consolidation may well be a lengthy process, it is possible to identify whether it is happening by various indicators, including the amount of political rights and civil liberties judged to be present in a country. This is the method chosen by the American organization, Freedom House, which publishes an annual survey of democratic progress covering all countries (see p. 11 and the appendix below for the Freedom House criteria and methodology).

Whereas there was much euphoria in the late 1980s and early 1990s that the world was witnessing an epochal shift to democracy, captured in the term 'new world order', by the end of the latter decade many observers were much less certain. After a decade of swift democratization, commentators' opinions varied about the chances of widespread democratic consolidation. A few saw evidence of continuing democratic progress around the world, believing that, while

Table 1.2 'Free' and 'partly free' new democracies, 1999

	'Free'		'Partly free'		
	No.	%	No.	%	Total no.
Asia (incl. Turkey)	4	40	6	60	10
Latin America	6	37.5	10	62.5	16
Africa	6	27.3	16	72.7	22
	16	33.3	32	66.7	48

Source: Freedom House.

consolidating democracy would be a long, arduous and highly problematic task, there was clear evidence of gradual democratic consolidation in many new democracies (Karatnycky 1999). Others saw something different: a widespread 'hollowing out', that is a diminishing, of democracy in many countries that had recently undergone democratic transitions. While multiparty competition was common, with, in some cases, a large degree of uncertainty over electoral outcomes, few new democracies showed much evidence of democracy becoming entrenched and embedded in ways commensurate with democratic consolidation. In fact, Diamond (1999) asserted, there was strong empirical evidence, not just of a failure of democracy to progress, but of something more serious: a 'reverse wave' away from democracy and back to authoritarianism.

1.2 The third wave of democracy and its ramifications

Contrasting assessments of widespread democratic consolidation are the starting point for this book. It is not principally about democratization and democratic transitions, although, because the nature of a transition is often thought to influence the chances of democratic consolidation, we focus on the issue in chapter 2. However, the main concern of the book is democratic consolidation – its problems and processes – in the new democracies of Latin America, Asia, Africa and the Middle East, an issue we turn to in chapter 3. It is worth noting in this context that the concept of 'third wave of democracy', originally coined by Samuel Huntington (1991), is actually rather meaningless. This is because it is used to group together *all* recognizably democratic systems outside Western Europe and the United States. The problem is that there are very few common features between the political systems of countries as politically, socially and economically different as those of Latin America, Asia and Africa. In addition, some third wave democracies, such as Chile, have a long history of democracy and recent, relatively short, periods of authoritarian rule; others, such as Jordan or South Korea, have no tradition of democracy. This is not irrelevant because a tradition of democracy is thought likely to make a significant difference to attempts to consolidate democracy, for example by affecting the level of party institutionalization, seen as an important contributory factor in democratic consolidation. The point is that some countries will build and consolidate democracy relatively easily, and others will not; and that countries that manage to consolidate democracy tend to have certain identifiable characteristics and features.

Chapter 3 is devoted to an examination of the theory and practice of democratic consolidation, and addresses the following issues:

1   What is democratic consolidation?
2   Why does it occur in some countries and not others?

My main hypothesis is that democratic consolidation is linked to:

1   the nature of the *structural conditions* that democratically elected regimes inherit;
2   *agent-led innovations* that can encourage or discourage democratic progress.

The interaction of these two sets of concerns is known as *structured contingency*.

The literature on democratization and democratic consolidation is clear about when to expect structural continuities or agent-led innovations. Many analysts favour *contingent explanations for democratic transitions*, that is, political outcomes seem primarily to be the result of the interplay and interactions between leading political actors. On the other hand, when attention turns to seeking to explain *democratic consolidation*, structural explanations are usually deemed of greater relevance to outcomes. This is because a contingent approach – one that focuses on what political actors *do* – cannot tell the whole story. To augment its insights, it is also necessary to be concerned with *patterns of institutional regularity* which significantly inform progress towards democratic consolidation. However, there is a complicating factor: while the insight that both structure and

agency are of importance to democratic consolidation may be analytically useful, we cannot know at the outset how much weight to
attach to each. Under what conditions will structure shape action?
Under what conditions will the opposite be true? It seems likely that
the relative importance of structure and contingency will differ from
country to country and reflect the importance of various factors, both
domestic and, given the importance attached to globalization, external. It may well be that some circumstances lead to political continuity, while others favour significant political innovations.

Using the explanatory insights offered by a structured contingency
approach, in chapters 4–8 I focus on democracy and democratic consolidation – or their lack – in Latin America, East and South East
Asia, South Asia, Africa, and the Middle East. Each chapter contains
two case studies. The main criteria for selection are that countries
should have interesting political histories, that they have made recent
attempts to consolidate democracy, and that they illustrate the role
of structured contingency in democratic outcomes.

Inevitably I will be making comparisons – and generalizations –
between a number of diverse countries in different parts of the world.
An obvious problem with this approach is that because these regions
and countries vary – for example, they have different historical
experiences, cultures and social, political and economic structures –
then, it might be argued, comparisons between them would offer little
in the way of general analytical guidance. To complicate matters
further, there were 'unexpected' democratic outcomes *within* regions,
for example the sudden emergence of democracy in the 1990s in
economically impoverished, multiethnic African countries, such
as Benin, Malawi and Mali. Consequently, attempting a comparative
examination of democratization and democratic consolidation could
throw up at least as many questions as answers. However, there is a
growing body of literature on democratic consolidation, and this will
help in attempting to pull things together when seeking to identify
and account for both universal and particularistic factors of regions'
and countries' democratic experiences. In sum, aware of the potential pitfalls of overgeneralization, I am nevertheless convinced that it
is possible to arrive at a reasonably well-informed judgement regarding what factors are most important in explaining why democratic
consolidation has occurred in some countries and not in others.

Before discussing the issue fully in chapter 2, it will be useful to
note here what are said to be the main signs to explain democratic
consolidation or its lack. The literature on democratic consolidation
highlights how important it is that certain conditions and factors
are present, including 'broadly consensual, political attitudes, social

structures and political institutions' (Pinkney 1993: 159). Other important factors are said to include a certain, relatively high, level of national prosperity; a robust, relatively unfragmented civil society; and an institutionalized, relatively unfragmented party system. International encouragement can only help, although it is rarely, if ever, pivotal for democratic consolidation. Certain factors, the converse of the above, are said to make democratic consolidation most unlikely: enduring economic crisis; lack of societal toleration among ethnically and/or religiously divided groups; a weak civil society; a highly fragmented party system; no or unsustained external encouragement.

1.3 Forms of authoritarian rule

While it is important to identify what democracy is, defining it is a very tricky task. Consequently, I shall start by discussing what it is *not*. I will do this by identifying four generic types of authoritarian regimes found either historically or currently in the regions examined in this book. Although by 2000 around 75 per cent of governments were elected, this obviously implies that around a quarter – about 50 regimes – were not. Four generic kinds of authoritarian regimes can be identified:

1 communist governments;
2 non-communist single-party regimes;
3 'personalist' governments, including autocratic monarchies;
4 military administrations.

Communist governments

After the demise of socialist regimes in Eastern Europe a decade ago, five communist governments remained worldwide, those of China, Cuba, Laos, North Korea and Vietnam, collectively home to nearly 1.5 billion people. The theoretical justification for communist single-party rule was that only the party had the capacity to organize the defence of the revolution against counterrevolutionary forces, plan and oversee expansion of the forces of production, and supervise the reconstruction of society. Consequently, the party, via the state, was to be the vehicle for building the framework for communism. Following the collapse of Eastern Europe's communist regimes, the remaining communist governments, to some degree affected by the global pro-democracy *Zeitgeist*, felt obliged to change tactics and, in some cases, alter national goals. For example, the communist government of China allowed capitalism to grow to previously unexpected heights, to the extent that it is difficult to believe now that it still envisages the development of a classless society. The governments of Vietnam and Cuba also allowed more capitalism than before, while both Laos and North Korea urgently sought increased international aid to shore up their crumbling economies. In sum, affected by the global trend towards free markets and, to a lesser degree, democracy, after the fall of the Soviet bloc the remaining communist regimes attempted to reform economically but without necessarily allowing more democracy than before.

Non-communist single-party regimes

While communist governments achieved power as a result of revolutionary change, non-communist single-party regimes typically came to power either by the ballot box or via a military coup d'état. Following decolonization in Africa and Asia in the 1950s and 1960s it was confidently expected that political parties would increasingly come to resemble those of the West. With the same forms and functions, they would be integral parts of multiparty systems offering an increasingly educated and discerning public organized electoral choice and channels of accountability. What actually happened, however, was in many cases somewhat different: after independence, multiparty systems soon gave way to single-party systems, especially in Africa. Between 1958 and 1973 multiparty governments in 12 African countries abandoned multipartyism, mostly for single-party rule (Doig 1999: 23). Some observers saw this as a broadly progressive development, as single-party governments were often judged to be the only 'modern' organizations, crucially important 'agents of national integration in states whose new and often arbitrarily imposed boundaries commanded less loyalty than "primordial" ties of language, religion or locality' (Randall 1988: 2).

But single-party regimes were not democratic in the sense of allowing citizens the periodic chance to elect their government. Their legitimacy was often rooted in the claimed ability to oversee economic development and national integrity, that is, to weld together often disparate peoples into a nation-state. While, initially, both tasks seemed within the grasp of many single-party regimes, over time their abilities in these regards were increasingly questioned. Popular demands for democracy in the 1980s and 1990s, especially in Africa, were often the result of the failures of single-party regimes to preside over acceptable levels of economic development or to engineer national integrity.

Personalist regimes and autocratic monarchies

In personalist regimes, a dominant figure wields a great deal of personal power. It is absolutist rule with virtually no limitations. The main justification for such rule is that it ensures political stability and enhances chances of economic development. Under such regimes, the 'luxury' of political parties or free and fair elections cannot be allowed because, it is argued, the resources and energy used to contest elections and fight political battles between parties detract from the development effort. In sum, under such regimes, most – if not all – democratic freedoms are denied, including freedom of expression, assembly and organization.

Military regimes

Military government is rule by the armed forces, commonly achieved by coup d'état. Until the recent shift to democracy, they were the most common form of non-democratic regime in Latin America, Asia and Africa, with about half the countries in these regions ruled by the military (Hadjor 1993: 196). Military regimes come in varying forms. Some of them are dominated by a charismatic senior officer and described as 'military dictatorships'. Others are governed by groups of military personnel in juntas. While military regimes can vary considerably, what they all have in common is a dislike of democracy and a suppression of civic freedoms. While military personnel nearly always claim to be only temporarily in power to deal with civilian corruption and the task of putting 'the ship of state back on an even keel', in fact, once there they tend to stay put, often for years. And while the number of overtly military regimes has declined in recent years, this does not mean that the political power of the military has necessarily fallen away. In fact, in many countries it remains great, to the extent that military support is often seen as fundamental to a regime's survival.

Summary of characteristics of authoritarian regimes

While the various kinds of authoritarian regimes differ, all have the following characteristics:

• A voice in politics is denied to the mass of ordinary people.
• Power is in the hands of a numerically small elite group.
• Regime legitimacy is measured in terms of economic success rather than accountability or representativeness.

1.4   Forms of democracy

It is widely agreed that democracy has two fundamental aspects: *democratic institutions*, including popularly elected legislatures; and *democratic principles*, including popular control of the government and political equality among citizens (Beetham 1999). Beyond that, while consensus is elusive, Robert Dahl's concept of 'polyarchy' is often cited as denoting a form of democratic system. 'Polyarchy' has seven main features:

1 free and fair elections;
2 elected officials;
3 inclusive suffrage;
4 the right to run for office;
5 freedom of expression;
6 alternative sources of information to those disseminated by the state;
7 associational autonomy. (Dahl 1989: 221)

I shall work from the premise that when these seven features are in existence in a polity then democracy is consolidated.

The American organization Freedom House, broadly making use of a Dahlian concept of democracy, compiles annual statistics pertaining to the degree of democracy in all countries. Freedom House ratings of a country's democratic position are judged in terms of 'political rights' (PR) and 'civil liberties' (CL). In both categories the highest level of freedom is rated '1', while the lowest is rated '7'. Thus the best score that a country can achieve under the Freedom House system is a '1' for PR and a '1' for CL. (See the appendix for more on Freedom House and its criteria in awarding its ratings.) Diamond

(1996) suggests that the Freedom House rating of 'free' is a 'rough' indicator of democratic consolidation in a country. Zakaria (1997) proposes a combined PR + CL total of between 2 and 4 to denote democratic consolidation, while Diamond suggests a range of between 2 and 5. Both Diamond and Zakaria suggest that PR + CL scores of between 5 and 10 amount to a 'partly free' state, that is, one where some aspects of democracy are present but not others, that is, a 'limited' democracy. For both authors, as well as for Freedom House, a combined PR + CL total of between 11 and 14 signifies a state which is 'not free', that is, there are very few, if any, indicators that a democratic regime exists.

I use Freedom House indicators in this book to judge whether democracy appears to be consolidated, that is, when a polity is described by Freedom House as a 'free' state. A second category, 'partly free', denotes in my terminology a 'limited' democracy – that is, it is a polity with a recognizably democratic system but with flaws. Third, 'not free' refers to a country with very few – if any – democratic characteristics.

1.5 Types of democratic regime

I refer to three kinds of democratic system in the chapters of this book:

1 'facade' democracy;
2 'limited' democracy;
3 'full' democracy.

They principally differ from each other in varying degrees of political and civil freedoms, although the dividing lines between the categories are rarely clear. 'Facade' democracies have few democratic characteristics, although periodic elections will be allowed. Examples are found in contemporary Africa and the Middle East. 'Full' democracy is at the other end of the democratic spectrum, but does not actually exist anywhere in the world at the current time. Consequently, it is an aspirational category. 'Limited' democracies fill the middle of the spectrum and are the most common form of post-transition regime in Latin America, Asia and Africa. They are hybrid regimes with a mix of democratic and non-democratic characteristics.

'Facade' democracy

Facade democracies exist when rulers have few real pretensions to democracy, yet allow regular, albeit controlled, elections and a very limited range of civil liberties. Historically, such regimes were common in some Latin American countries and are currently found in certain Middle Eastern and African countries. In Latin America they were the result of elections held primarily to impress external observers: that is, 'for the English to look at' (or, in the original Portuguese, 'para os ingleses ver') (Whitehead 1993: 316). In contemporary Africa, 'figleaf' elections in various countries, such as Togo, Burkina Faso and Cameroon, fulfil a similar role (Bayart 1993: xii–xiii).

The contemporary Middle East offers the most egregious examples of facade democracies. Leaders such as Saddam Hussein (Iraq), the late Hafiz al-Assad (Syria) and Hosni Mubarak (Egypt) have regularly won presidential elections with unfeasibly large majorities – often more than 90 per cent of the popular vote. Moammar Gadaffi (Libya) takes things one step further: he does not bother to put himself before the electorate, despite the fact that he grabbed power in 1969 and has *never* asked Libyans formally to endorse his rule. His justification is that he is merely the conduit for popular decisions taken at lower levels via elections; a claim, many observers judge, that does not stand up to serious scrutiny (Bill and Springborg 1994).

During the Cold War (*c*.1948–89), facade democracies were often encouraged by Western governments anxious to thwart the perceived desire of the Soviet Union to expand its global influence. Friendly regimes lacking most democratic attributes were supported if they appeared to be important bulwarks against the spread of communism, not least because they denied left-wing forces any chance of coming to power. Under conditions of political repression, reformist movements often had great difficulty in making headway, being routinely labelled communists. This repression was rarely a bar to friendly regimes receiving aid, developing trade links and instituting military pacts (Gills et al. 1993). While the end of the Cold War opened up the possibility of transitions to more authentically democratic regimes, democratic progress often proved elusive, a consequence of the historic entrenchment of unrepresentative, undemocratic political systems under the domination of unrepresentative, often tiny, elites.

Summary of 'facade' democracy

- Common historically in Latin America, this form is currently found in Africa and the Middle East.
- Rulers have few real pretensions to democracy, yet allow regular, controlled elections.
- Facade democracies were often encouraged during the Cold War by Western governments anxious to combat the global influence of the Soviet Union.
- Leaders of facade democracies manage to retain power when there is insufficient pressure to compel them to change.

'Limited' democracy

Limited democracies are hybrid regimes, political systems with a mix of democratic and non-democratic characteristics. They differ from facade democracies in satisfying certain formal procedural criteria of democracy, especially periodic, relatively free and fair elections – that is, with meaningful rules and regulations to determine their conduct and content – and a range of political and civic freedoms. However, limited democracies lack a full array of liberal freedoms. They have a relatively narrow range of civil liberties, often limited concern with the processes of law and, other than at election times, low levels of political participation in politics.

Limited democracies typically have their roots in political competition or collaboration among numerically small elite groups, sometimes exclusive oligarchies dominated by 'informal, permanent, and pervasive particularism (or clientelism, broadly defined)' (O'Donnell 1996: 120). Under such regimes, elections are not necessarily designed to produce the conditions where a change of government is plausible, but rather to 'change *the form* in which political actors pursue control of the state apparatus and its resources *but not the logic of their behaviour*' (Bratton and van de Walle 1997: 235–6, emphasis added).

Limited democracy, Zakaria suggests, is 'a growth industry. Seven years ago [that is, 1990] only 22 per cent of democratizing countries could have been so categorized; five years ago that figure had risen to 35 per cent.' The point is not that limited democracies are a point on a forward trajectory to consolidated democracy; few have reached that stage. As Zakaria observes,

far from being a temporary or transitional stage, it appears that many
countries are settling into a form of government that mixes a substantial degree of democracy with a substantial degree of illiberalism.
Just as nations across the world have become comfortable with many
variations of capitalism, they could well adopt and sustain varied
forms of democracy. Western liberal democracy might prove to be
not the final destination on the democratic road, but just one of many
possible exits. (1997: 24)

Political stability in a limited democracy is often based less on respect
for democratic values than on the personal power of the state's leader,
his or her immediate circle of confidants and the security services.
There will typically be only limited institutional constraints on executive power, with power effectively personalized, constrained only by
the 'hard facts of existing power relations and by constitutionally
limited terms of office' (Zakaria 1997: 22).

Finally, unequivocal civilian control over the military is likely to
be absent. This is either because the military is institutionally too
strong to be controlled by an elected civilian regime, or that the latter
recognizes the crucial importance of having a supportive military. In
both scenarios, elected leaders forge alliances with senior military
personnel. Military leaders publicly profess support for elected governments while resisting civilian efforts to control the armed forces'
internal affairs, to dictate security policy and to make officers subject
to the judgement of civil courts.

Summary of 'limited' democracy

- Limited democracies have certain formal procedural criteria of
  democracy.
- There is a lack of *liberal* freedoms, a relatively narrow range of
  civil liberties and, except at election times, low levels of popular
  involvement in politics.
- Political control is often in the hands of small elite groups and
  military support is cultivated.

'Full' democracy

Full democracy is an ideal: it does not exist anywhere in the world.
It is, however, useful to discuss it briefly as it represents an important aspirational goal towards which, no doubt, many ordinary

voters would like to see progress. The concept of full democracy extends the democratic ideal beyond the formal mechanisms of limited democracy to a point where there is widespread, continuous citizen participation in politics, and government rules with much transparency and accountability. A full democracy would have a real and sustained, as opposed to rhetorical and intermittent, stress on individual freedoms and the representation of citizens' interests, a consistently high degree of equity and justice for all, and a full array of civil liberties and human rights. All citizens, regardless of social or class position, would have easy, regular access to governmental processes and, as a result, a real say in collective decision-making. This would be accomplished, not only via elected representatives in national and subnational legislatures, but also via other methods of group participation and public forums. The armed forces would be consistently and unequivocally subservient to civilian rule. Those traditionally lacking power – such as the poor, minority ethnic and religious groups, women, young people – would have a real say in political outcomes.

Summary of 'full' democracy

- The concept of full democracy extends the democratic ideal beyond the formal mechanisms of electoral democracy to include continuous citizen participation in politics.
- Government rules with much transparency and accountability.
- The military is unequivocally under civilian control.
- Those formerly lacking political power would enjoy some.

1.6   Overall conclusions

Democratically elected governments have appeared in large numbers of previously undemocratic countries in recent years. Initially, scholarly attention was devoted to democratic transition, assumed to lead typically to democratically elected governments. It was widely expected that democratic consolidation would follow, but optimism was dashed when limited democracies developed in many countries. Consequently, there was a shift in scholarly interest towards the problems of the survival and stability of new democratic regimes, or, in the terminology adopted in this book, problems of democratic consolidation.

Most transitions led to limited democracies, where basic democratic institutions and practices coexisted with weakness of political accountability and often fragility of civil and political rights. The large number of enduring limited democracies made it clear that democratic consolidation could not be understood simply as regime durability. Rather, it was a question of the democratic content of regimes: measuring the degree to which basic rights were respected and comparing countries' democratic performances. It became clear that accounting for democratic outcomes depended on structural and agency factors, and these differed from country to country, a reflection of individual political histories and characteristics.

2

Democratic Transitions and Structured Contingency

2.1 Democratic transitions in comparative perspective

Introduction

Democratic transitions from authoritarian regimes are a necessary prerequisite for democratic consolidation. This chapter is concerned, first, with theories of transition, and, second, with the notion of structured contingency, briefly introduced in chapter 1. The chapter has two aims: (1) to survey the relevant literature, including important theories and arguments about democratic transition; (2) to set up a framework of enquiry for the theoretical and empirical chapters that follow.

From authoritarian rule to democratic transition

At a certain, variable stage, leaders of authoritarian regimes may judge that their hold on power is more threatened by trying to maintain the status quo than by agreeing to political changes which they might be able to control. Typically, however, tensions soon emerge, centring on the pace and precise direction of political changes. There is likely to be polarization between those wanting as little change as possible ('conservatives', 'hardliners') and those believing that because change is either desirable or inevitable, then it is wise to get in the best position possible to profit ('reformers', 'softliners'). Such tensions lie at the root of the dynamism and uncertainty that characterize all democratic transitions and highlight how the transition period, while varying in length of time, is always characterized by great political uncertainty. This is because there is an absence of predictable 'rules of the game' during democratic transitions that serves to expand the boundaries of contingent choice open to political actors. The transition's dynamics revolve around the strategic interactions and tentative arrangements between actors with uncertain power resources.

Democratic transition is the period between an authoritarian and an elected government, an empirically verifiable, self-contained phase of democratization. It can occur quickly or slowly: Argentina's is an example of the former, Brazil's of the latter. Whatever the duration, transitions typically create, or help speed up, a dynamic of change, a process centring on the interactions between the leading political players. Pridham and Vanhanen explain that transition is a 'stage of regime change commencing at the point when the previous non-democratic system begins to collapse, leading to a situation when, with a new constitution in place, the democratic structures become routinized and the political elites adjust their behaviour to liberal democratic norms' (1994: 2). And, as Bratton and van de Walle point out, the 'motivations, preferences, and calculations' of political actors are of great significance at this stage: 'one agent's initiative prompts another actor's response and . . . political events cascade iteratively from one to another' (1997: 24).

There is always a considerable risk of reversion to authoritarianism during transition. This is because political institutions of the old regime necessarily coexist with emerging post-authoritarian ones, while authoritarians and democrats share power either as a product of conflict or by tentative agreement. In other words, transition is a stage with varied forms, 'subject to unforeseen contingencies, unfolding processes and unintended outcomes' (Karl and Schmitter 1991: 270). The cut-off point dividing authoritarian from democratic rule is usually identified as the first free and fair elections that symbolically found the new, post-authoritarian order. In sum, whether short or long, transition is characterized by:

1 intense political uncertainty;
2 struggle between competing political forces over the rules of the political game, and the spoils of victory and its attendant resources;
3 the nature of future political competition.

What may begin as a limited concession from rulers to opposition can eventually lead to comprehensive negotiations between rival factions over future political arrangements. Within authoritarian regimes tensions can emanate principally from domestic or external factors or from a combination of the two. But whatever the precise causes and directions of change, authoritarian regimes experience growing problems of legitimacy prior to transition. The fact that few, if any, authoritarian regimes were entirely untouched by recent calls for democracy implies that there was more to the global process of democratization during the third wave than simply a range of unconnected political decisions taken by disconnected elites around the world. Other factors played an important role in pressuring elites to introduce political changes. These factors include economic upheavals and associated popular demands for fundamental reforms, because authoritarian regimes typically rely on good economic performances to legitimize themselves. If a sustained economic downturn occurs, they are vulnerable to popular demands for change. Indonesia offers a good example in this regard: prolonged economic progress under the authoritarian rule of President Suharto (1965–98) helped keep demands for democracy muted. A period of sustained economic downturn occurred in 1997–8 followed by loud demands – from students and other civil society actors – that Suharto should stand down. Eventually, in 1998, sustained popular pressure hounded him and his regime from office, leading to a prolonged period of democratic transition and the inauguration of a democratically elected government (Liddle 1999; Tornquist 1999).

While the recent example of Indonesia highlights the importance of political elites for democratic outcomes, it should be noted that what elites do politically has been an important analytical focus of analysis for decades. One of the most influential contributions in this vein was that of Dankwart Rustow. In his article, 'Transitions to democracy', published in 1970, he started from the premise that all democratic countries by and large followed the same route to democratic consolidation. He argued that barriers to democracy can be overcome – *providing political leaders agree to bury their differences, unite behind a drive for democracy, agree to abide by democratic rules*. For Rustow democratic progress goes through five stages. First, there is a phase when national unity is established in a polity. Second, the now nationally oriented polity goes through a period of prolonged and inconclusive political struggle. Democracy is born as a result of often intense and prolonged political contestation, but the struggle can be so intense that a fledgling democracy will collapse. Third, there is the first transition phase, a highly significant moment, when leading political players decide to compromise, to adopt democratic rules and allow each some stake in the new democratic order. At this stage, crucially, political leaders must agree to adopt and adapt to democratic political rules. Fourth, there is a second transition when democracy is constructed – that is, the beginning of consolidation. This is the stage during which democratic rules become habituated among leading political players. The final stage, when democracy is consolidated, is judged especially problematic because it involves paths that are both complex and uncertain. Consequently there will be success *only* if all major political actors are fully committed to democracy: that is, while presenting opposing policies, they must agree to work together politically and neutralize non-democrats. This is important so as to avoid facilitating the return of authoritarianism. O'Donnell calls this the 'great accord or pact of the second transition' (1992: 24).

In sum, during transition the role of political agency is crucial: political elites, parties and civil societies have a 'direct impact upon political outcomes', dwarfing that of 'deep structures' (Bratton and van de Walle 1997: 22). Pinkney observes that, during the transition, it 'would require an extremely deterministic approach to attribute government control, or lack of it, over transitions, simply to immovable traditions or power structures' (1993: 139–40). Later, however, structures strongly reassert themselves and have a major bearing on democratic outcomes. I hypothesize that, after transition, a renewed focus on the impact of structures is necessary to explain differing outcomes in countries whose socioeconomic position is apparently similar. However, it is also crucial to factor in what political actors *do*, because, during attempts to consolidate democracy, 'the initiatives and interplay of purposive political actors' are also important (Bratton and van de Walle 1997: 223). Before we examine this notion – structured contingency – in detail we need to identify types of democratic transition to see what impact they have on what follows.

2.2 Characteristics of democratic transitions

What forces principally propel the dynamic of transition, and how are the chances of democratic consolidation affected? Huntington (1991) identifies four modes:

1 'transformation', when transition is primarily initiated by the government acting more or less alone;

2 'transplacement', where transition is a joint initiative between power-holders and leading opposition figures;
3 'replacement', when popular pressure principally inaugurates a transition;
4 'foreign intervention', when a transition is instigated by a foreign government.

Transformation

Transformation is often a fairly lengthy process. It occurs when an authoritarian regime, without undue pressure from opposition forces or the wider society, decides, following internal debate, that it is in its own best interests to inaugurate political changes. This mode of transition may result in the retention of an armed forces' veto on future political arrangements, as well as preferential treatment of the military at the hands of the new government. The result of such a transition is likely to be, at best, a limited democracy notable for the continued political dominance of a relatively small number of elite figures, often those who enjoyed power under the ancien régime. Transformation was a common mode of transition in many Latin American, African and some Asian countries (Lievesley 1999; Vanhanen 1998).

Fundamental to this mode of transition is the truism that those who rule authoritarian societies do not voluntarily surrender power; and nor are they generally willing to modify systems of rule to jeopardize their hold on power (Doig 1999: 29). The wider point is that decisions about basic democratic institutions in this mode of transition are taken by existing power-holders motivated primarily by their own personal and group interests. This is emphasized by Lijphart and Waisman when they note that 'political self-interest, that of both politicians and their parties, is the dominant motivation behind the choice of institutional designs.' Such actors tend to be both 'self-interested thinkers [and] short-term thinkers . . . the institutions that are adopted are mainly expedient bargains' (1996: 244).

While institutional outcomes reflect the struggle between competing interests, they (the institutions) do not necessarily contribute, over time, to the strengthening of democracy. For this, as White notes, 'political leadership of a broader, more visionary kind may well be essential' (1998: 44). However, as Kasfir observes, 'members of dominant classes have paid attention to state power in order to gain it, not reform it. They may solicit support from underclasses at elections, but they rarely promote their interests when in power' (1998a: 5). In order to make it as difficult as possible for the mass of ordinary people profoundly to alter the prevailing social and material circumstances, on coming to power 'new democratic governments . . . must set about demobilising those forces in civil society that may have been instrumental in driving the transition process' (Ginsburg 1996: 78). Not to do so would be to leave intact socially orientated groups and movements who may see democracy as the opportunity to deal with problems of underprivilege and deprivation. This would, for elite groups, unavoidably lead to an unwelcome loss of power and influence.

Transplacement

The importance of elites is also highlighted in the transplacement mode. Diamond argues that 'the only absolute requirement for transition (short of foreign conquest and imposition) is a commitment to democratization on the part of the strategic elite' (1993: 58). For Linz and Stepan (1978) the 'political creativity' and 'leadership' of the political elites are of vital significance. Such concerns are encapsulated in strategic elite theories of transition whereby government and opposition elites discover common cause in a drive for limited democratic outcomes. In the transplacement mode, the primary aim is rarely to encourage popular political participation; rather, it is to resolve elite differences with the objective of strengthening elite influence so as to channel political actions in ways favourable to their interests.

The key to a successful conclusion of negotiations is that reformers in the authoritarian regime and moderates in the pro-democracy opposition join forces and manage to arrive at a consensual outcome. Eventually (1) 'softliners' become dominant, both in government and among opposition forces; (2) rulers and opposition challengers agree to draw a veil over the past, even when there were serious human rights abuses during authoritarian rule; and (3) there is broad agreement that, unlike in the past, future policy directions will be consensual. It is imperative that the position of traditional power-holders, such as senior military figures and large-scale landowners, is not fundamentally imperilled in the new order. Consequently, the post-transition regime 'must be strong enough to govern effectively, but weak enough not to be able to govern against important interests' (Ginsburg 1996: 76). Merkel notes how important it is for political stability after the transition fully to integrate 'elites into a stable framework of efficient democratic institutions which do not threaten their interests' (1998: 56). But if elites do not judge their interests sufficiently protected in the new order, they will not accept its legitimacy and will do all they can to undermine it. (For a review of the relevant literature, see Shin 1994.)

As in the transformation mode, choices made by leading political actors are central to transplacement – and for the same reasons: to ensure that post-authoritarian political arrangements benefit, as far as possible, the existing elites, both in government and outside it. On the other hand, transitions via transplacement tend to be more fluid and less government controlled than in the transformation mode. While the nature of the resulting 'pact' between government and opposition is variable – such as a series of unwritten understandings, or a sealed document – it always reflects a relatively stable settlement between government and opposition. Once the parties are seated at the negotiating table, the most significant items on the agenda are the institutional forms and parameters of democracy. If an acceptable compromise is reached, it amounts to a bargain expressed in and through institutions that not only insulate the post-authoritarian government from the broad mass of people but also, typically, allow pre-existing power-holders to retain a considerable degree of power under the new, democratically elected, government. As Shin notes, 'in the real world of new democracies, the elites more often than not collude rather than co-operate in order to seek the best personal outcome' (1999: 199). The implication is that even if power officially shifts to a different group of people, the pre-existing power structure will be an important factor moulding attempts at democratic consolidation.

A typical catalyst for this kind of transition is when a government begins to lose its authority – perhaps after initiating hesitant liberalization. The opposition moves to exploit the situation, and expands its support among ordinary people. This, in turn, encourages it to intensify its campaign for change. Alarmed, the government tries to contain the opposition, but fails. However, a stalemate ensues at this point: the opposition is not powerful enough to force the changes it wants, while the government lacks the power to put into practice its chosen solutions. Eventually, however, both groups recognize the reality of the situation and agree to negotiate to try to resolve the crisis. Hardliners within both the government and among the opposition initially wish to pursue maximalist solutions by provoking, or intensifying, an all-out conflict. However, for reformers within the authoritarian ranks (recognizing that the retention of power requires, to some degree, power-sharing) and for moderates within the pro-democracy movement (recognizing the futility of inheriting only the ruins of a once viable society) the scenario of post-transition political chaos is not attractive. Consequently, in the face of impending or actual disorder, most 'political actors calculate that whatever difference in their welfare could result from a more favourable institutional framework is not worth the risk inherent in continued conflict' (Przeworski 1991: 85). As Linz and Stepan (1996) note, the constitutional compact, defining the new regime's main laws, procedures and institutions and favouring democratic consolidation, constitutes a crucial condition for solving existing social conflicts pacifically.

In sum, according to the transplacement scenario, progress towards democratic consolidation will only occur when transitions involve negotiations and deals between elites in the government and the opposition. However, there is likely to be a democratic price to pay: because future stability is founded on guarantees secured by the old ruling elites, striving to protect and maintain privileges and impatient to escape judgement for any crimes committed during their rule, such agreements will lead to clearly limited democracies.

Replacement

The genesis of the replacement mode is likely to be a serious national crisis of some kind which the government is unable to resolve. It is a kind of transition that is not elite dominated. Instead, change comes primarily – at least, initially – from bottom-up pressures, and elites are compelled to accede to the popular will. In other words, popular demands underpin and galvanize this mode of transition, rather than elite pacts. This is when 'ordinary' men and women often aid the 'assault [on] the seats of power' (Linz 1990: 152).

This mode of transition – whereby incumbent elites are basically forced from office by popular pressure – is unlikely to lead to stable democratization (Bratton and van de Walle 1997). This is because the absence of pacts during transition will be a serious impediment to the emergence of the necessary climate of moderation and compromise characterizing democratic consolidation. The arrangements consolidation logically embodies – that is, a shift in power from pre-existing elites to new power-holders – are likely to be strongly resisted by those who have the most to lose from change.

In sum, while authoritarian regimes may be overthrown by mass mobilization, this is not likely to result in their replacement by stable liberal democratic regimes. Instead, new governments may regress into, or be replaced by, new forms of authoritarianism (Huntington 1991; Karl and Schmitter 1991; Bratton and van de Walle 1997).

Foreign intervention

As the name of this transition mode suggests, 'foreign intervention' is a transition catalysed by the intervention of an outside power. In recent times, however, it has become the least common method of political transition. Examples include democratic transitions in Haiti, Panama, and an attempted one in Somalia, all in the 1990s under the auspices of the government of the United States. In the cases of Panama and Haiti, incumbent strongmen were overthrown by the actions of the US government, while in Somalia a similar strategy was attempted but failed. Some analysts also include Grenada in this category, although this is to overlook the fact that the tiny Caribbean island – with a population of fewer than 100,000 people – already had a democratically elected regime in power when the United States invaded 'to oust the Cubans' in 1983.

There is another, less forceful type of foreign intervention relating to democratic transitions to be noted. The influence of foreign aid donors was of great importance in the decision to democratize some economically poor authoritarian regimes. Following the significant oil price rises of the 1970s and associated international indebtedness, the ability of such regimes to maintain adequate programmes of political and economic development dropped sharply in the 1980s and 1990s. The result was that it became increasingly difficult for developing states – especially for those without oil – to balance their budgets. Many became increasingly dependent on loans and aid from the West. Aid donors argued that the situation would be remedied by democratization, part of a general process of improving governance. Increasingly, the continuity of foreign aid was made dependent on the agreement of aid-hungry regimes to democratization. In this way, many economically poor, authoritarian regimes were strongly encouraged to shift to democracy. In addition, in a linked move, Western governments encouraged the installation of market-based economic programmes to the extent that they were 'intrinsic' to democratic openings in economically impoverished Africa and Central America (Joseph 1998: 10; Karl 1995: 77). In short, external encouragement to democratize – linked to the supply of aid and loans – was often of major significance for poor countries.

Rueschemeyer, Stephens and Stephens note that the 'external imposition of any kind of regime is difficult, and particularly so of democratic rule' (1992: 279). This is a way of saying that external actors, however economically or diplomatically powerful, cannot for long impose their choices of political systems on unwilling countries or precisely dictate political outcomes. Short-term external intervention may – for a while – tip the balance in favour of democratization, and its absence can certainly be an advantage for the forces of authoritarianism. But democracy will only take root and prosper when certain domestic criteria are fulfilled. Evidence for this comes from the experiences of Greece, Spain and Portugal, all countries that swiftly democratized from the mid-1970s. While external encouragement to democratize, especially from the European Union, was of great importance, democratic consolidation was dependent on (1) domestic consensus that democracy was more desirable than any alternative political arrangement; and (2) an absence of serious ethnic, religious or class schisms (Pridham 1991). The lack of such conditions in most Latin American, Asian and African countries suggests that democratic consolidation would be hard to achieve.

In sum, while there are several recent examples of external actors encouraging democratic transition, whether by direct military intervention or via aid packages, there is little or no evidence that such initiatives have a strong bearing on eventual political outcomes.

Summary of democratic transitions

- Transition is characterized by dynamism and uncertainty.
- Lack of predictable 'rules of the game' during transition serves to expand the boundaries of contingent choice open to political actors.
- Transitional dynamics revolve around strategic interactions and tentative arrangements between actors with uncertain power resources.
- Democratic consolidation is promoted when transition involves negotiations and deals between the outgoing elite and the leading representatives of the democratic opposition. Elite pacts typically lead to limited democracies.
- Future political stability is linked to guarantees secured by the old ruling elites, including the armed forces. Their aim is to protect privileges and, in some cases, to escape judgement for any crimes committed during authoritarian rule.

- The absence of a pacted transition is likely to serve as a serious impediment to the emergence of the necessary climate of moderation and compromise characterizing democratic consolidation.
- External encouragement may aid democratization but the eventual political outcome is fundamentally linked to domestic structures and processes.

2.3   Structured contingency

Democratic consolidation involves quite different challenges to political actors than those encountered during transition and, consequently, requires different analysis. After transition, the main challenge is to institutionalize democratic competition between groups and organizations with conflicting interests and aspirations, previously united in opposition to authoritarian rule. To facilitate democratic consolidation, political actors must now agree to subordinate their strategies and divisions so that, at the very least, a return to authoritarian rule is not facilitated. This places considerable demands on political actors' skills and commitment to democracy, for they must now demonstrate the 'ability to differentiate political forces rather than draw them into a grand coalition, the capacity to define and channel competing political projects rather than seek to keep potentially divisive reforms off the agenda, and the willingness to tackle incremental reforms . . . rather than defer them to some later date' (Karl 1990: 17). But this outcome is often difficult to achieve as, post-transition, political actors will settle back into largely predictable positions, competing with each other for power. And the underlying distribution of power in the society will be an important factor in determining post-transition outcomes when politics again becomes routinized, following largely predictable patterns. At this stage, typically, 'the same configuration of institutional forces' conditioning 'the process of transition will regain saliency at increased levels' (Bratton and van de Walle 1997: 274). All political actors work within a framework of political restraints and opportunities that not only limit the range of plausible alternatives open to them but also make it highly likely that certain courses of action will be selected over others. After transition a polity's 'immovable traditions [and] power structures' – that is, its *structural characteristics* – will be important in determining political outcomes (Pinkney 1993: 139–40). This is because structures impose limits on the range of choices available to political actors, predisposing them to opt for certain courses of action over others. Decisive factors generating medium-term political outcomes are strongly linked, O'Donnell suggests, to 'various long-term factors . . . that newly installed democratic governments inherit', such as socioeconomic problems (1994: 65). This is a way of saying that the starting point of democratic consolidation will differ from region to region and from country to country.

Structures

What structures are politically relevant? First, there are *formal* political institutions – that is, the permanent edifices of public life, such as, laws, organizations, public offices, elections and so on – found in virtually all states. Second, there are various *informal* institutions that also affect outcomes, including the 'dynamics of interests and identities, domination and resistance, compromise and accommodation', that may run parallel or counter to formal democratic ones (Bratton and van de Walle 1997: 276). It is the interaction of such aspects, coupled with agency factors, that, I hypothesize, will determine the outcome of democratic consolidation in a polity. The relative weight of these factors, as well as the factors themselves, will differ from country to country. However, certain structural characteristics always have a significant impact on democratic outcomes. The likelihood of democratic consolidation is linked to

1 the specific character of a polity's social and economic system;
2 constellations of power at the state and lower levels;
3 the effectiveness of civil and political societies in influencing political outcomes.

Relationships between class divisions and state power are analytically central to a structural perspective, with the specific relations between various classes – such as big capitalists, middle classes, industrial workers, landlords, peasants – profoundly affecting democratization outcomes. In other words, a country's historical trajectory towards or away from democracy is shaped by structures of class, state and transnational power, driven by particularist histories of capitalist development (Cammack 1997). Also of importance is the overall economic position of a country and the degree of social polarization inherited by the democratically elected government. It is often said that democracy requires a rough balance of power between the state, on the one hand, and societal interests organized in political and civil society, on the other. Democracy is unlikely to be the result when the state is either excessively powerful in relation to traditionally subservient social classes, as in many Middle Eastern countries, or is overdependent on powerful landed classes that benefit from the control of labour-repressive agriculture, as in many Latin American nations. Finally, external factors – such as background conditions, influential actors and individual, decisive events – can be important in helping determine the trajectory of democracy. For example, the importance of influential external actors was noted in the democratization of Greece, Portugal and Spain from the mid-1970s. Encouragement from the European Union in particular was seen as vital (Pridham 1991).

While the precise mix differs from country to country, structural factors of general importance to democratization and democratic consolidation include:

- the legacy of personalistic rule, typically with a lack of relevant political institutions;
- national political cultures that do not value democracy more highly than other forms of political engagement;
- weak or declining economies, heavily dependent on international financial assistance;
- serious religious, ethnic and/or ideological conflicts;
- weak and/or fragmented civil societies;
- a highly politicized military intent on maintaining the existing structures of power;
- government regarded as illegitimate and unaccountable by most citizens;
- unrepresentative, undemocratic political parties, dominated by powerful leaders;
- a numerically small, politically powerful, landowning elite denying large numbers of landless people access to the land they need for agricultural purposes;
- a monopolistic electoral and economic hold on power at the local level by 'bosses' or 'big men';
- religious traditions, such as Confucianism and Islam, which some observers regard as hostile to democracy.

In sum, a polity's structural legacies are important during attempts to consolidate democracy, a period when political actors are searching for binding rules of political competition and engagement. In other words, there is no *tabula rasa*. No incoming regime, whatever its stated ideological proclivities or goals, democratically orientated or not, can erase historically produced societal behaviour and the structures that accompany it. On the other hand, a myopic focus on structures alone would lead to us overlooking the important role of human agency in helping to determine political outcomes after transition. In other words, we must be aware that structures are only part of the story, as we cannot ignore what individual political actors *do*. This raises the issue of *contingency*, to which we turn next.

Contingency

A consolidated democracy requires that democratic institutions are not only built but also valued. Democracy can be installed without democrats, but it cannot be consolidated without them. Political actors may initially see a founding election as the 'least worst' alternative to solve an intractable political standoff or to induce political movement in an ossified regime. Democracy may even survive in the short run under the force of these kinds of strategic calculations, but democracy will truly last only when political actors learn to love it. Until elites and citizens alike come to cherish rule by the people and exhibit a willingness to stand up for it, in Africa as elsewhere, there will be no permanent defence against tyranny. (Bratton and van de Walle 1997: 279)

This is the closing paragraph of Bratton and van de Walle's book on democratic transitions in Africa. It highlights the importance to democratic consolidation of contingent factors, that is, the role of human agency in helping determine political outcomes. Implicitly, however, they are suggesting that it is impossible to construct a handy checklist of contingency factors to which we can turn when wishing to assess the chances of democratic consolidation in an individual country or region. This is because the events that can send things in a democratic direction, or reduce that possibility, are simply too varied to list.

Africa provides several recent examples to illustrate the importance of contingency to political outcomes. One is the well-known role of the former president of South Africa, Nelson Mandela, whose decision to enter into political negotiations with the apartheid government following his release from prison was widely judged to be a pivotal event in the shift to democracy. Another, less well-known example is from the East African country of Uganda. There, the government introduced democracy, albeit an unconventional 'no-party' variation, known as the 'movement system', in 1986 (Hansen and

Twaddle 1995). The interesting question is why the regime didn't
decree a multiparty route like most others in Africa? The issue gains
piquancy when we note that there was little doubt that the regime
would have won elections had it chosen to allow a multiparty system.
One interpretation is that the country's powerful leader, Yoweri
Museveni, sincerely believed that multipartyism was the root cause
of the evils of tribalism and religious prejudice which had led to two
decades of conflict in Uganda prior to his rule. The point is that
Museveni's personal decision to pursue an unconventional form of
democracy highlights the importance of both structure and contingency to Uganda's political outcomes from the mid-1980s.

A third African example highlighting the importance of contingency comes from Nigeria. The election to power of a former military leader, Olusegun Obasanjo, in early 1999 led to optimism that
the country would finally put behind it a long history of military governments. President Obasanjo was seen as fervently pro-democracy
and, as a result, the government of the United States focused much
development assistance on the country. However, it soon became
clear that Obasanjo could not easily or quickly overcome anti-
democratic structural legacies, including serious ethnic, religious and
regional frictions and the entrenched political role of the military
(McGreal 2000). The point is that the president's personal desire for
democracy, bolstered by US financial assistance, was not necessarily
sufficient to set the country in a political direction where democracy
would be privileged over non-democratic ways of doing politics.

African political heritages are different from those of other countries and regions. For example, not only in most Latin American, but
also in some Asian countries, notably South Korea and Taiwan, the
authoritarian legacy took on a particular bureaucratic form, known
as 'bureaucratic authoritarianism'. Consequently, attempts at democratic consolidation commenced from a different starting point than
those in Africa. At the same time, political outcomes were also linked
to human agency. For example, a long period of democratic rule in
Venezuela – beginning in 1958 – did not lead to democratic consolidation, as the political scene was dominated for decades by the
carving up of power between the country's two leading political
parties. Eventually, in the late 1990s, power was won via the ballot
box by Hugo Chavez, a charismatic politician and former coup
leader. Chavez could have simply continued with the old regime and
retained the existing power equation. Instead he claimed that he was
instituting a new form of popular democracy that would take away
power from the old, discredited parties in order to 'pass it to the
people'. While critics claim that he is presiding over a new form of

charismatic authoritarianism, the point is that Venezuela offers a good example of a political environment where both contingency and structures are important for political outcomes.

Uganda's Museveni, South Africa's Mandela and Hugo Chavez in Venezuela are three major political figures whose *personal* decisions were of great importance to democratic outcomes in their countries. These examples highlight the essence of structured contingency, and suggest the following hypothesis: *While inherited structures form the context within which political leaders act, individuals are not slavishly bound by structures: agency is also of great importance for political outcomes.*

Summary of structured contingency

- All polities have historically established, informal and formal, structures of power. They are reflected in established rules and institutions that limit the available – that is, realistic – alternatives open to political actors; consequently, actors will tend to select certain courses of action over others.
- Because political outcomes are not entirely random but reflect to a large degree institutionalized patterns, as a concept structured contingency is concerned with 'the interaction of the uncertainties of politics with persistent institutional structures' (Bratton and van de Walle 1997: 278).
- The concept of structured contingency highlights that (1) all polities have structures – that is, inherited rules and institutions and recurrent patterns of behaviour – to which those engaged in political competition are attuned; and (2) that political outcomes are also linked to what individual political actors do.

2.4   Overall conclusions

Successful transitions to recognizably democratic regimes are often thought to be most likely through pacts, especially when 'softline' reformers in the ruling party and 'moderate' opposition leaders cut a deal (Huntington 1991). Such a process – constrained by the need to make trade-offs, to compromise, to protect property rights and the interests of the armed forces – emphasizes the crucial role of leadership in delivering democratic transition. However, the outcome, as Kiloh notes, is 'likely to be a minimalist democracy which is essentially procedural and conservative rather than one which undertakes a fundamental transformation of society' (1997a: 312).

Seeking to judge whether stable forms of democracy are more likely to emerge from government–opposition cooperation, pacts, consensus, moderation and gradual change, or from opposition, revolution, conflict and radical and rapid change, it would be difficult not to accord greater plausibility to the former set of factors. Much of the relevant literature points to the likelihood that gradual, as opposed to sensational, gains in levels of democracy will prove most sustainable over time, not least because they allow political elites time to get accustomed to new political arrangements. Where underlying conditions exist favouring factors essential to democracy – such as cooperation, consensus and gradual, moderate change – and where there are enough political actors of an adequate stature to give a high priority to democratic objectives, and with the skills to pursue them robustly, then such assets are always important. If these conditions are absent, democratic consolidation is unlikely. This is where *structured contingency* comes in: democratic outcomes are not only linked to an array of structural factors, but also to the decisions taken by individuals and groups of political actors. Distinctive institutional legacies – for example, bureaucratic authoritarianism in Latin America and African personalist regimes – will have an impact on democratic outcomes, but the role of agency in individual contexts must be analysed in order to understand democratic outcomes or their lack.

3

Explaining Democratic Consolidation

3.1 What is democratic consolidation?

Introduction

In chapter 2 we looked at various kinds of democratic transition from authoritarian rule, and saw that it was a necessary stage towards democracy and democratic consolidation. We also examined the concept of structured contingency. I suggested that, once a democratically elected regime exists, chances of democracy and democratic consolidation are closely linked to an array of structural and contingent factors. In the current chapter I survey the democratic consolidation literature and identify factors thought to make democratic consolidation plausible. Everything else being equal, the more factors encouraging consolidation, the more assured the process will be.

In the first part of the chapter, we examine theories of democratic consolidation linked, first, to political issues, second, to economic concerns, and third, to international issues. The purpose is not only to survey the literature and theories and arguments, but more specifically to set up a framework of enquiry for the empirical parts of the book, chapters 4–8, concerned with regional democratic consolidation. I will refer to these theories and arguments in the historical analyses and democratic prognoses of the regions and countries in later chapters, and, suggesting which seem central in each case, examine conditions linked to democratic consolidation. While all are drawn from the same list, some will be more central to democratic outcomes in Latin America, others of most relevance to those in Africa, and so on. Armed with this knowledge, we will then be in a position, in the succeeding chapters, to answer the question: what is the hope, first, of democratic survival and then of democratic consolidation for new democracies in Latin America, Asia, Africa and the Middle East?

Democratic consolidation in comparative perspective

How have the new democracies of Latin America, Asia, Africa and the Middle East fared in trying to consolidate democracy? The short answer is that the picture is mixed, illustrated in the data presented in table 1.2 above (p. 5). Evidence suggests that while a few polities managed to consolidate democracy quickly, most did not. Table 1.2 shows that Freedom House judged 17 (35.5 per cent) of 48 new democracies in Latin America, Asia and Africa to be 'free' states in 1999, that is, where democracy could be said to be consolidated *at that time* (don't forget that democratic consolidation can decline!). On the other hand, 31 (64.5 per cent) were categorized as 'partly free', that is, they were limited democracies. Before seeking to explain democratic outcomes in the regions under review, we need to examine the concept of democratic consolidation.

Democratic consolidation is a contested term. For Huntington (1991), democracy is said to be consolidated when a polity passes the 'two-turnover test': that is, a government loses an election, the opposition wins it and then, next time, loses it, so that a new government from the opposition is formed. This test of democratic consolidation has the virtue of being empirically easy to verify but it has the vice of not being nuanced enough. For example, Japan did not fulfil the criteria of the test until 1993: was it not a democracy until then?

Mainwaring, O'Donnell and Valenzuela suggest that democracy can be said to be consolidated when 'all major political actors take for granted the fact that democratic processes dictate governmental renewal' (1992: 3). Linz and Stepan (1996) argue that democratic consolidation does not depend on electoral results; rather the concept amounts to a particular, *institutionalized* form of democracy. It is a procedural system with open political competition, multiple parties freely competing, and an impressive array of civil and political rights – guaranteed by law. Political accountability is crucial, and operates primarily via the electoral relationship between voters and their representatives. For Linz and Stepan, democratic consolidation comprises *behavioural, attitudinal* and *constitutional* aspects. First, *behaviourally,* democracy is said to be consolidated when 'no significant national, social, economic, political, or institutional actors spend significant resources attempting to achieve their objectives by creating a nondemocratic regime or turning to violence or foreign intervention to secede from the state'. Second, *attitudinally,* when most citizens believe that democratic procedures and institutions are the best means 'to govern [their] collective life'; and where support for 'antisystem alternatives is quite small or more or less isolated from the pro-democratic forces'. Third, *constitutionally,* 'governmental and nongovernmental forces . . . become subjected to, and habituated to, the resolution of conflict within the specific laws, procedures, and institutions sanctioned by the new democratic process' (1996: 6). In sum, for Linz and Stepan, democratic consolidation amounts to the institutionalization of democratic practices and processes. It is in place when the great majority of political actors and citizens concur that such a democratic arrangement is the *only* acceptable way to resolve societal conflicts.

Some observers have argued that a combination of a penetrating state and an elite-dominated party system constitutes the most realistic institutional arrangement to facilitate democratic consolidation, albeit at a relatively 'modest' level. This is a way of saying that a recognizably democratic system – one with a stable democratic order and a good range of secure civil liberties and political rights – will develop only when popular sovereignty is *somewhat* circumscribed, although not excessively so. This is because democratic consolidation is said to be dependent on the protection of elite interests, not their demolition. Political stability is a vital aspect of democratic consolidation – and its embedding will depend on whether political elites and their allies in the military are willing to follow constitutional rules and, more generally, accept the legitimacy of a democratic system. If they do not, democracy will be seriously endangered since authoritarian attempts to grab power would be likely, for example via military coups d'état. When their position is not threatened, elites gradually become accustomed to a democratic regime, realizing that it does not hurt as much as they initially feared, and move from grudging acceptance to full endorsement of democracy. If this happens, democracy becomes not an expedient alternative to authoritarian rule ('negative' consolidation), but the preferred political order ('positive' consolidation).

In sum, democratic consolidation initially involves ad hoc patterns of democratically orientated behaviour that eventually develop into the accepted way – both for political elites and the mass of ordinary

people – of 'doing' politics. 'Democratically legitimate' political
actors are admitted into the system according to previously established, legitimately coded procedures, and anti-democrats are politically neutralized. The system is underpinned by legal guarantees and
extensive protections for individual and group freedoms, secured by
and through the workings of an independent, impartial judiciary.
Unequivocal civilian control of the military and a competent state
bureaucracy – necessary to carry out state policies – are vital. In short,
a consolidated democracy requires:

1   generally accepted, democratically orientated political rules;
2   stable, durable, democratic institutions;
3   a wide range of state-guaranteed civil and political rights, upheld
    by the rule of law.

3.2   Democratic consolidation: political, economic and international dimensions

Chances of democratic consolidation are said to hinge on the interaction of three sets of factors:

1   *Political factors*, including colonial traditions and foundations;
    political culture and elites; legitimacy and post-authoritarian
    regimes; political society; civil society; and the form of govern-
    ment, whether parliamentary or presidential.
2   *Economic factors*, including economic growth and social welfare.
3   *The international dimension*.

Let us look at each in turn.

Political factors

Colonial traditions and foundations

Beneficial colonial legacies, it is sometimes suggested, have been
important for some countries in helping develop pro-democracy
political cultures. Rueschemeyer, Stephens and Stephens (1992)
suggest that democratic longevity in various former British colonies
– including Jamaica, Trinidad and Tobago – was facilitated by inher-

ited colonial traditions, supplying foundations on which post-colonial political elites could build democratic structures. The process was said to be facilitated by lengthy preparations for independence because they allowed sufficient time for democratic values to be inculcated by native counter-elites. However, comparative evidence suggests that such colonial experiences did not necessarily leave beneficial legacies for democracy to develop. For example, other former British colonies, including Pakistan, Sri Lanka, Burma, Ghana, Nigeria and Malaysia, experienced British colonial rule over long periods – yet none managed to retain democratic governments over time. Further evidence for the variability of colonial traditions is suggested by the fact that 'there is little reference to nineteenth century Spanish and Portuguese colonialisms in Latin America in the analysis of democratization there in the late twentieth century' (Potter et al. 1997: 267). In sum, first, the importance of the colonial experience for subsequent political development can fade over time, even when it is deemed, as in the case of British colonial rule, to be a facilitating factor for democracy. Second, lengthy preparations for democratic rule are not sufficient for democratic consolidation when other factors, such as serious ethnic or religious divisions, turn out to be more important.

Political culture and elites

As Pinkney observes, democratic consolidation depends heavily on 'rather precarious sets of delicate relationships' between, on the one hand, political elites and, on the other, between the latter and the mass of ordinary people (1993: 86). The nature of these relationships is linked to a polity's predominant political culture, a concept defined as *a set of values and beliefs within which political action is embedded and given meaning.* As Dahl notes, 'it is obvious . . . that the emergence and persistence of a democratic government among a group of people depends in some way on their beliefs' (1989: 30). A pro-democracy political culture need not exist at the outset of a democratic regime, but for democratic consolidation it is crucial. Emerging from what might be decades of authoritarian rule, polities are unlikely, initially, to have many democrats (Shin 1999; Ottemoeller 1998). How to increase their numbers?

It seems plausible that the degree to which a pro-democracy political culture evolves will be linked both to structural and agency factors. Regarding the former, the development of a pro-democracy political culture is likely to be particularly difficult to achieve if a country has serious ethnic or religious hostility, major ideological splits, or gross economic inequalities. To overcome such drawbacks would require enlightened political leadership. Several long estab-lished democracies – those in India, Mauritius, Trinidad have been noted in the literature – appeared to develop pro-democracy politi-cal cultures despite the existence of major ethnic and/or religious divisions and serious economic inequalities (Ayoade 1988; Mitra and Enskat 1999; Premdas and Ragoonath 1998). To achieve this goal, government and opposition must work together consensually, animated by a shared belief that consolidating democracy is a normatively desirable goal. Put another way, political contest must not become a zero-sum game.

Mauritius offers a good example. Since independence in 1968, 'class and ethnic loyalties [have] criss-crossed one another', helping to prevent politics becoming a zero-sum game (Pinkney 1993: 90). An intricately plural society, the country managed to build a demo-cratic consensus among rival politicians within a stable political system. Successive governments showed tolerance for political rivals in the opposition, a trend set in 1982 when Seewoosagur Ram-goolam, the founding father of independence, lost gracefully to the opposition. In addition, the adoption of a 'best loser' system ensured 'the representation of ethnic minority interests on a partially pro-portional basis in parliament' (Ayoade 1988: 113). In Trinidad, too, political elites have united across ethnic divides to resist radical chal-lenges, in particular the attempted 'Muslim coup' of 1988 (Haynes 1996c: 109–11).

Legitimacy and post-authoritarian regimes

The nature of the former authoritarian regime is sometimes thought to play an important role in the survival chances of new, post-author-itarian democracies. Linz and Stepan (1996) argue that the single most important explanatory variable in democratic transitions in Southern Europe, Latin America and Eastern Europe in the 1970s and 1980s was the degree of political repression under the authori-tarian regime. When political repression was severe – or when there was participation in war, or economic performance was persistently negative – then the legitimacy of the authoritarian government would be likely to be seriously eroded. Harsh authoritarian experiences help facilitate the signing of political and social pacts, as well as a rela-tively vigorous civil society. The democratically elected replacement regime would be widely regarded as legitimate – if for no other reason than that it was not the old, discredited one. This is known as 'inverse legitimation', that is, the new regime is validated simply because it is not the former, failed one. But inverse legitimation is unlikely to last beyond a brief honeymoon period. It must be followed by 'positive' legitimation of the post-authoritarian regime for democratic consolidation to develop.

Political society

Linz and Stepan (1996) regard a strong and independent political society as crucial for democratic consolidation. It is characterized by certain types of interaction among political actors, competing legitimately to exercise the right to control power and the state apparatus. Political society can be defined as the 'arena in which the polity specifically arranges itself for political contestation to gain control over public power and the state apparatus', notably parliament and political parties (Stepan 1988: 3).

Previous democratic experience and democratic consolidation   To consolidate democracy it is necessary to construct – or reconstruct if there has been a previous democratic experience – core political institutions: elections, electoral rules, political parties, political leadership, intraparty alliances, legislatures. Some recent democratic transitions took place after previous institutions of democracy had been demolished, while in other cases some institutions were maintained during authoritarian rule – although their functions may have been distorted. Karl (1991) argues that the second scenario should offer a better outlook for consolidation than the first, emphasizing the advantages for a country that has retained some democratic mechanisms against one that introduces them *de novo*. Some observers suggest that *only* countries that previously experienced democratic rule would be capable of democratizing now (for example, most Latin American nations had democratic regimes at some time in the past). This is because democratically relevant intermediate structures and democratic routines can crucially aid the re-emergence of previous alliances among parties and groups, as well as the return to the political scene of interest groups, unions and other important pro-democracy organizations. In addition, a prior democratic experience may encourage the mass of ordinary people to believe that, once democracy is reinstituted, then future political decisions will be broadly in accord with democratic norms. However, such a view condemns polities that have not experienced democracy to an unremittingly undemocratic future. As we shall see later, an earlier experience with democracy can help redemocratization, but it is not necessarily crucial for a democratic regime.

Political parties   The chances of democratic consolidation, Sartori (1991) argues, are bolstered when there are relatively few, ideologically unpolarized, parties. In addition, autonomous, democratically organized political parties can help to keep the personal power aspirations of political leaders in check. Morlino (1998) argues that such political parties are a crucial key to consolidation, especially when there is no pervasive legitimacy during democratic transition. He also contends that the more rapidly the party spectrum forms during transition, then the more likely eventual democratic consolidation will be. When party systems become institutionalized in this way, parties typically orient themselves towards the goal of winning elections through focused appeals to voters. But when the party structure is only slowly or indeterminately established, then citizens may respond better to personalistic appeals from populist leaders than to those of parties. This scenario tends to favour the former, who may attempt to govern without bothering to establish and develop solid institutions underpinning their rule.

The point is that institutionalizing party systems matters a great deal as they are much more likely to help sustain democracy and to promote effective governance than the alternative: amorphous party systems dominated by populist leaders. An institutionalized party system can help engender confidence in the democratic process in four main ways. First, it can help moderate and channel societal demands into an institutionalized environment of conflict resolution. For example, in both India and Costa Rica, the party system helped over time to prevent 'landed upper class[es] from using the state to repress protests' (Rueschemeyer et al. 1992: 281). Second, it can serve to lengthen the time horizons of actors because it provides electoral losers with the means periodically to mobilize resources for later rounds of political competition. Third, an effective party system can help prevent the grievances of disenchanted groups from spilling over into mass street protests, likely to antagonize elites and their military allies and to facilitate a return to authoritarian rule ('the need for strong government'). Finally, an effective party system, linked to a capable state, can be important in helping imbue the mass of ordinary people with the idea that the political system is democratically accountable.

Civil society

It is often suggested that a robust civil society is important for democracy and democratic consolidation. The term 'civil society' crept quietly and largely unexamined into the literature on democracy in the 1980s, influencing the discourses of many leaders of movements for political reform. While there are many conceptions of civil society and its relationship with the state, Stepan's (1988) is useful. He defines civil society as the arena where social groups and movements – including community associations, women's groups, religious bodies and various professional organizations (lawyers, journalists, trade unions, entrepreneurs and so on) – express themselves and seek to advance their interests vis-à-vis the state, challenging the latter's tendency to seek ever greater amounts of power. In short, according to Stepan, civil society, comprising organizations which both limit *and* legitimate state power, functions as the citizen's curb on the power of the state and its tendency to try to dominate. When institutions and supporting bodies comprising civil society are strong enough to keep the state within substantive and procedural confinement, then the chances of democratic consolidation should be enhanced. Strong civil societies nearly always stem from strong societies. Risse-Kappen argues that ' "strong societies" are characterized by a comparative lack of ideological and class cleavages, by rather "politicized" civil societies which can be easily mobilized for political causes, and by centralized social organizations such as business, labor or churches' (1995: 22). On the other hand, when civil society organizations are collectively weak it will be easy for the state to incarcerate, coopt or buy off troublesome leaders and activist opponents. Under such circumstances, the state will 'shape, define, create or suppress civil society and popular reactions thereto' (Manor 1991: 5).

In sum, the political effectiveness of civil society is linked to:

1   its *cohesiveness*, a factor that depends on the nature and extent of extant class, ideological, ethnic and/or religious divisions;
2   *a country's level of economic development*: it is suggested that, *ceteris paribus*, the more modernized a country, then the more likely it is to have a strong civil society;
3   *how long a country has been independent*: this is said to be important because it takes time to build up the power and organizational capacity of civil society. For example, civil societies tend to

be more robust in Latin America than in Africa. States in the former region tend to be comparatively more modernized, richer and less societally polarized than in the latter.

Presidential and parliamentary government

The relative effectiveness of presidential and parliamentary forms of government is also central to the debate about democratic consolidation and how to achieve it. While Mainwaring (1999) argues that presidentialism may offer advantages for democratic consolidation, Przeworski, Alvarez, Cheibib and Limongi (1996) aver that representative institutions of the parliamentary type are often better for democratic continuity. In a multiparty regime, a president typically relies on an interparty coalition for support, yet under presidentialism such coalitions are very often fragile and transitory. This makes it important that appropriate, robust political institutions are in place. Presidentialism can lead to legislative paralysis when a legislature is controlled by a majority hostile to the president but not numerically dominant to the point of being able systematically to overcome presidential vetoes. The problem is compounded if the party system is fragmented, exacerbating the executive–legislative deadlock. Stepan and Skach, drawing on a wide variety of comparative data, suggest that, *ceteris paribus*, parliamentarianism provides an institutional framework more conducive to democratic consolidation than presidentialism. This is because the former embodies a greater propensity for governments to have parliamentary majorities to implement their programmes and a 'greater tendency to provide long party-government careers, which add loyalty and experience to political society' (1993: 22).

In sum, democratic consolidation is likely to be encouraged: (1) when party systems are broadly based, organized along programmatic rather than personalistic or narrowly sectional lines; and (2) *ceteris paribus*, and according to some views, by parliamentary, rather than presidential, political systems, although there is no clear evidence either way. Much depends, almost regardless of what system is in operation, on the qualities of those at the apex of the political system and their commitment to democratic politics and accountability.

Conclusion

Various political factors are seen as important for democratic consolidation. They include:

1 potentially beneficial colonial legacies providing viable foundations for post-colonial democratization;
2 a pro-democracy political culture informing the political behaviour of both elites and the mass of ordinary people;
3 the legitimacy of post-authoritarian regimes and what they can do to bolster it;
4 forms of political and civil societies conducive to democracy;
5 the form of government.

Economic factors

The literature suggests that political factors intimately interact with economic factors in the context of democratic consolidation. Two important economic factors are often identified:

1 sustained economic growth, with the benefits reasonably equitably spread among citizens;
2 an institutionalized system of social welfare encompassing most citizens.

Sustained economic growth

For Przeworski (1991), a country's wealth is of great importance to democratic consolidation. Economic growth at stable and moderate levels of inflation is, he believes, a key criterion in sustaining democratic regimes over time. Once a democratic regime is established, then the chances of democratic consolidation are likely to be greater if a country is relatively rich because wealth and economic growth can decisively ease the embedding of democratic institutions. But the level of *current* wealth is not crucial: if poor countries succeed in generating reasonable levels of economic growth and economic prosperity and, for most citizens, there is an overall developmental benefit, then democracies may survive in even very poor countries. If economic expansion helps reduce societal conflicts resulting from inequality or other cleavages, and serves to diminish any tendency to political alienation, polarization and destabilizing social violence, then democratic consolidation is plausible. On the other hand, economic decline poses a severe threat to democratic sustainability: a prolonged governmental failure to address effectively challenges of growth and equity will be likely to undermine the depth and stability of societal support and perhaps encourage authoritarian alternatives. In sum, sustained economic growth and development, coupled with only moderate price inflation and growing, relatively widely spread economic prosperity can be important to chances of democratic consolidation.

The classic starting point for the link between economic growth and democracy was the early work of Seymour Martin Lipset (1963). Using contemporary data he surveyed selected (democratic) Western and (at the time, authoritarian) Latin American countries. He found that in the former there were consistently higher mean levels of socioeconomic development than among the latter. Thus Lipset's famous dictum: 'the more well-to-do a nation, the greater the chances that it will sustain democracy.' However, Lipset established a correlation between prosperity and democracy; he did *not* propose that democracy is the *inevitable* result of a certain level of socioeconomic development. In fact, it is empirically easy to see that there is no *inevitable* connection between the level of economic development and the degree of democracy. If this *was* a rule of general applicability, how would economically impoverished India's half century of democracy be explained, or recent shifts to democracy in poor countries like Ghana or Nepal? As table 3.1 shows, some of the world's poorest countries – with GNP per capita of less than $1,000 a year in 1998 – are currently democracies. Other countries, such as Turkey, have democratically elected governments and a relatively low per capita GNP (Turkey's was $3,160 in 1998), whereas oil-rich Gulf states, such as the United Arab Emirates ($19,720) and Saudi Arabia ($6,790) have undemocratic political systems. In sum, there is no 'simple relationship between socio-economic modernization and the development of liberal democracy' (Kiloh 1997a: 387).

Social welfare

When a privileged elite minority is perceived to consume an inappropriate proportion of available resources then popular satisfaction with democracy may fail to develop. To avert this, it may help if a democratically elected government presides over sustained economic growth and convinces the mass of people that it is shared with *relative* equity. Przeworski et al.'s (1996) comprehensive survey of evidence – covering 1950–90 – indicates that the chances of democratic survival, and ultimately consolidation, increase when a government: (1) manages to develop its country's economy in a sustained fashion; and (2) gradually, yet consistently, manages to reduce socioeconomic inequalities via effective welfare policies.

Table 3.1 Poor countries and democratic status

	Political rights	Civil liberties	Annual growth of GNP per capita, 1985–95	GNP per capita ($)	Human development index (HDI) 1998	Freedom rating 1998
Malawi	2	3	−0.7	170	0.334	Free
Mali	2	2	0.8	250	0.226	Free
Mongolia	2	3	−3.8	310	0.593	Free
Sao Tomé e Principe	1	2	−2.1	350	0.563	Free
Benin	2	2	−0.3	370	0.378	Free
Bolivia	2	3	1.8	800	0.593	Free
Cape Verde	1	2	n.a.	960	0.591	Free

High human development > 0.8; medium > 0.5; low > 0.1.
Source: Karatnycky 1999; World Bank 1997.

Linz and Stepan (1996) argue that increasing welfare expenditures played a central role from the mid-1970s in the process of democratic consolidation in Spain, Portugal and Greece. Their governments increased tax revenues and these were used in part to expand social policies and enhance societal welfare. Przeworski (1986) claims that the maintenance of an adequate system of public assistance has a positive influence on consolidation since it both reduces the inequalities among different social groups (a factor said to promote democratic collapse), and can help curb social unrest. However, many recent democratic transitions in Latin America, Asia and Africa were galvanized by economic crisis. It was often difficult under circumstances of societally painful economic reforms to introduce or maintain effective social policies to protect those whose subsistence was threatened.

Evidence for the political efficacy of sustained policies to reduce economic inequality come from India and Botswana. India, a democracy for more than 50 years, is said to have certain complex conditions facilitating the survival of 'the institutional legacy of post-colonial democracy' (Rueschemeyer et al. 1992: 24–5). Mitra suggests that of particular importance in helping maintain support for the democratic system was the 'steady and substantial improvements in the physical quality of life' for most Indians (1992: 10–11). India's example suggests that the chances of democratic consolidation are enhanced when there is a conscious attempt to share out national wealth, with a concern for ameliorating the plight of the poor via welfare and taxation policies. In addition, in Botswana, a rare example of an African consolidated democracy, 'the egalitarian impact of government expenditure [was] a means of consolidating support for the political system' (Thomas 1994: 76).

In sum, chances of democratic consolidation are said to be linked to: (1) sustained economic growth, relatively equitably spread, even if it starts from a low base; and (2) governmental focus, via welfare policies, to ameliorate the plight of the poor and underprivileged.

The international dimension

To what extent is democratic consolidation influenced by extraneous actors and factors? Democratization is facilitated when no foreign power hostile to this development interferes in the political life of a country with the intention of subverting the political system. White-head (1993) argues that in recent democratization attempts the influence of international actors has always been secondary to domestic factors. Huntington (1991) suggests that foreign actors may hasten or retard – but not fundamentally influence – democratic outcomes. However, he also notes that foreign encouragement to democratize can actually hinder overall chances of democratic consolidation. This is because such encouragement can, on the one hand, lead to democratization *before* countries reach a suitable economic and social level, while, on the other hand, it could deter democratization in countries where chances of democratization seem more plausible. Generally, international support for democratization grew in the 1980s and 1990s, but its impact was often unclear (Carothers 1999).

The United States has long been a key international actor: both the government and various state-linked bodies, such as the National Endowment for Democracy, have actively supported democratization. Such a development is not new: in the 1950s newly democratic governments, for example those in Costa Rica, Venezuela and Colombia, received support from the US for democratization. More recently, the evolution of US foreign policy – from President Carter's human rights policy in the late 1970s, through President Reagan's promotion of democracy as a counter to perceived communist expansionism in the 1980s, to President Clinton's less ideologically linked support for democracy in the 1990s – supported democratically elected governments.

Since the late 1980s the US government has provided more than $700 million to over a hundred countries to aid democratization (Carothers 1999). Carothers argues that such assistance was focused according to 'a standard democracy template', involving financial support to underpin the electoral process and democratic structures: constitutions, political parties, state institutions, the rule of law, legislatures, local government structures, better civil–military relations, and civil society organizations. Leftwich points out that it takes more than money to develop democracy, because it is not easy to create and firmly establish concrete manifestations of what he calls 'good governance'. Such an outcome is 'not simply available on order', but requires 'a particular kind of politics' . . . 'to institute and sustain it' (1993: 612). This raises an important issue: external funding for democracy will be insufficient to achieve its aims if target regimes are content to 'acquire democratic legitimacy internationally *without substantially changing their mode of operation*' (Lawson 1999: 23, emphasis added). Superficial democratization is encouraged when external actors limit their scrutiny of the democratic process to elections alone; often, critics argue, the international observation of elections seemed to be the only meaningful test for judging a shift from authoritarianism to democracy. However, when elections are complete and the attention of the corpus of international observers shifts, then 'democracy' may be little more than rhetorically achieved, as elite hegemony resurfaces with a narrow base of political systems and 'authoritarian clientelism and coercion' (Karl 1995: 74).

In sum, external actors, especially those in possession of large financial resources to encourage democracy, like the US government, are often important at the transition stage of democratization but less central to efforts to institutionalize and sustain democracy. This underlines how democratic consolidation is always a long-term project, dependent for success on an array of domestic, especially political and economic, developments, including the spread of a pro-democracy political culture, the building of democratically-accountable institutions, and sustained economic growth and general welfare provision. The inference is that, especially in the early stages, democratic consolidation is fraught with obstacles, constantly threatened with reversal.

3.3   Theoretical perspectives and hypotheses on democratic consolidation

Having surveyed a variety of political, economic and external factors thought in the literature to be important to chances of democratic consolidation, we are now in a position to propose a number of hypotheses that stem from the analysis. We can take them forward

into the empirical chapters that follow to assess the chances of democratic consolidation in a selection of individual country case studies.
It is important to note that, while all are drawn from the same list,
not all hypotheses have universal validity. For example, some are
more central to Latin American than to African or Asian countries.

- *The national political culture must value democracy over authoritarianism* The likelihood of this developing is linked both to
  structural and agency factors.
- *The post-authoritarian regime will need to establish its own
  legitimacy* Legitimacy will be enhanced, at least in the short
  term, by the degree of political repression under the preceding
  authoritarian regime. But over time, this will fade unless the
  new democratic regime takes necessary steps to build its own
  legitimacy.
- *The institutionalization of a strong and sufficiently representative
  political system is required to ensure broad political participation
  by channelling and regulating societal demands* Important
  here is a strong and cohesive party system, without 'excessive'
  ideological polarization, as well as a robust, unfragmented civil
  society.
- *The presence of either a presidential or a parliamentary regime
  is not significant for democratic consolidation* Much seems to
  depend on the individuals at the apex of the political system and
  their willingness to rule within agreed democratic parameters.
- *Sustained economic growth and a developed welfare system are
  crucial* These conditions help to enlarge the basis of popular
  support for a democratic regime, while their absence will be likely
  to undermine it.
- *Various external factors, including diplomatic pressures, economic reform attempts and aid programmes, cannot determine
  democratic consolidation on their own* These can be important,
  especially at the commencement of democratic consolidation but
  are rarely, if ever, fundamental in the longer term.

4
Latin America

4.1 Introduction

The background to the recent regional wave of democratization was the widespread assumption of power by military rulers in most Latin American countries in the 1960s and 1970s, which took on a particular form, known as bureaucratic authoritarianism. While specific characteristics of military rule differed from country to country, what they all had in common was a political scene where civil and political societies were comprehensively repressed. Prior to the regional wave of democracy, regime legitimacy had plummeted in many of these countries, the consequence of political repression and poor economic performance. Encouraged in many cases by the government of the United States and pressurized by rejuvenated civil and political societies, democratically elected leaders came to power proclaiming a willingness to try to make democracy work.

Regional democratic transitions in Latin America in the 1980s and 1990s led to a situation whereby, in 2000, all 35 members of the Organization of American States, except Cuba, were run by popularly elected leaders. In mid-2000, the Mexican presidential elections brought to an end 71 years of rule by the Institutional Revolutionary Party (PRI), confirming what appeared to be a clear trend towards more democracy and pluralism in Latin America. On the other hand, concerted allegations of fraud in the June 2000 presidential poll in Peru, coup attempts in Ecuador and Paraguay, the declaration of martial law to quell a popular uprising in Bolivia, and Colombia's undeclared civil war suggested that, in some cases, progress towards democratization and stability was highly problematic.

In this chapter, we examine, first, general regional factors relating to democratic consolidation. This will enable us to put the case studies into a theoretical perspective. Second, we turn attention to two politically interesting countries – Mexico and Venezuela. Neither had military governments prior to the recent round of democratization when most of their regional neighbours did. Instead, Venezuela was one of the few regional countries to retain a democratic system over time, while Mexico had a de facto one-party system for seven decades (1929–2000) under the domination of the Institutional Revolutionary Party, until a non-PRI candidate won the presidential elections in mid-2000. The main question relating to Mexico concerns the comparative importance of structural and contingent factors in accounting for the country's recent political revolution. A further question arises as to the ability of the new president, Vicente Fox, an avowed democrat strongly encouraged by the US to democratize and liberalize the economy as part of the continuing development of the regional economic grouping, NAFTA, to overcome the entrenched anti-democratic structural characteristics of Mexico's political system.

Unlike Mexico, Venezuela has been a democracy for over four decades, since 1958. For this reason it is a regional rarity which, many observers believed, had successfully managed to consolidate its democratic system. However, it became increasingly clear over time that its efficacy was, in fact, problematic: power was firmly in the hands of two main political parties, AD and COPEI, which had embedded a cosy system of power rotation which effectively denied other parties the possibility of achieving power. However, the election of a former military officer and anti-system politician, Hugo Chavez, as president in December 1998 led to fundamental political changes. Enjoying much popular support, especially among the poor, Chavez pledged that he would fundamentally reform Venezuela's political and economic system to the benefit of the less privileged. The issue here is the ability or willingness of Chavez to shift those entrenched structural characteristics of the country's political system which had ensured that power remained in the same hands for decades. In other words, to use the terminology adopted in this book, would the contingent factor of Chavez be able to overcome inherited structural inhibitions?

4.2 Structural impediments to democracy in Latin America

Three main structural impediments to democratic sustainability in Latin America are noted in the literature:

- *Lack of governmental legitimacy and accountability*   Intent on pursuing the interests of civilian and military elites, most regional governments have ruled with scant concern for the interests of ordinary people.
- *The nature of agrarian class relations*   Large-scale landowners are an important constituency among civilian elites in many Latin American countries. They have often used their influence with governments to help resist significant land reforms. The outcome was huge numbers of economically impoverished and politically impotent landless rural labourers.
- *The political relationship between state and military power*   In many regional countries, a close relationship developed between civilian and military elites from the days of regional colonial independence in the early nineteenth century. The armed forces were seen as *the* main defenders of the state from external (foreign governments) and internal (class-based political actors) attack.

The consequence of these structural factors is that regional political systems are said to be rooted in a 'culture[s] of repression and passivity that is antithetical to democratic citizenship' (Karl 1995: 79). That is, a complex of anti-democratic structures are said generally to inhibit chances of democracy and democratic consolidation in the region.

To what extent have Latin American countries been able to reconcile a desire for democracy with their own largely undemocratic histories? Latin America's post-transition outcomes reflect both continuity and discontinuity with the past. *Continuity* is reflected in: (1) unrepresentative, elite dominated political systems; (2) a continuing significant political role for the military in many countries; (3) gross inequalities between haves and have nots; and (4) a lack of liberal freedoms for ordinary people. *Discontinuity* is reflected in: (1) strong external pressure, especially from the United States government, for sustained economic and political reforms; and (2) emergence of a certain kind of strongly reformist leaders – for example, Mexico's

Table 4.1 Latin America's new democracies, 1989–1999

	Political rights (PR)		Civil liberties (CL)		PR + CL average	PR + CL average	Freedom rating
	1988–9	1998–9	1988–9	1998–9	1988–9	1998–9	1998–9
Uruguay	2	1	2	2	2	1.5	Free
Bolivia	2	1	3	3	2.5	2	Free
Chile	5	3	4	2	4.5	2.5	Free
Dominican Rep.	1	2	3	3	2	2.5	Free
Ecuador	2	2	3	3	2.5	2.5	Free
El Salvador	3	2	3	3	3	2.5	Free
Nicaragua	5	2	4	3	4.5	2.5	Free
Panama	6	2	5	3	5.5	2.5	Free
Argentina	2	3	1	3	1.5	3	Partly free
Honduras	2	3	2	3	2	3	Partly free
Brazil	2	3	3	4	2.5	3.5	Partly free
Guatemala	3	3	3	4	3	3.5	Partly free
Paraguay	6	4	6	3	6	3.5	Partly free
Peru	2	5	3	4	2.5	4.5	Partly free
Haiti	7	5	5	5	6	5	Partly free

Source: 'Annual survey of Freedom country scores, 1972–73 to 1998–99',
http://www.freedomhouse.org/survey99/method/

Vicente Fox and Hugo Chavez of Venezuela – who achieved power on a platform of systemic improvement.

Table 4.1 sums up the democratic position of 15 new democracies in Latin America at the end of the 1990s. Freedom House judged eight to be 'free', with six at the interface level of 2.5 between 'free' and 'partly free'; seven were categorized as 'partly free'. Overall, regional democratic trends were unclear: six 'free' countries – Uruguay, Bolivia, Chile, El Salvador, Nicaragua, Panama – saw an improvement in the position of the combination of political rights and civil liberties in the 1990s, and one – the Dominican Republic – saw a decline. On the other hand, five 'partly free' countries – Argentina, Honduras, Brazil, Guatemala, Peru – saw a *reduction* in the combined level of political rights and civil liberties, and two – Paraguay and Haiti – registered improvements.

Despite the lack of clear regional democratic trends, some observers believe there is evidence of progress. What is happening is said to be more than just another event in the traditional cycle of alternations between democracy and authoritarianism: a new historical stage characterized by regular, free and fair elections, broaden-

Table 4.2 Percentages of those voting in elections between 1970 and 1997 in new Latin American democracies

	For president						For parliament					
	% voting			% spoilt			% voting			% spoilt		
Uruguay	88	93	93	–	–	–	96	97	95	5	4	3
Chile	82	87	–	4	3	2	82	87	–	1	5	6
Argentina	80	83	76	2	–	4	80	78	89	4	7	7
Bolivia	51	65	59	12	13	10	62	50	51	–	5	10
Panama	70	56	57	–	4	12	70	53	–	–	–	4
Paraguay	33	56	64	1	1	–	45	54	64	4	2	1
Brazil	77	80	–	19	6	–	77	77	70	6	5	4
Dominican Rep.	61	63	49	1	2	–	62	31	46	2	–	2
El Salvador	42	48	40	4	7	6	82	51	44	–	–	9
Honduras	64	76	78	1	3	4	64	76	78	4	3	4
Nicaragua	76	78	74	5	6	6	76	73	74	5	6	7
Ecuador	72	68	71	11	16	–	68	66	65	22	16	17
Guatemala	26	33	32	4	6	5	15	41	50	12	14	13
Peru	66	66	65	18	10	13	58	57	65	44	21	12
Haiti	29	54	36	13	–	–	33	53	–	–	–	–

Proportion of the voting age population voting in new Latin American democracies in the last two, or if held, last three, elections, with the most recent elections listed first; percentages are rounded up or down.
Source: IDEA 1998.

ing electoral participation, respect of oppositional rights, enhanced civil liberties and media freedoms. In sum, this is said to amount to gradual, yet emphatic, democratization, to the extent that future would-be authoritarians would find it very hard to do away with the democratic gains (Remmer 1993; Whitehead 1993; Wiarda and Kline 1996; Munck 1997).

The popularity of democracy is said to be reflected in the recent relatively high voting turnouts (IDEA 1998). Table 4.2 shows that percentages of those voting in recent parliamentary and presidential elections in Latin America were, typically, high or higher than in many Western consolidated democracies: in the former, voting turnouts of 50–70 per cent were commonplace, while in the latter, notably the United States, only about 50 per cent of voters have bothered to vote in recent presidential elections.

Democracy pessimists are less convinced that there is a *genuinely* democratic trend in the region. For Diamond, 'Latin America has not made significant net progress toward greater democracy' (1996: 61).

This is because, Philip (1999) argues, power has remained firmly in the hands of populist presidents, often men with little time for democratic institutions. Typically, they have risen to political prominence by skilful manipulation of the media – rather than through leadership of strong, representative parties. This point underlines that, generally speaking, political institutions have remained underdeveloped in Latin America, despite the recent round of democratization. Political competition is still in most cases controlled and delimited by privileged minorities. O'Donnell points to the existence of what he calls 'semi-democratic political systems' – in our terminology, limited democracies. Such polities are found in Argentina, Chile, Bolivia, Brazil, Ecuador, Nicaragua, Panama, Peru and Uruguay. They are said to be 'informally institutionalized' polyarchies, with a mix of – both 'formal electoral' and 'informal particularistic' – political institutions (1996: 35). Concerned that such polities would find it difficult to retain citizens' confidence, Huber, Rueschemeyer and Stephens suggest that their political limitations would result in a 'rapid decline in popular faith in the efficacy of democracy' in the context of 'a vicious cycle of inegalitarian policies and growing poverty and social problems, such as marginalisation and crime' (1997: 323–4). In several regional countries – Bolivia, Ecuador, Peru, Haiti, Brazil, Guatemala – there were relatively high (greater than 10 per cent) proportions of spoilt ballot papers in recent elections, suggesting some popular dissatisfaction with the political status quo.

In sum, for the democracy pessimists, while flagrantly authoritarian rule abated, limited democracies typically followed. They reflected the region's anti-democratic political cultures, of personalism and successful lawlessness (grabbing power via coup d'état), which, combined with economic strictures – often linked to 'Washington consensus' policies – have in many cases delivered clearly limited democracies. Put another way, despite the introduction of democratic institutions, continuing weaknesses in the rule of law and the lack of professionalisation of governments has resulted in political systems not necessarily in transition to anything at all.

4.3 Democratic consolidation in Latin America

Having identified various factors linked to democratic consolidation in chapter 3, we will now examine the importance for democratic outcomes in Latin America of the following issues:

- political culture and regime legitimacy;
- political participation and institutions;
- economic and international factors.

The first two sets of factors – political culture and regime legitimacy, and political participation and institutions – will have primarily reflected the importance of structural characteristics, while the latter – economic and international factors – will often have been informed by contingent factors. After discussing the regional importance of these issues, we will be in a position to focus on the case studies in the second half of the chapter.

Political culture and regime legitimacy

Striving to shake off the legacy of colonial rule in the early 1800s, many post-colonial republics adopted constitutional orders based on the nearly contemporaneous American Constitution. The latter prescribed a federal structure, an elected president and Congress, and an independent judiciary. This was testimony to the perceived importance of liberal thinking within at least one part of the political class in Latin America. To such people, the United States (another new nation at the time) was *the* role model for *all* new, modern nation-states. However, over time, outcomes were often quite different in Latin America: the interests of unelected figures – typically large-scale landowners and the military – took clear precedence over those of other groups and classes.

Over time, a generic regional political culture emerged, antithetical to democracy. This was bolstered by the fact that most Latin American countries experienced long periods of rule by *caudillos* (personalist dictators) and/or military governments which served to strengthen elite power. Elites often claimed that democracy was inimical for the well-being of the nation and, as a result, the mass of the people were to be excluded from political decision-making. Groups expressing contrary conceptions of the public good and claiming to embody it, such as leftist guerrillas, were strongly resisted by the armed forces, the proclaimed defenders of national independence and guarantors of national well-being. Under such circumstances, it was hardly surprising that non-elite civilians often found it difficult to express their political preferences. The result was that, until recently, civil society was underdeveloped in many regional countries.

Political participation and institutions

It is suggested that one of the most important structural characteristics relating to democratic sustainability is whether a country has past experience of democracy. Some regional countries, such as Chile and Uruguay, have a long – albeit intermittent – history of democratic rule, interrupted by periodic military government, which suggests that democratic institutions can be relatively easily resurrected. The point is that while institutions may be suspended or immobilized by authoritarian regimes, their outlines can reappear when the latter exit; and their characters are likely to have an important bearing on chances of democratic consolidation. Put another way, political *institutions* – for example, parties, legislatures, presidencies – can be created or destroyed at will but political 'structures' – stable, recurring patterns of behaviour – can survive authoritarian rule.

Political society

A strong, independent political society is often seen as crucial for chances of democratic consolidation as it facilitates interaction among political actors competing legitimately to exercise the right to control power and the state apparatus. The perceived positive role of an institutionalized party system in democratic consolidation was outlined in chapter 3. It was noted then that countries with a past history of democracy, during which political parties managed to put down deep societal roots, are best placed to establish or re-establish a viable party system after authoritarian rule. We also saw that a strong and cohesive party system is a fundamental component of democratic sustainability. A weakly institutionalized, fragmented party system makes that task impossible to accomplish. In the latter scenario, voters tend to respond to personalistic appeals from populist leaders – more concerned with staying in power than with developing democratic institutions, including political parties. As we shall see, the characteristics of their party systems were of great importance in explaining democratization or its lack in our case studies, Mexico and Venezuela.

Civil society

Linked to urbanization and industrialization, many regional civil societies gradually developed a greater coherence and sense of purpose. Focusing on the desirability of democracy and economic reforms, and relatively undivided by ethnic and/or religious polarization, regional civil society organizations, including politically active working classes and well-organized trade unions, gained in importance in many countries in the region. More generally, industrialization and urbanization, together with swift population growth, combined to generate strong societal demands for increased social spending and a greater say in political outcomes. But when such demands became too vociferous, as in the 1960s and 1970s, ruling elites, in tandem with the military, proceeded to abolish democracy. When it was reinstated throughout the region in the 1980s civil societies were often important forces in encouraging the withdrawal of military rule. The absence of military rule – for example, in Mexico and Venezuela – did not mean that governments were necessarily more responsive to societal demands expressed through civil society organizations. As we shall see, the structural characteristics of power in both countries were closely linked to the ability of state/party to undermine civil society actors – either by incorporation or repression.

Presidential and parliamentary systems of government

We noted in chapter 3 that a country with representative, parliamentary-type institutions is often thought to have a better chance of democratic consolidation than those with unrepresentative presidential systems. This is because presidentialism is often associated with legislative paralysis, for example when a legislature, controlled by a majority hostile to the president, is nevertheless too divided among many parties to overcome presidential vetoes. A second problem with presidentialism is that under-used state institutions can become both atrophied and corrupt. Third, the independence of courts is crucial – especially in the absence of strong, stable party systems and legislatures willing and able to take on the president and form a counterweight to his power. Lievesley (1999) notes that the trend has been towards the growing marginalization of the courts in some regional countries under presidential forms of government. Some presidents, such as Alberto Fujimori in Peru and Hugo Chavez in Venezuela, sought brazenly to override elected legislatures, courts, judges and other institutions in their attempts to reform their polities (Philip 1999). Finally, Nagle and Mahr point out that support from the armed forces can help bolster the position of an elected president to the extent that he or she can be 'dependent on the good will of the military to back even more concentration of power', encouraging the president to act as an autocrat, 'via "state of siege" or "state of emergency" declarations' (1999: 248). For example, the 'anti-system', former military man Hugo Chavez won power via the ballot box in Venezuela in the election of December 1998 and proceeded to build his own personal power, supported by the military.

The main point to note is that the institution of president in Latin America tends to be synonymous with unrepresentative political systems. What might be done to control excesses of presidential power? Observers have noted the difficulties in trying fundamentally to reform one of the region's most enduring political institutions: the 'strong' president. Nohlen (1992) argues that the presidential tradition in most Latin American countries is simply too strongly anchored to be abandoned and, as a consequence, the only realistic course of reform is to stick with the existing system, attempting to reform it via pressure from political and civil society. But not all regional countries have the requisite structural characteristics – including various cultural and developmental factors – which, currently, emphatically support democratic political mechanisms. Consequently, it seems unrealistic to put too much emphasis on the independent role of political institutions when there is no clear indication that newly democratized institutions would be able to overcome traditionally undemocratic ways of 'doing' politics. Regional political systems still generally lack what many would see as the essence of democratic politics: adaptability, complexity, autonomy and coherence, in short, the competitive pluralism capable of constraining government power through peaceful means. It is doubtful to what extent the latest batch of elected Latin American presidents accepts the political wisdom of democratizing their polities – if for no other reason than that it might well result in an unacceptable loss of personal power. In a comment about Peru, but one that could be applied to most contemporary Latin American countries, de Soto and Orsini aver that 'the only element of democracy in Peru today is the electoral process, which gives Peruvians the privilege of choosing a dictator every five years' (quoted in Wiarda and Kline 1996: 59).

In sum, *nouveau presidentialismo*, while ostensibly utilizing the procedures of polyarchy, often in practice reinforces a huge concentration of power in the figure of the chief executive. On the other hand, we should note recent regional challenges to what was perceived as inappropriate or excessive use of presidential power. Brazil's Congress and courts removed an elected president, Fernando Collor de Mello, from office for corruption in the early 1990s. But the fact that Brazilians then voted to continue a strongly presidential form of government – over other suggested models – made it likely that it was

primarily Collor himself, not the institution of the 'strong' president
per se, which many Brazilians saw as the problem.

Economic and international factors

Demands for democracy in Latin America were frequently linked to
economic problems and popular pro-democracy movements typically
built support partly as a result of economic malaise. When authoritarian governments were replaced by democratically elected alternatives the issue was the extent to which the new regimes would be able
or willing to alter the inherited structural economic characteristics of
their polities in line with popular demands.

The literature suggests that a country's chances of democratizing
and of sustaining democracy are linked to increasing national prosperity and a relatively equitable distribution of the fruits of growth.
As O'Donnell puts it, the continued appeal of democracy is likely to
'depend . . . in part on [its] capacity to be translated into concrete
meanings for the majority of the population' (1992: 21). This is
because economic expansion 'should' reduce the conflicts arising as
a result of inequality or other social cleavages and lessen the likelihood of 'excessive' political alienation, societal polarization and
destabilizing social violence. Cammack notes that the political and
economic structures of countries in Latin America are rooted in its
peripheral capitalism and less than central position in the world economic system (1994: 186). Most regional polities do not have the
resources to provide steady material gains to all citizens and, as a
result, struggle to bring all the citizens into the political mainstream.
Some people prefer not to vote, or they may join anti-system guerrilla movements.

According to many observers, neoliberal economic policies introduced in the 1980s did not enable Latin America to transcend its traditionally peripheral and dependent status in the global economic
order or to provide more social justice and income equity for most
of its people. But at this point contingency must be taken into account
for an understanding of regional democratic outcomes. Encouraged
by the United States government, virtually all Latin American countries sought to liberalize their debt-ridden and statist economies in
the 1980s and 1990s under the direction of the International Monetary Fund and the World Bank. The drive to construct 'Washington
consensus' policies – that is, to build a global trading system in the
free market image of the US, with appropriate political and economic
structures – was of considerable importance to political outcomes in

Latin America. In order to raise new capital and avoid debt defaults, Latin American governments, encouraged by the US government, engaged in successive rounds of economic marketization and privatization. Regimes sold off state-owned enterprises and, in many cases, drastically curtailed social spending on education, health care, public transport and subsidies for basic consumer goods. The strategy hurt the poor most, leading to yet greater social inequalities and depriving more of those at the bottom of the pile of the chance to develop the skills most needed for gaining access to the opportunities of the newly marketized economies. But it is an ill wind that blows no one any good: economic liberalization and selling off state-owned assets was highly beneficial both to incoming foreign capital and to local elites. In the 1980s, in various regional countries, including Brazil and Mexico, privatization, carried out by the reform-minded presidents Fernando Collor de Mello and Carlos Salinas de Gortari, enabled those within the old party-state power axis suddenly to expand their already considerable wealth.

In sum, US encouragement to regional governments to introduce reforms often dovetailed with popular desires for change. However, in terms of generating broad-based prosperity and enhanced welfare, 'Washington consensus' measures, while not necessarily worse than extant statist-nationalist alternatives, enjoyed at best only patchy success. Rising levels of societal inequality and very unequal opportunity structures in the newly liberalized and privatized economies in Latin America generally during the 1990s (Buxton and Phillips 1999) raised a serious question about the long-term stability of the region's new democracies, since a high level of social polarization is surely inimical to democratic sustainability. The quandary for regional rulers was clear: while a democratic political system should allow for the articulation of popular demands for economic justice, in order to get economic recovery programmes to work and to qualify for foreign aid, loans and investment, such demands must be suppressed in pursuit of economic growth. As Castañeda put it: 'a necessary condition for equity in Latin America appears to be democratic rule, but democracy seems incompatible with growth under actually existing circumstances' (1994: 398).

Conclusions

In terms of the hypotheses relating to democratic consolidation suggested at the end of chapter 3, how was Latin America placed at the end of the 1990s? In many countries, the legacy of transition, elite pacts, served to deliver (only) limited democracies. National political cultures in the region rarely seemed emphatically pro-democracy, being the result of decades of authoritarian rule by civilian *caudillos* and military personnel, while party systems were only patchily institutionalized and representative. Civil societies had become more robust in pressing for reforms but there was no guarantee that they would not fragment under democracy.

Turning to economic growth and prosperity, the region's recent experiences were that economic reform programmes hit the poor the hardest, while often enhancing the position of the wealthy. The democratic consolidation literature would anticipate that this would lead to a drop in support for democracy among those who did not benefit economically. Finally, the impact of external factors – especially Washington consensus policies – was a contingent factor which, at least theoretically, could encourage political leaders to take the democracy road. In sum, the factors having an impact on democratic outcomes in Latin America turn out to include both structural and contingent issues.

We turn next to the chapter's case studies – Mexico and Venezuela – in order to see the impact of structured contingency on recent political outcomes in particular countries. What lessons do their experiences offer us regarding democratic consolidation?

4.4   Case studies: Mexico and Venezuela

Neither Mexico nor Venezuela are 'typical' regional countries, as both avoided military governments in recent years. For decades until 2000, Mexico had a de facto one-party system, while Venezuela was a regional rarity – a long-term democracy, albeit with characteristics which led observers to question how democratic it actually was (Lievesley 1999).

Each has distinctive structural and contingency characteristics. While Mexico had a one-party state for seven decades from the 1920s, constructed on the proceeds of oil sales, a gradual process of democratization started in the late 1970s. This culminated in the election of an opposition candidate in the presidential elections of mid-2000. As well as the presidency, the previously hegemonic party, the Institutional Revolutionary Party (PRI), also lost control of big cities and various regions of the country at this time. The interesting question is whether these changes imply a diminution of the power of structural factors to determine political outcomes and, if so, what kind of democracy might the new president seek to develop? In other words, would the new president, Vicente Fox, an apparently strong supporter of democracy, be able to overcome the entrenched anti-democratic structural characteristics of Mexico's political system? Could contingency outweigh structure in defining political outcomes?

Like Mexico, Venezuela is a major oil producer; unlike Mexico, Venezuela has been a democracy since the late 1950s. However, over time, the quality of its democracy was increasingly questioned (Buxton 1999). The regime of President Hugo Chavez, elected in December 1998, introduced a different form of democracy which clearly bore the imprint of Chavez himself: he would wield much personal power – not for personal aggrandizement, he claimed, but in order to redress a democratic imbalance between the classes. This proclaimed political revolution reflected the importance of agency in determining political outcomes in Venezuela.

—

Mexico

Regionally, Mexico is triply unusual: (1) its political system is a presidential/party system; (2) the military has traditionally had little political clout; and (3) this relatively wealthy and modernized country (with a GDP in 1998 of $3,970) 'ought' to have been a democracy long since. But entrenched structural conditions – linked to the long-term pre-eminence of the PRI – helped delay democratization. The PRI achieved power in 1929, following a civil war, and did not lose it until 2000, more than 70 years later. The party's hold on power was facilitated by Mexico's modernization, which, based on strong economic growth rooted in expanding oil exports, allowed the party to preside over increases in living standards for most ordinary people. While for years this served to mute political challenges, the PRI's ability to deliver relatively broad-based development gradually waned, resulting in the recent election of Vicente Fox, candidate of the National Action Party (PAN).

While successive PRI governments claimed to emphasize democratic values in public education and to employ democratic forms of constitutionalism and elections (Pendle 1976: 198), most recent analyses concur that, in fact, Mexico under PRI rule was an authoritarian polity. After reviewing a substantial literature, Booth and Seligson characterized Mexico as politically authoritarian (1993:

131), while Foweraker asserted that 'Mexico . . . cannot claim to be democratic' (1998: 651). However, while most informed observers concurred about the undemocratic nature of the political system, few believed that significant political changes were on the horizon. While Hall suggested that Mexico looked set 'to remain a single-party state' (1993: 284), the PRI's hold on power was soon to be broken. How did this happen? The answer is linked to both structural and contingent factors. Democratic progress is likely to depend on the extent to which President Fox can reform the political and economic systems to make them more representative and equitable.

Political culture and regime legitimacy

The structural characteristics of Mexico's authoritarian political culture were for decades conducive to the entrenchment of authoritarian rule. The role traditionally played by the PRI in the civic life of Mexico is hard to overestimate. It was a cradle-to-grave party, with control over everything from schools to health care, broadcasting to real estate. But this came at a political price: under PRI rule, Mexico's post-revolutionary political culture was moulded by the powerful, centralized state and party system, with civil and political rights underdeveloped. Latinobarometer surveys in the 1990s consistently showed that only around 5 per cent of Mexicans had 'much confidence' in several key state institutions, such as the police and judiciary, the lowest figures in the eight regional countries surveyed (Turner and Martz 1997). For many poor Mexicans the rule of law in relation to basic individual rights continued to deteriorate – to the point that even minimal socioeconomic rights did not exist for millions of people. As one anti-PRI, Zapatista rebel stated: 'We have nothing, absolutely nothing – not decent shelter, nor land, nor work, nor health, nor food, nor education. We do not have the right to choose freely and democratically our officials. We have neither peace nor justice' (quoted in Vidal 1996).

Political participation and institutions

Mexico's slow democratic transition was far more ambiguous than that of most other regional countries, 'hard to encapsulate in a single performative act' (Philip 1999: 4). Some observers suggest that the slow pace of democratization was linked to the fact that Mexico's single-party system had traditionally been less repressive than many of the region's military dictatorships, being characterized by a more inclusive and pragmatic political system than that found in many other contemporary single-party regimes, such as that of the Soviet Union (Ortíz 2000). While there was certainly widespread electoral fraud, the PRI also enjoyed a substantial level of popular support. Recently, however, as the PRI's hold on power weakened, poorly restrained paramilitary groups and unprosecuted human rights abuses by the army and the police became common.

Demands for democracy emanated from both domestic and external sources. From the late 1970s, Mexico became subject to the changing global trend towards democracy. With the encouragement of the United States, Mexico began a series of electoral reforms which, over time, 'cumulatively developed a momentum that favoured the opposition' (Wallis 1999: 3). After two decades of gradual political reforms, the PRI lost control of one of the two houses of Congress, the Chamber of Deputies (the national legislature) to opposition parties in the mid-term federal elections of 1997. This was a considerable watershed: no longer was the PRI electorally invincible. This not only encouraged the anti-PRI opposition to redouble its efforts but led to increased pressure on the PRI government from the United States government to democratize the political system further. Wallis suggests that by this time, it was probable that the PRI, harried by domestic and external pro-democracy actors, no longer had the capacity – or, perhaps, the willingness – 'to deny the electorate's will on anything like a large scale' (1999: 5).

The PRI's electoral decline began slowly but later speeded up. In 1979 the party received 85 per cent of the votes, falling to 60 per cent in 1991 and 38.5 per cent in 1997 (IDEA 1998: 73). However, 38.5 per cent of the popular vote still allowed the PRI to acquire 239 of the 500 seats (that is, 47.8 per cent), and the opposition parties were highly fragmented. Thus while it lost majority control, the PRI comfortably remained the largest party in the legislature. The PRI's loss of a majority in the Chamber suggested to some that the party was being punished for the decline in numbers of state jobs, an integral part of an economic liberalization programme introduced under the auspices of the International Monetary Fund. The point, however, is that the structural dominance of the PRI had begun to decline in the 1980s – because of growing domestic and external pressures for significant changes – and economic liberalization helped compound its problems.

As discussed in chapter 2, the concept of structured contingency implies that structural factors help set and mould political agendas while allowing for the possibility that individual actors or factors can also significantly affect political outcomes. To what extent have structural factors moulded recent political outcomes in Mexico? Did the direction and content of political reforms depend more on the willingness of political leaders to introduce and preside over real changes? Or were such actors unable fully to control outcomes because of structural factors?

Much attention has traditionally been focused on the political role of the president, the figure at the epicentre of the Mexican system. The Mexican president has traditionally enjoyed high levels of power, a consequence of a combination of constitutional powers with long-term PRI control both of the presidency, enabling him to act through the party, and of both houses of Congress (Weldon 1997: 227). Other political institutions – including Congress – have often been perceived as largely superfluous. However, as we saw in chapter 3, the development of a sustainable democracy would be likely to require a clear shift in power from president to legislature, which would be evidenced by an increased ability to propose and amend legislation as well as by mechanisms for scrutinizing the executive.

Full analysis of recent political changes in Mexico would not only focus on institutional reforms, but also highlight the importance of enhanced political participation in encouraging political leaders to reform the system. That is, in our terminology, the importance of contingency must not be overlooked. Over time, increasing challenges from both political and civil society, encouraged by pressure from the US, helped persuade the Mexican government to introduce political reforms, including relatively free and fair elections. Regarding civil society, of particular importance was the rise both of an assertive, relative autonomous business community, and also of an array of new social movements (Morris 1995; Foweraker and Landman 1997; Cornelius 2000). Developments in political society not only centred on the increasing electoral clout of opposition parties, but were also affected by growing political conflict between the state and rebels, especially in the Zapatista stronghold of Chiapas, where there were large numbers of unresolved political murders during the 1990s (Haynes 1997: 90–2).

Economic and international aspects

While the structural significance of the long-term pre-eminence of the president and the PRI has already been noted, it is also important to highlight the importance of contingent factors in relation to recent political and economic changes. Mexico's protracted process of democratic transition and economic liberalization was strongly encouraged by the United States government, with membership of the North American Free Trade Association (NAFTA) as the prize. The interest of the United States in Mexico as a prospective economic partner grew in the 1980s, while the Mexican government eventually came to regard NAFTA as the best available means for increasing economic growth. The reasons for American enthusiasm seem straightforward. After the Cold War, the State Department's global view was that democracy and free trade were the new ideological buzzwords of the emerging 'new world order'. This was Washington's consistent message, not only to Mexico but to Latin America more generally, from the time that Bill Clinton took office in January 1993.

Despite serious doubts, the PRI government was willing to reform both political and economic systems in order to win the support of the US Congress for Mexico's membership of NAFTA. Founded in 1994, NAFTA was the United States's regional blueprint for the economic-strategic set of relationships it wished to build as part of its post-Cold War global strategy of democratization and economic liberalization. However, both goals were politically explosive in Mexico, as they would work to undermine PRI hegemony built on central control and state monopoly. In sum, NAFTA was the regional model for President Clinton's ambition of building a 'Washington consensus' (Philip 1999: 5).

The election of Vicente Fox as president in mid-2000 was strongly welcomed by the Clinton government, which saw in him a kindred spirit with whom it could do business. However, it remained to be seen whether President Fox could actually put into practice his proclaimed policies. Fox promised deregulation, competition and a balanced budget, together with an ambitious social agenda that included a pledge to double education spending, increase subsidies for farmers and build health clinics; in short, a raft of policies and programmes to address the enormous disparity between rich and poor. However, to enact such policies would obviously require a sea change in long-established policies and, as a result, Fox would be unlikely to have things all his own way politically. Despite losing the presidency, the PRI would have sufficient congressional seats, in tandem with smaller parties, to block Fox's crucial constitutional and structural reforms. The PRI also retained control of half of the country's 32 state governorships and numerous municipalities. Whether Fox will be able to dismantle the inherited structures of PRI rule remains to be seen.

Conclusion

In Mexico, a lengthy democratic transition was accomplished in 2000 when the PRI's candidate, Francisco Labastida, lost the presidential election to the National Action Party's candidate, Vicente Fox, by a landslide: 43 against 36 per cent. This confirmed a trend that had begun more than 20 years earlier: eroded by stronger electoral laws and processes, and growing support for opposition parties, public support for the PRI and its de facto single-party system fell away to the point that its presidential candidate failed to be elected to office. However, as Linz and Stepan note, to achieve democratic consolidation, both 'civil and political society must be ... embedded in and supported by the rule of law' (1996: 10). It is clear that Mexico needs urgent progress in a number of areas, including the rule of law to be upheld throughout the country; better civil and human rights; less poverty and inequality (S. Morris 1995; Philip 1999). But significant problems lie ahead for Fox – not least because to reform the political and economic system in the ways he has outlined would require stepping on a lot of powerful toes. This is because Mexico's political structures and system have long centred on the role of the PRI in the context of a powerful, centralized state. Whether such an important structural factor can be overturned as a result of bold and imaginative decisions by the new president remains to be seen.

Venezuela

As with the example of Mexico, recent political outcomes in Venezuela also provide a good example of the importance of both structural and contingency factors in political changes. The accession to power in late 1998 of a charismatic maverick, Hugo Chavez, came in the midst of serious economic problems. It resulted in a novel kind of political system which Chavez and his supporters claimed to be an unconventional, yet profound form of popular democracy. It differed from the past in that the former two-party system, established 40 years earlier, would give way to a form of popular representation which would seek to represent the interests of the mass of ordinary people, who in many cases, like their counterparts in Mexico, had seen declines in economic well-being and political rights.

A democracy since 1958, Venezuela is also one of the world's leading oil producers. While the country has the highest per capita income in Latin America, national wealth is very unevenly distrib-

uted, with a tiny elite taking the lion's share. Millions of poor people
are condemned to what must seem like eternal impoverishment.
During the boom years of the 1960s and 1970s rich Venezuelans
earned an international reputation as the region's leading exponents
of 'conspicuous consumption'. The 1980s saw a sharp economic
downturn, with a period of nationally unprecedented negative
growth reaching its lowest point in the late 1980s, with −5.3 per cent
growth in 1987–9. The serious economic position not only threatened the country's fiscal stability but also led to stringent austerity
measures that prompted widespread unrest and two unsuccessful
coup attempts in 1992 – one of which was led by Hugo Chavez.
Already a national hero to many among the poor, Chavez was able
to exploit widespread concerns among Venezuelans concerning the
nature of the country's political and economic systems and structures.
On coming to power in 1998, it appeared that Chavez, a former
paratrooper, would be a strong-minded president who, like Mexico's
Vicente Fox, had unconventional ideas about how to remould the
political and economic landscape to the benefit of the mass of ordinary people. Chavez promised a 'peaceful revolution', which would
amount to a complete reform of Venezuela's entrenched political
system and a popular form of democracy, via reformed political institutions, to replace extant yet poorly functioning political institutions.
The new order would aim to tackle the country's main political
problem, a lack of representation, and its chief economic flaw,
extreme inequalities of wealth.

The political impact of an oil-dominated economy

Recent political changes in Venezuela are intimately linked to the
country's economic and developmental characteristics and, as a
result, we will start the analysis with a brief survey of these issues.
In the late 1990s, a time of falling GDP and soaring inflation, the top
10 per cent of the population received about half of the country's
earnings, unemployment was at 17 per cent and, despite having the
largest oil reserves in the western hemisphere, 9 million Venezuelans
were without sanitation, over 4 million were without safe water, and
42 per cent of rural people and nearly a third of urban dwellers lived
in absolute poverty; overall, around 75 per cent of Venezuelans were
afflicted by moderate or severe poverty at this time (UNDP 1996:
170; Bellos 1999b, 1999c).

The political system created in 1958 was built on the premise of
a rotation in power between the two main political parties, AD

(Acción Democrática) and COPEI (Partido Social Cristiano/Comité de Organización Electoral Independiente). As long as successive governments met societal demands financially via structured clientelistic mechanisms – that is, by way of personalistic relationships through which individuals could count on rewards for supporting the government – the limited nature of the democratic system was not seriously challenged from below. As Buxton puts it, a 'clear trade-off between political autonomy and economic well-being [was] revealed in the fact that 58 per cent of peasants claimed to have affiliated with a political party for patronage considerations' (1999: 252). Linking the political system to economic redistribution, the COPEI–AD pact underpinned a primarily material, rather than necessarily normative commitment to democracy. When this was arrested by fiscal crisis in the 1980s and 1990s, disaffection with the dominant parties mounted – but because of the restricted nature of the political system, opposition could not be effectively mobilized or institutionalized against the entrenched hold on power of the two parties.

The point is that the parties' clientelistic ability to maintain voters' loyalty was underpinned for decades by the wealth flowing from impressive oil revenues. It is hard to overestimate the importance of oil to Venezuela's economic well-being, as oil sales typically account for over 90 per cent of export revenues. In the early 1970s, Venezuela enjoyed an economic boom as the global price of a barrel of oil rose sevenfold – from $2 to $14. Average per capita income doubled to nearly $3,000 a year, leading to a burst of consumption and the characterization of Venezuela as the 'Saudi Arabia' of Latin America. But this was temporary opulence. Domestic demand rapidly exceeded local production capacities, imports grew swiftly and non-oil exports collapsed, leading to chronic balance payments of problems in the 1980s. To maintain the legitimacy of the model of *partidocracia* (or 'dual control'), governments were unwilling or unable to rein in state expenditure levels and, when the price of oil fell in the 1980s, the result was a swift accumulation of foreign debt, which rose to $31 billion in 1988. Despite the economic downturn and rapidly rising indebtedness, there was no immediate change in the expansionary orientation of economic policy. 'On the pretext of encouraging private sector development, taxation remained chronically low and domestic interest rates sharply negative. The result was intensive capital flight, steep recession and chronic debt problems' (Buxton 1999: 257). The result was that average per capita income declined by 25 per cent, poverty among the poor greatly increased and the country's welfare system collapsed (Bellos 1999a; World Bank 1999).

Seeking to respond to the imperatives of the debt crisis, a newly elected leader, President Pérez, took the unprecedented step in 1988 of introducing a package of neoliberal stabilization and structural adjustment measures (*el paquete*, the package). However, the application of *el paquete* was met with unprecedented social disturbances, principally from the poor and the middle classes who expected to take the brunt of decreases in state employment and removal of subsidies on some basic goods, including foodstuffs: an estimated 1,000 people died in riots against economic liberalization in the capital, Caracas, in February 1989. Despite favourable macroeconomic results, including a resumption of economic growth, *el paquete* was consistently opposed by all sectors, including the president's own AD party. The point is that although the Pérez government sought to break the cycle of economic malaise, the imposition of neoliberal economic reforms undermined the redistributionary legitimacy of the state and the monopolistic position of the parties. This explains the resistance – both socially and politically – to *el paquete*, and highlights the importance of Venezuela's structural economic conditions and their impact on political outcomes. The government was unable to construct a coalition of potential beneficiaries from the package of neoliberal reforms because all social groups had vested interests in maintaining the intermediary role of the state. After initial macroeconomic successes, the economy later fell back into serious disarray. Agreement was reached with the IMF in 1996 on an economic stabilization package, 'Agenda Venezuela', involving both stabilization and adjustment measures. But progress was limited, not least because a mini-boom in oil prices in 1997 prompted the government to stake its reputation on expansionary measures. But bust followed boom: oil prices fell to $11 a barrel, well below the budgeted $15.50, leaving a huge hole in the government's finances (Banks and Muller 1998: 1013).

Political culture and regime legitimacy

Three years after the Caracas riots, the country was further rocked by two serious military coup attempts. The first, in February 1992, gained widespread public sympathy, with contemporaneous opinion polls indicating 'a precipitous decline in state institutions, with government and parties registering in particular little popular confidence' (Buxton 1999: 257). These events highlight how political developments in Venezuela, in focusing power in the hands of a select group of elites – while permanently excluding others from power or even the *prospect* of power – gradually called into question the desirability of the maintenance of the prevailing system. Put another way, structures of power in Venezuela, despite the official existence of a long-term democratic regime, did not deliver a *consolidated* democracy. As we have seen, such a democracy is characterized by democratically orientated behaviour that eventually develops into the accepted way – both for political elites and the mass of ordinary people – of 'doing' politics; and the admittance of 'democratically legitimate' political actors into the system according to previously established, legitimately coded procedures, together with the political neutralization of anti-democrats. Underpinned by legal guarantees and extensive protections for individual and group freedoms, such a system's democratic nature is also secured by and through the workings of an independent, impartial judiciary. Unequivocal civilian control of the military and a competent state bureaucracy – necessary to carry out state policies – are also vital for democratic consolidation.

It is ironic that, for decades, Venezuela's political system was hailed as *the* regional model of policy restraint and political consensus. This stemmed from an intra-elite pact, enacted in 1958. Under the terms of the pact, three main parties (later reduced to two) agreed that each would have a share of government posts *in perpetuity* – irrespective of which party or combination of parties actually won elections. Consequently, the structural characteristics of Venezuela's political system was for four decades rooted in the perpetuation in power of a small group of political elites and a stable party system distinguished by a high degree of consensus among the main parties. Under the terms of the pact, 'extremist' parties and groups were marginalized. Over the next two decades, the apparent 'success' of the system was marked by peaceful turnover of administrations, consistently high levels of voter participation and, for most voters, clear partisan alignments. Under the terms of the agreement, each party agreed not only to pursue consensually oriented national development goals but also to keep communists from power (McCoy 1988: 88). This latter policy in particular earned successive regimes strong support from US governments.

Political participation and institutions

Over time, the structural attributes of the political system became institutionalized. In effect, the 1958 pact served to frame 'the limits of policy change and effectively tied [the parties] into the democratic process by guaranteeing that they would all have a stake in the government and that neither they nor their supporters would ever lose too much' (Leftwich 1997: 529). However, it became increasingly clear that many ordinary Venezuelans were dissatisfied with the lack of openings for change at the core of the pacted political arrangement. Whereas some 70 per cent on average voted in elections in the 1970s and 1980s, this figure dropped to less than 50 per cent in presidential and parliamentary polls in 1993 (IDEA 1998: 85, 100). The inference is that Venezeula's heavily pacted system gradually alienated many ordinary people from political life. The system served the interests of a small group of elites and their supporters while failing to deal with the country's growing economic problems and lack of avenues for protesting against the political arrangements.

Venezuela's political experiences since the late 1950s support Merkel's claim that 'one of the most urgent, and developmentally crucial, elements of democratic consolidation is for wide sections of society to improve their political access, to be involved in the process of institutional "crafting"' (1998: 32). This is a way of saying that democratic consolidation is only manifested when voters believe that *their* vote can make a difference to political outcomes. Venezuela is a good example of a polity where many voters lost faith in the political system. The country's elite-pacted democracy, with its closely controlled parties, monopolized the political process and penetrated state and organizational life to the extent that interest groups excluded from the triptych of the state and the two parties no doubt felt robbed of political efficacy. No space was left for the incorporation of 'new, marginal, or alienated constituencies into democratic politics' (Diamond 1999: 97). But this was not all: an examination of Venezuela's political system restricted to the procedural political mechanics would fail to uncover what made the political system tick. That is, the operational realities and the political relations sustaining the traditional 'democratic' model underestimate the capacity of dominant parties to sustain 'transitionary relations through structural bias and interest distortion' (Buxton 1999: 264–5).

One of the main dangers of pacted democracy noted in the literature is that the elites carve things up for their own ends, and work assiduously to prevent changes which might undermine their predominant position. In Venezuela, the cosiness of the elite-dominated, pacted democracy meant that powerful vested interests, with a strong interest in the maintenance of the political status quo, managed for decades not only to obstruct measures to improve representation and accountability but also to delay increasingly urgent economic reforms. The nature of the system encouraged the development of state paternalism and of rent-seeking behaviour (that is, attempting to gain profit from becoming the sole producer and/or distributor of a good or service), while many ordinary people became locked into dependent relationships, whether with the state or the hegemonic parties. The pacted system also worked against a wider redistribution of economic resources to the lower strata of society because changes in relations of production were structurally precluded. Paralleling broadly similar developments in Mexico, the cumulative effect of these policies was to underpin the development of 'a skewed pattern of rent dispersal, which favoured the wealthiest sectors of society while limiting the ability of labour to mobilise for a more equitable distribution of the economic rewards' (Buxton 1999: 259).

In sum, established by the two main parties, AD and COPEI, Venezuela's system of *partidocracia* ('dual control') was central both to democratic sustainability *and* to the system's eventual decline. *Partidocracia* amounted to a situation whereby AD and COPEI were 'converted into virtual monopolisers of the political system which is formally competitive and open' (Buxton 1999: 247). In other words, Venezuela's twin hegemonic parties were so centrally placed and apparently immovable that the pact became the chief obstacle to democratic evolution. The electoral system itself assisted in the structuring of the bipolar hegemony since it seriously diminished the mobilizing potential of minor parties. This paralleled the situation in Mexico, with one difference: Mexico's system was maintained by and served the interests of one party – the PRI – rather than two, as in Venezuela.

Economic and international factors

The government came under strong pressure from the US to reform both its political and economic systems. However, when political change did come it was in a form viewed by the US with trepidation: the election to power of Hugo Chavez, friend of Saddam Hussein and Moammar Gaddafi. Chavez, a populist, a former paratroop officer and leader of a coup attempt in 1992, was elected to power on an 'anti-system' ticket in December 1998. His platform, an anti-corruption, populist-nationalist stance, enabled him to win nearly 60 per cent of the popular vote, with much support coming from the poor and middle classes, an outcome which unnerved 'the local business community and foreign investors' – the main beneficiaries of the prevailing political system (Hoag 1998).

Chavez's outbursts against the iniquities of the political and economic situation not only helped channel popular frustration and anger at the traditional political elite, who seemed to many to have brought the country to its knees, but were also instrumental in helping secure his election. Once in power, Chavez called for a new popularly elected assembly which would override or dissolve the opposition-controlled Congress, an institution whose senators had rejected his proposals to promote dozens of military officers to positions of political power. He called for the convocation of what he called an 'organic', rather than party-based, constituent assembly to create the appropriate circumstances for a 'peaceful revolution'. Chavez held a referendum in December 1999 on the desirability of several fundamental social and political reforms: a new constitution, abolition of Congress and its replacement by a new assembly, an end to IMF-dictated neoliberal policies, restrictions on privatizations, and improvements in social equity. In effect, this was a referendum on the nature of Venezuela's political and economic system, and Chavez won it with over 60 per cent of the popular vote (albeit on a low turnout).

Chavez's election to power and subsequent referendum victory not only underlined the political system's inability to reform from within, but also indicated its vulnerability to charismatic challenge from outside. Economic mismanagement, lack of systematic renewal, serious state-level corruption, and demobilization of civil society were all factors facilitating his rise to power. The lack of satisfaction that Chavez claimed many Venezuelans felt with the political system was endorsed by a poll carried out by a local organization, Fundación Pensmiento y Acción. Half of those interviewed saw justice as the most important aspect of their desired social and political system, 'followed by employment (40 per cent), freedom (28 per cent) and equality (27 per cent)'. Suggesting a less than fulsome belief in democracy Venezuelan-style, only 'six per cent cited elections, two per cent consensus and 13 per cent participation [as very important]. All of which correlate[d] directly with the approach, platform and appeal of Chavez' (Buxton 1999: 264).

It was clear that the former paratrooper struck a popular chord when he claimed that Venezuela's political system had been fatally undermined by the long-term dominance of the AD and COPEI. Analysing why many Venezuelans held the established political parties in such low esteem, it was clear to him that the political ramifications of the original power-sharing pact were the root cause: the pact had established a strictly limited democratic system – limited in terms of accountability, popular input and participation – while legitimizing and strengthening the parties' anti-democratic tendencies. The consequence, according to Chavez, was that the system could not respond adequately, because of its structural characteristics, when fundamental change became necessary. To sustain consensus it had been necessary to restrict ideological debates, which had helped the narrowly based political elite to retain power. Negation of internal party democracy had led to serious decay in the wider political system, with a shrinking and detachment of civil society organizations. A reliance on clientelistic disbursement of state resources to build and maintain support attenuated the parties' dependence on their grassroots both for fund-raising activities and for political mobilization. In this respect, the central nature of the parties in the political system and their legitimacy had been highly contingent on redistribution. This weakened an important point of linkage and accountability between the party base and the leadership. As Buxton notes, 'in the absence of internal feedback mechanisms, the parties and their sectoral affiliations – specifically the unions – became increasingly removed from sectoral interests' (1999: 253).

Conclusion

Venezuela is a good example of a political environment where both contingency and structures are important for political outcomes. A long period of democratic rule in Venezuela – beginning in 1958 – did not lead to democratic consolidation because the political scene was dominated for decades by the carving up of power between the country's two leading political parties. In 1998 power was won through the ballot box by Hugo Chavez, a charismatic politician and former coup leader. Chavez could simply have continued with the old regime and retained the existing power equation. But he claimed that he wanted to institute a popular democracy in order to take away power from the old, discredited parties and 'pass it to the people'. When he made it clear he wanted a fundamentally different system, critics claimed that he was intent on introducing and developing a new form of charismatic authoritarianism.

But Chavez was highlighting what millions of ordinary Venezuelans believed: that the consequence of a closed political structure in Venezuela was a blocked, heavily overinstitutionalized party system, notable for the corruption, arrogance and lack of responsiveness of its leading players. While a high degree of party control may initially have been necessary to gain the support of the economic elites, the arrangement was eventually instrumental in limiting the ability of state agencies to deliver the necessary collective goods to elicit the mass of the people's commitment to the political system.

This analysis of Venezuela's political and economic characteristics has sought to highlight how the system, while meeting *functional* prerequisites of democracy – such as regular elections – was insufficient for either governmental legitimacy or systemic stability. Venezuela's pacted democracy was notable for the ability of hegemonic parties to prevent change by restricting the inputs of ordinary people into the political system. The consequence was that at the end of the 1990s, four decades after its democratic transition, Venezuela's democracy under AD and COPEI leadership had fundamentally *de*consolidated, with plummeting support for political institutions and rising voting abstention (from 6 to 40 per cent from 1958 to 1993) (IDEA 1998: 85). The rise of the populist maverick, Hugo Chavez, gaining an emphatic victory in the referendum to approve a new constitution and other major economic and political reforms in 1999, highlighted popular dissatisfaction with the extant political and economic arrangements and focused the popular desire for fundamental reforms.

4.5   Overall conclusions

In Venezuela a popular, populist president gained power in 1998 in response to the deficiencies of a supposedly democratic system which had actually failed to deliver clear benefits to the mass of ordinary people. Mexico also saw the collapse of long-term electoral hegemony: the PRI lost power in 2000 when an opposition candidate, Vicente Fox, won the presidential election – the first time in seven decades that a PRI candidate had failed to be elected. To some extent these political developments can be traced to the economic failures of successive governments in both countries. Economic reform programmes were introduced in the 1980s in both Mexico and Venezuela, but the societal impact involved serious costs for millions of ordinary people – not least from reductions in the numbers of state jobs. It is worth noting that the experiences of hardship in Mexico and Venezuela were by no means unique in the region: an estimated three-quarters of the region's population – some 300 million people – suffered from some indication of malnutrition in the 1990s, a clear indicator of mass poverty (Black 1993: 545). In sum, the apparent inability of successive Mexican and Venezuelan governments to reduce the gross inequality between numerically small elite groups and the mass of the people suggests that, despite macroeconomic growth in some cases, unemployment and underemployment remained a serious problem in both rural and urban areas.

The experiences of both Mexico and Venezuela underline a further, more general point: limited democracies are notable for their maintenance of elite privileges, a price for the elite's support for democracy. Nothing in the foregoing suggests that limited democracy will not endure in the region. If a return to the past seems unlikely, and a leap into the consolidation of full democracy equally improbable, what lies ahead for the countries of Latin America? In the 1970s and 1980s divisions among economic, political and military elites led them to promote democratization. This was not necessarily or even primarily for the purpose of facilitating popular participation but more as a means of resolving their differences, strengthening their own influence and striving to channel political action along lines which would enable them to retain as much power as possible in the post-authoritarian order. In other words, political reforms championed by civilian and military elites alike created the opportunity for limited democracies. However, what ultimately determined whether such regimes endured or evolved in a more participatory direction was the extent to which political and civil society could put pressure on governments to move in the latter direction. Where such factors were relatively strong, as in Chile and Uruguay, democracy seemed to advance. When they were not, it did not. As the examples of Venezuela, and to an extent, Mexico, indicate, limited democracies were the outcome, with no guarantee that such systems would eventually evolve into more conventionally democratic polities. In other words, limited democracy in Latin America is not necessarily a temporary or transitional stage, but could well be an enduring form of government that mixes a substantial degree of democracy with a substantial degree of authoritarianism.

5
East and South East Asia

5.1 Introduction

Taken together, recent democratic changes in a number of countries in the region in the 1980s and 1990s – including South Korea, Taiwan, Thailand, the Philippines and Indonesia – indicate that East and South East Asia became part of the third wave of democracy. In the Philippines, a 'People Power' movement forced President Ferdinand Marcos and his government from power in 1986, while, nearly contemporaneously, pacted transitions in South Korea and Taiwan ushered in new democracies. Popular pressure was also instrumental in two other regional examples of political reform: (1) the 'May 1992 events' in Thailand which led to the ousting of the government of Suchinda Kraprayoon and its replacement by a new regime; and (2) the student-led protests in Indonesia in 1998, which catalysed wider societal unrest and culminated in the downfall of President Suharto and his regime. Generally, across the region, pro-democracy campaigners, focused in a variety of civil society groups – encouraged by external actors including the government of the United States, wishing to see clear manifestations of the 'Washington consensus' model – helped undermine the legitimacy of political authoritarianism. The result was that, with differing degrees of decisiveness, authoritarian rule was widely rejected (Tornquist 1999).

Contrary to the claims of some authoritarian leaders that pro-democracy groups were instigated by foreign actors, Hewison pointed out that 'demands for the opening of political space, with calls for increased democracy in Southeast Asia, are not originating in the West

or among western-influenced actors but have domestic causes' (1999:
231). Authoritarianism and suppression of political opposition had
long been justified and legitimized by governments as a price for often
impressive economic growth. But that legitimation took a major knock
in 1997–8 when many of the region's economies experienced serious
– albeit short-lived – economic downturns. It began with a currency
collapse when the Thai government stopped defending the national
currency – the baht – against the US dollar. A domino effect was
triggered of collapsing currencies throughout South East Asia. The
regional economic malaise made it plain that authoritarian development models were fallible. This was also consequential for the claimed
trade-off – economic growth and prosperity, but little political freedom
– which regional governments had explicitly or implicitly invoked as
a justification for their styles of rule. In sum, the financial crisis in the
region helped increase the revealed new weaknesses in regional authoritarian developmental models and helped strengthen the legitimacy of
pro-democracy discourses.

Analysis of recent political changes in East and South East Asia is
made complex by the fact that, while a large number of countries are
conventionally identified as belonging to the region, other than in the
sense of the countries' physical proximity to each other, they share
few characteristics. There is no obvious way to delimit the East
and South East Asia region in terms of geography, politics, economy,
history or culture. Unlike in Africa, with its common, colonially
derived European languages, English and French, or in Latin
America, with Spanish and Portuguese, in East and South East Asia
there is no common language to bind together the diversity. Instead,
there are many very different regional languages written in different
scripts. In addition, unlike the ubiquitous Christianity of Latin
America, East and South East Asia has a variety of profoundly different religious traditions. Finally, unlike Africa or South Asia, the
region of East and South East Asia does not share a colonial history.
While many regional countries were colonized at one time or another
by various powers (including Britain, France, Spain, the Netherlands,
the United States, Japan), not all were. For example, there was a distinctive non-colonial form of authoritarianism – royal absolutism –
in Thailand. The overall point is that East and South East Asia is
marked by more political, historical and cultural diversity than
perhaps any other region examined in this book. It seems plausible
to suggest that this factor will have implications for political outcomes. Not least, it is likely to make them variable.

Because problems of democracy and democratization will reflect,
on the one hand, distinctive structural legacies and variables, and, on

the other, the actions of agents, in this chapter we are primarily concerned with the *interaction* of structural and contingent factors. South Korea and the Philippines are the case study countries for reasons explained later.

The region's political diversity is manifested in the fact that, apart from various examples of (mostly limited) democracies, East and South East Asia also had various kinds of non-democratic political systems in 2000. These included communist governments (Vietnam, North Korea, Laos, China), non-communist authoritarian regimes (Cambodia), a military administration (Burma), civilian absolutist rule (Brunei), a restricted 'communitarian' democracy (Singapore) and a dominant-party system (Malaysia). Freedom House categorized all these countries' political systems as either 'not free' or at the interface between 'not free' and 'partly free'. Various kinds of political structures and processes were utilized for the purpose of underpinning authoritarian rule, with often strongly centralized regional states developing a variety of measures for societal control. These included hegemonic single-party systems (Indonesia, Malaysia), vote-buying (Thailand), ethnic affirmative action (Malaysia), restrictions on the right to organize, debate and voice opinions (Singapore, Malaysia, *inter alia*), and cooption of civil society activists along with emergency laws to restrict opposition activities (most of the region's countries at various times).

Among the region's non-authoritarian regimes, two regional countries – South Korea and Taiwan – were classified 'free' by Freedom House in 1999. While, in our terminology, this would suggest that they might have managed to consolidate their democratic systems, Shin (1999) counsels caution before drawing such a conclusion. He argues that political systems in several regional countries, including South Korea and Taiwan, conform to what he calls a 'Confucian model of democratization'. As I shall explain below, this is a political system with both liberal and illiberal characteristics rooted in the traditional philosophy of Confucianism. Both Thailand and the Philippines were categorized by Freedom House in 1999 as being at the interface between 'free' and 'partly free'. In our terminology, this characterizes them as limited democracies. East and South East Asia's new democracies are shown in table 5.1.

In sum, several countries in the East and South East Asia region have undergone recent democratic changes. However, the inherited weight of authoritarian characteristics makes it difficult in all cases to see unproblematic progression to clearly consolidated democracies. The reasons for this state of affairs are explored in the next section.

Table 5.1   New democracies in East and South East Asia, 1989–1999

	Political rights (PR)		Civil liberties (CL)		PR + CL average	PR + CL average	Freedom rating
	1988–9	1998–9	1988–9	1998–9	1988–9	1998–9	1998–9
South Korea	2	2	3	2	2.5	2	Free
Taiwan	5	2	3	2	4	2	Free
Philippines	2	2	3	3	2.5	2.5	Free
Thailand	3	2	3	3	3	2.5	Free

Source: 'Annual survey of Freedom country scores, 1972–73 to 1998–99',
http://www.freedomhouse.org/survey99/method/

5.2   Structural impediments to democracy in East and South East Asia

While differing from country to country, four main *structural* impediments to democracy are noted in the literature on East and South East Asia. They include:

- *The nature of agrarian class relations*   Traditionally, regional countries have been influenced, both politically and economically, by elite groups of large-scale landowners. Such elite groups were typically strongly opposed to significant political reforms as they believed that these would threaten their privileged positions, not least because they might lead to the dissolution or diminution of their land holdings and a handover to landless rural labourers. Significantly, two regional countries that have seen recent democratic progress – South Korea and Taiwan – undertook significant land reforms in the 1950s. Two others, Thailand and the Philippines, did not: land ownership patterns have remained substantially unreformed despite recent shifts to democratically elected regimes.
- *A mutually supportive relationship between the state and the armed forces*   Most regional countries have traditionally had a close relationship between those in power at the state level and senior military figures. Often sharing a similar class outlook with civilian power-holders and suspicious of democracy, senior armed forces personnel have traditionally seen themselves as the key defenders of the state against domestic and foreign attacks.
- *Lack of governmental accountability*   Most regional regimes were, until recently, rooted in authoritarian political systems. It is

suggested that many ordinary people were prepared to accept less than democratic regimes as long as the latter could preside over rising economic prosperity. But when economic and developmental problems developed, civil society organizations turned to democratic alternatives.

*   *Authoritarian legacies*   Throughout the region, development of democratic regimes would depend on the ability to overturn or overcome authoritarian political legacies, typically state repression and societal passivity.

Several *contingent* factors have also been noted relating to regional chances of democratization. First, some see the recent economic problems as giving a fillip to democracy's chances by encouraging civil society to exercise its voice. Second, democracy was encouraged by governments of foreign countries, such as the US and Japan. Such governments had long regarded democracy as dangerous to strategic interests as it might allow communists or socialists to achieve power via the ballot box. However, the demise of the Soviet Union and other communist countries in the late 1980s and early 1990s encouraged the US to see democracy in a different light: as the core of its post-Cold War 'Washington consensus' policies which highlighted the importance not only of democracy but also of free markets. Third, the emergence of pro-democracy political leaders would be expected to have an impact on political outcomes.

Reflecting a concern with the comparative importance of both structural and contingency factors, opinions about the future of democracy in the region are mixed. Some observers argue that, despite their differing characteristics, most regional political systems are notable for traditions of strong, typically authoritarian political leaders and associated political systems, with, at best, only a veneer of democracy lying over decidedly non-democratic structures. For this reason, Thompson (1993) is highly sceptical about chances of widespread democratic progress in the region. He points to a continuing tight hold on power by undemocratic political elites, a corresponding lack of resolve to democratize political systems and only intermittent pressure from domestic and external pro-democracy forces to change things. Pei (1995) suggests that various cultural factors, such as Confucianism in South Korea or 'bossism' in the Philippines, are a serious barrier to the advance of democracy because their collective legacy is to encourage social and political passivity in relation to the rule of authoritarian governments.

Other commentators, such as Leftwich (1993), see a reasonably promising outlook for democracy and democratic consolidation in certain regional countries, including Malaysia, Indonesia, Thailand, Taiwan and South Korea. Such an assessment is based largely on the fact that these countries were in the regional vanguard of economic growth at the time of the analysis, the 1990s. The point, Leftwich argued, was that strong economic growth would facilitate democratization for the reasons that Lipset noted four decades ago: modernization would create a new middle class who would demand a say in political outcomes.

Hewison highlights a further factor linked to recent democratization in the region: the enhanced robustness of civil society in various countries. He notes that in some cases 'political space' – that is, the 'arena created through struggle with the state and involving activist groups' – has expanded in recent years (1999: 225). In addition, Moody (1988) points to growing instances of political opposition in many regional countries. On this basis, he argues that popular pro-democracy sentiments have now reached the point where they have often significantly affected the characteristics of local political cultures. The result is that a return to the *status quo ante*, characterized by traditional expressions of authoritarian rule and associated forms of politics, is practically impossible.

The various issues raised in this section suggest two analytical questions of interest in relation to the comparative importance of structural and contingent factors in explaining political outcomes in East and South East Asia. We shall pursue answers to them in the remainder of the chapter, first, in relation to general regional issues, and second, in a focus on recent political developments in South Korea and the Philippines. The questions are as follows: First, to what extent do structural impediments to democracy suggest that there are clear limits to democratic progress in the region? Second, if this is the case, what can pro-democracy actors do about it?

5.3 Democratic consolidation in East and South East Asia

Democratic transitions in the region were either through elite pacts or popular uprisings. In South Korea and Taiwan they were the result of elite pacts, while popular pressures led to the downfall of authoritarian governments in the Philippines, Thailand, and Indonesia. From the literature, it would be expected that limited democracies would be the result in the first two countries, while in the latter three, where transitions were inaugurated by popular pressure without elite agreements, post-authoritarian regimes would be unstable, with uncertain democratic outcomes.

We noted in chapter 2 that what happens during the transition can affect the chances of democratic consolidation. For example, democratic consolidation 'should' be promoted when transitions involve pacts between an outgoing authoritarian elite and leading representatives of the democratic opposition. But there will be a democratic price to pay: future political stability is seen as linked to the guarantees secured by the old ruling elites, striving to protect and maintain privileges and perhaps to escape judgement for any crimes committed in power. Consequently, pacted transitions are thought likely to lead to limited democracies. On the other hand, the absence of transition pacts is thought likely to serve as a serious impediment to democracy, making more difficult the emergence of the necessary climate of moderation and compromise among elites.

But this cannot be the whole story. Post-transition regimes will reflect the influence of more factors than those emerging from the nature of the transition itself. It is suggested that post-transition structural factors are likely to reassume central importance for democratic outcomes, while allowing a role for those connected to contingency. To examine this issue in relation to East and South East Asia we turn next to an assessment of the impact of structural and contingent factors under the following headings:

1   political culture and regime legitimacy;
2   political participation and institutions;
3   economic and international factors.

It is suggested that in many post-authoritarian regimes the importance of the first two sets of factors – political culture and regime legitimacy, and political participation and institutions – will primarily reflect inherited structural characteristics. On the other hand, the latter set of components – economic and international factors – while also to some degree reflecting structural legacies, will also be likely to be informed by contingency. To pursue the analysis, we examine first these issues in relation to the region as a whole, before, second, turning attention to the chapter's case studies.

Political culture and regime legitimacy

Various kinds of authoritarian factors that are said to inform political cultures of various regional countries, and are linked to specific varieties of non-democratic regime, are noted in the literature. Three will be briefly examined here: (1) 'Asian values'; (2) 'bossism'; (3) Confucianism. Each is said to be linked to regional political cultures that are collectively not conducive to the development of Western-style *liberal* democracy, that is, democracy with a focus on the individualistic aspects of political freedoms. Zakaria (1997) notes the frequent regional occurrence of what he calls 'illiberal democracies'. Illiberal democracies are political systems with periodic, relatively free and fair elections, and some meaningful rules and regulations to determine their conduct and content, but without a 'full' array of liberal freedoms. In such systems, rulers wield power with little reference to other political institutions, ordinary citizens enjoy only a narrow range of civil liberties and, other than at election times, there are low levels of popular political participation. In sum, illiberal democracies have a mix of political characteristics, including 'democracy, liberalism, capitalism, oligarchy and corruption', which coexist much as they did in 'Western governments circa 1900' (Zakaria 1997: 28).

'Asian values' in Malaysia and Singapore

Some regional political leaders, such as Malaysia's current prime minister Muhammad Mahathir and Singapore's former prime minister, Lee Kuan Yew, have claimed that liberal democracy is 'culturally alien' to the region. Instead, East and South East Asian countries are said to have different kinds of political cultures and histories that, while differing from country to country in precise details, nevertheless reflect an important collective factor: the societal significance of the community or group, rather than the individual. Such a concern is said to be at the heart of the concept of a generic 'Asian culture', embodying an array of 'Asian social and political values' – including harmony, consensus, unity and community – that differ significantly from 'Western culture' and its individualistic, self-seeking values. In Mahathir's view, societies such as Malaysia's are imbued with such 'Asian social and political values'. The result is that government is popularly regarded as legitimate *only when it reflects values associated with the community's particular cultural contours.* The political consequence is that the claimed appropriateness of the Western-style 'universal' is simply wrong. Instead, national political institutions and practices of democracy are necessarily adjusted to 'fit' local cultural values. The result, for Mahathir, is a regional style of politics based on consensus rather than the conflictual adversarial approach characterizing Western political competition (Maravall 1995: 16).

'Bossism' in the Philippines

A second kind of political authoritarianism is found in the Philippines, and known as 'bossism'. The legacy of US colonialism (between 1898 and 1946) is seen as an important structural factor that served to prevent the embedding and development of representative institutions and democracy (Gills et al. 1993). Although democratic institutions were introduced during the period of American control, they were quickly hijacked by powerful local landowning oligarchs (known in the Philippines as 'bosses'). Since then, such 'bosses' have been of central political importance, functioning as both electoral and economic powerbrokers and enjoying virtually monopolistic control over entire localities. Although the Philippines democratized in 1986 this did not fundamentally change the system. Patronage politics linked to bossism still dominated the Philippines political system, both at national and local levels. The outcome was that the results of electoral contests remained dependent on the ability of politicians to influence the voting process, primarily by their comparative ability to buy votes. Attempts at various times to change the political system by creating an effective party system failed, unable to overcome the legacy of irresponsible factionalism and landowner power.

Confucianism in South Korea

Confucianism, the third authoritarian legacy, associated with the name of Confucius, a Chinese philosopher who lived from 551 to 479 BC, is said to have a significant impact on political outcomes by affecting the nature and characteristics of political systems in various regional countries, including South Korea. Fukuyama regards 'hierarchical and inegalitarian' Confucianism as a 'value system most congruent with Oriental authoritarianism' (1992: 325, 217). Confucianism in Korea developed strongly between the seventh and tenth centuries AD, a philosophical system strongly affecting social, cultural and political aspects of the nation's life. Later, in the 1960s and 1970s, a period of strong modernization in South Korea, the country's Confucian heritage was regarded by modernizing leaders as a root cause of developmental backwardness. Consequently, political leaders committed themselves to eradicating this traditional cultural value and to replacing it with Western-style modernization. However, 20 years later, in the 1980s, broadly the same group of elites became concerned about the social effects of 'too much Westernization' and, as a result, began a programme of re-education in Confucianism and other traditional values. This was accompanied by officially sponsored excursions into political philosophy, with Confucianism harnessed to desirable prescriptions for politics and government – based on limited conceptions of democracy. The result was what some observers have identified as 'Korean-style democracy', based on Confucian principles of harmony, consensus and order. The overall aim was to try to eliminate or at least reduce the kinds of adversarial oppositional activity that Korea's then military leaders associated with liberal democratic practices. In sum, various kinds of authoritarian legacies have informed recent attempts to democratize political systems in many of the region's countries.

Political participation and institutions

What do regional variants of authoritarian systems amount to in terms of their impact on political participation and institutions? Are they any more than opportunistic attempts by anti-democratic leaders to justify their styles of rule by allusion to the claimed cultural attributes of their countries? Many observers are unimpressed by the arguments of figures like Mahathir, and suggest that the region's authoritarian governments are, collectively, regimes with high levels of social control dominated by authoritarian leaders that are unwilling for mostly self-interested reasons to open up political systems to democratic structures and processes (Tremewan 1994; Jesudason 1996; Case 1997; Putzel 1997).

Such claims were given credence when two countries with Confucian cultures, Taiwan and South Korea, underwent democratic transitions from the late 1980s. Henceforward, some observers noted, these countries' political systems were characterized by competition for state power via regular, free and fair elections; real opposition parties and developing party systems; and expanding civil and political liberties, including increased freedom of expression and the press, the right to demonstrate and to strike (King 1993: 141). For some, this was evidence that an authoritarian past could be overcome provided there was sufficient commitment on the part of democrats to change things fundamentally. Others contended, however, that things were not as clear-cut as this suggested: post-authoritarian political systems not only in South Korea and Taiwan, but also in the Philippines and elsewhere, were seen as notable for incomplete democratization (Hewison 1999; Putzel 1999; Kelly and Reid 1998; Van Ness 1999).

Observers suggest that, rather than underpinning culturally attuned and dynamic forms of local democracy, such political systems were little more than restricted political systems under the control of still authoritarian leaders anxious to legitimate their own authority in the face of growing challenges (Rodan and Hewison 1996; Callahan 1996). In sum, there was controversy as to what degree post-authoritarian political institutions were truly democratic.

Economic and international factors

Economic and international issues are dealt with together because they are so often interrelated in the context of the region's political outcomes.

As we have seen, authoritarian legacies of the past make it likely that related structural factors are of significance for democratic outcomes. But two further sets of factors – related to economic and international issues – also suggest the importance of contingency in the region. Substantive international encouragement to democracy could be important – although probably not important enough on its own to outweigh less helpful factors. What might help would be a degree of economic wealth. Some regional countries, for example South Korea, were, prior to democratization, judged to be good candidates for democratization because of their relative wealth. Other regional countries, such as the Philippines, were much poorer, and hence seen as unlikely candidates. In sum, many observers would anticipate that in South Korea democratization would be facilitated by its level of economic growth, while democratization in the Philippines would be unlikely, or at least unlikely to endure, because of the country's relative poverty.

Much of the theoretical literature would accept that, while in poor countries it is often difficult to democratize, in wealthy countries democracy has 'already occurred. In between there is a "political transition zone": countries in this middle economic stratum are those most likely to transit to democracy, and most countries that transit to democracy will be in this stratum' (Huntington 1991: 31). In East and South East Asia, sustained economic growth over time in many countries, as well as periodic economic malaise, for example connected to the regional financial crisis in 1997–8, encouraged democrats to demand fundamental political reforms. But whereas international support for pro-democracy actors, most notably from the government of the United States, had earlier encouraged many local democrats to call for reforms, the events of 1997–8 led to external pressure becoming more muted. This was because the US government, concerned with 'Washington consensus' goals – that is, a free market framework as the basis of globalization – was more concerned to see political and economic stability than democracy. In other words, in the late 1990s the contingent factor of external pressure to reform gradually took second place to a stronger concern with stability.

The point is that external factors can be as important as domestic factors for chances of democracy and democratic consolidation, but that their influence and impact can differ over time. However, as Burnell argues, an adverse external environment – for example, a 'global economic slump or international financial crisis' – can help facilitate 'significantly . . . chances of democratic deconsolidation, or failures to consolidate' (1998: 12). While international pressures may help persuade economically privileged elites that democratic transition will not seriously harm their interests, and so help turn aside their opposition, 'by further entrenching such groups in the economy, these same international forces are possibly dimming the longer term prospects for greater social and political equality' (Burnell 1998: 23).

This suggests that in an increasingly globalized economic system, the economic prospects and outcomes of individual states are not only the result of local decisions but are also linked to international factors. The latter can operate either to aid or to hinder democracy. One view is that the advance of economic neoliberalism in the form of a 'Washington consensus' – expressed via the coordinated actions of international financial institutions, such as the IMF and the World Bank, and, more generally, through global market pressures – helps promote economic (and perhaps political) *liberalization* while necessarily restraining democratization, as it is likely to encourage opposition leaders to call for social empowerment and expenditure, as well as participation by the poor in demanding fundamental political changes.

A further aspect of these international factors related to democratization noted in regard to East and South East Asia is when foreign governments, anxious to pursue their own strategic agendas, do their utmost to *deter* democratization. Gills, Rocamora and Wilson (1993) claim that the nature of democratic changes in some East and South East Asian countries has long been linked to the interests of important external actors, notably the government of the US. Over time, they suggest, the US government, in cahoots with local conservative elites, worked to limit the chances of regional democratization. This is because both parties were said to share an interest in limiting the extent of political changes. The outcome was 'low intensity democracy' (LID): a democratic veneer overlaying an otherwise unreformed political structure, with power staying in more or less the same hands as before – with the *illusion* only of democracy. This is a theory of democracy and democratic consolidation that highlights the limited significance of democratic advances in the East and South East Asian region, in part because of the contingent effect of certain powerful external actors. In short, the LID argument is that external forces helped dictate and control processes of political change in the East and South East Asian region for their own aims and those of entrenched authoritarian elites. This was a strategy which was intimately connected to their continued economic control and the survival in power of local allies.

In this section we have examined the importance of structural and contingent factors in explaining and accounting for the varied regional political outcomes. Next we turn to the case studies to examine such issues in the context of two regional countries: South Korea and the Philippines.

5.4   Case studies: South Korea and the Philippines

Some observers suggest that in regional terms, and despite its structural legacy rooted in Confucianism, South Korea has – along with Taiwan – moved farthest to democratize and even to consolidate democracy, following its pacted transition in the 1980s. Chances of democracy are said to be facilitated by South Korea's highly developed economy and its social homogeneity, yet diminished by relatively weak civil societies, leaders wary of allowing 'too much' democracy which might be destabilizing and, finally, the inherited structural legacy of Confucianism.

There is a different situation in the Philippines. There, democratization, while contemporaneous with South Korea's shift from authoritarian rule, was by way of unpacted transition. That is, democracy was propelled by popular pressure. Later, however, when elites regained political control, democratization lost its dynamism and as a consequence democratic consolidation was elusive. This state of affairs was said to be facilitated by the poor economic position of the Philippines, wide divisions between rich and poor, lack of social homogeneity and, in particular, serious ethnic and religious divisions, and a fragmented civil society (Aglionby and Denny 2000). In sum, it is important to note that South Korea and the Philippines are very different. Our account will focus on the problems for democracy in each country through analysis of the respective impact of structural and contingent factors.

South Korea

Political culture and regime legitimacy

South Korea is of particular interest in a regional survey of democracy and democratic consolidation because, some argue, it appears to have found the 'holy grail': clear democratic advances and sustained economic growth. South Korea began displaying what Przeworski (1986: 55) calls 'the signals of opening' in the mid-1980s, characterized by mass rallies and popular demands for political change. Eventually, however, an elite-dominated pacted transition from authoritarian rule ensued. Given this pacted transition, the theoretical literature would expect that the chances of limited democratization would be relatively good. Huntington (1991) suggests that democratization and eventual democratic consolidation will *only* be promoted if transitions involve negotiations and deals between the outgoing elite and the leading representatives of the democratic opposition. Linz and Stepan (1996) argue that the constitutional compact reflected in pacted transitions, in defining the new regime's main laws, procedures and institutions, is a necessary condition for resolving existing social conflicts peacefully and favours democratization. But, as both studies acknowledge, there will be a democratic price to pay. Because future stability is founded on guarantees secured by the old ruling elites, striving to protect and maintain privileges, impatient to escape judgement for any crimes committed during their rule, then stable yet limited democracies are likely to be the result of pacted transitions.

Korea's political transition had long roots. Pursuing a strategy of forced developmentalism from the 1950s, the state had managed to impose a coercive break with the traditional economy and lifestyles of its citizens. As a result, the democratic transition of the 1980s was from an authoritarian, some would say draconian regime, highly adept at suppressing the personal liberty and political freedoms of Koreans. Consequently, in order to democratize significantly it would have to overcome structural characteristics of authoritarianism which had been instrumental in enabling successive governments to transform society.

To understand the process of democratization in South Korea over time we need to take account of two important structural factors: (1) significant land reforms in the late 1940s and early 1950s; and (2) the impact of a highly authoritarian regime prior to democratization. One of the prerequisites for democracy often noted in the literature is fundamental land reform, necessary in order to beak the power of large-scale landowners and hence remove them as a fundamental impediment to political change (Cammack 1997; Rueschemeyer et al. 1992). Land reform was undertaken in South Korea in the late 1940s and early 1950s and, with the encouragment of the government of the US, the class of large-scale landlords was eradicated as a political and economic force. Following the Korean War (1950–3), land reforms provided an important foundation for political reforms, although democratization did not take place until more than 30 years later. South Korea's experiences underline that historical changes in the balance of power between the state and rural class structures do not automatically or by themselves lead quickly to democracy.

However, it is highly plausible to suggest that South Korea might not have democratized at all were there still a powerful class of anti-democracy, large-scale landlords which, allied to the state, would have fought tooth and nail to prevent it. But this does not explain the *timing* of democratization. It was inaugurated in South Korea because of a specific conjunction of developments at a particular time – the late 1980s – which highlights the contingent factor of political agency. That is, leaders, informed by the growing sociopolitical stresses and strains encouraged by speedy economic development, encouraged by the government of the US and domestic popular pressures to reform, chose to introduce democratic reforms (Cummings 1989).

A second structural factor is linked to South Korea experiences with authoritarian dictatorships for decades prior to democratization. While specific characteristics of regimes differed, generally speaking all were governments that put a high value on swift, enforced industrialization as the key means to modernize the country. Managed by a comprehensive state bureaucracy, and enforced and underpinned by a cohesive and ruthless military and secret police apparatus, the desired modernization, it was believed, would not be achieved without the strong repression of political freedoms – to a degree rarely seen outside communist Eastern Europe. The 18-year dictatorship of Park Chung Hee (1961–79) was especially notable for regime-directed terror against opponents. To some degree this was explicable in the international and ideological context: faced with the threat from the neighbouring Stalinist regime of Kim Il Sung in North

Korea, the Park regime manifested a Cold War paranoia which saw enemies everywhere, real, imagined or artificially constructed. Laws against subversion – for example, banning extreme left-wing parties and prohibiting political activities, including pro-democracy agitation – were broad enough to intimidate any substantial social, religious or political opposition, seen as aiding the North Korean communist enemy and thus endangering national security (Oh and Park 1999: 3).

However, the fear of North Korea did not end with the demise of military rule, and was used throughout the 1990s – that is, well after the democratic transition – as justification to repress opposition activists. For example, in 1992 the first democratically elected president, Kim Young Sam, ordered the arrest of more than 1,000 opposition leaders and in 1997 nearly 1,500. In the same year there was a 'massive crackdown on the Hanchongryun, the pro-unification student movement'. In addition, in early 1999 there were 'daily arrests of [pro-unification] student and labour leaders', linked to an 'explosion of social issues [focused in] new social movements, including human rights, environmental, feminist, and gay movements' (Oh and Park 1999: 4–5). In sum, the legacy of authoritarian rule was to keep democratic progress under control so as not to further the interests of North Korea.

Political participation and institutions

The legitimacy of the post-authoritarian regime was to some degree linked to its ability to deal with the perceived threat from North Korea. However, as Shin notes, compared to Latin America, 'South Korea began its transition to democracy with much less painful and fearful memories of its own non-democratic past. Memories of political repression, economic poverty and social inequality were neither pervasive nor deeply ingrained in Korean minds to the extent to which they were in the citizenry of most Latin American countries' (1999: 248).

A relative lack of fear of the consequences of democratic transition probably encouraged South Korea's authoritarian rulers to agree to democratize. The transition itself was based on a compromise between government elites and pro-democracy forces (Gills 1993: 238–9). The first relatively free and fair elections were held in 1988, at both central and local levels. Prior to this elections had been held regularly since 1967 but were tightly controlled affairs. During President Park's rule, political competition was restricted in a tightly controlled, two-party system. On the one hand, there was the centre-right Democratic Republican Party (DRP), formed in 1963 as an electoral mechanism for the ruling military junta, and, on the other, there was the centre-left New Democratic Party (NDP), founded in 1967 as the vehicle of anti-junta opposition groups. The DRP eventually became the personal vehicle of President Park until his assassination in 1979, while the NDP was relatively inconsequential. After Park's death it briefly appeared that the NDP would acquire the electoral upper hand, but it did not happen: the existing parties were dissolved in 1980 following a constitutional referendum, to be replaced by a new – still strongly controlled – multiparty system for the 1981 parliamentary and presidential elections.

Following the 1981 elections, in a move which some have identified as the first sign of political liberalization, eight parties obtained legislative representation. The new president, Roh Tae Woo, announced the popular election of local, municipal and provincial assemblies, with political parties able to nominate candidates for the first time for elections at these levels. In the 1985 elections the Democratic Korea Party (DKP) emerged as the largest party with 35.3 per cent of the popular vote on a high voting turnout: 84.6 per cent (IDEA 1998: 70). Later, in 1987, a powerful opposition grouping finally emerged when two leading dissidents, Kim Dae Jung and Kim Young Sam, joined a group of opposition politicians to announce the formation of a new party, the Reunification Democratic Party (RDP). However, this coalitional group later subdivided, before bipartisan politics returned in 1991 with the expansion of the opposition Democratic Party to accommodate Kim Dae Jung and his party. The first democratic election for a national president followed in 1992.

These events, Shin argues, were characteristic of a *limited* democracy. This was because the plethora of – presidential, parliamentary and local – elections from the 1980s were not fought in the context of 'a truly democratic party system'. As during the authoritarian period, parties were still primarily vehicles of individual politicians, rather than representative bodies with 'broad and reliable ties' with the mass of the people (1999: 191). The point is that this reflected the traditional nature of parties in Korea, a society with its roots in Confucianism, and until this changed it would be difficult to develop the democratic system further. For Shin, the main problem was that the age-old principles of Confucianism venerating individual leaders over representative organizations were still paramount for many Koreans. Consequently, for the foreseeable future, Korea would be unlikely to transform itself into the type of culture that could underpin 'a fully democratic party system' (Shin 1999: 191–2).

Economic and international factors

South Korea's democratic transition in the 1980s took place against a background of sustained economic growth. Whereas in 1950 South Korea had an annual GNP per capita of just $146, by the late 1990s the country was an impressive economic and industrial power with a GNP per capita of nearly $8,000, a 54-fold increase (World Bank 2000: 230). After colonialism, economic growth was guided by the authoritarian state, a legacy of Japanese colonialism. A decision, taken in the 1960s, was particularly important: to place economic decision-making in the hands of a technocratic elite, insulated from societal pressures, especially from labour. The technocrats, allowed considerable economic powers, set about forcefully encouraging export-oriented industrialization. In addition, the government not only established a close alliance with the country's large business groups, the *chaebols*, but also restructured the state bureaucracy and, generally, brought about an institutional transformation.

As the Cold War intensified in the 1950s and 1960s, Korea's main international ally, the US government, was content with a staunchly anti-communist regional ally. Later, in the 1980s, when the communist threat was seen to dissipate, the Reagan government began to promote democracy to its authoritarian allies. It created the National Endowment for Democracy, the main vehicle of US support for democracy at the global level. To this end more than $700 million was provided to over a hundred countries, including South Korea, to assist democratic transitions. But US support for Korea's democratization was not entirely disinterested. Changes in the world economic and political circumstances suggested that Korea should pay less attention to its traditional strategy – the authoritarian, statist development model – and more concern to developing a domestic consensus about future economic and political directions. In addition, both the American and Japanese governments argued that for Korea to become a full member of the international community it would be necessary to have a recognizably democratic system. In sum, contingent – international and economic – factors were instrumental in Korea's democratization, especially during the 1980s.

Ten years later, in October 1997, Korea experienced severe, albeit brief, financial difficulties and applied to the IMF for an emergency rescue package. Later, in December, a $57 billion agreement was signed – the largest ever negotiated with the IMF. At this time, the bankruptcy of one of the largest *chaebols* – the Hanbo steel and construction conglomerate – generated a financial scandal and led to the prosecution of a number of individuals on fraud and embezzlement charges. Among those prosecuted were the founder of the conglomerate Hanbo and the son of Kim Young Sam, the president of the country, who was sentenced to three years in prison. While the economic crisis turned out to be short-lived, the government implemented a series of IMF-mandated reforms of the economy (Elliot and Denny 1999). Significantly, the brief economic crisis illustrated that, to some extent, democratic institutions were becoming embedded in Korea by the late 1990s: unlike in the past, influential figures could not ensure that they would escape prosecution because of who they were or whom they knew.

Conclusion

Nagle and Mahr argue that, because South Korea's Confucian culture still appears to be an important cultural determinant of political behaviour, the country has developed an authoritarian and communitarian version of democracy different from the generic Western model based on individual freedoms (1999: 261–3). Diamond suggests to the contrary that the weight of changes associated with the country's recent democratization and modernization will quickly transform South Korea – he suggests, 'within a generation' – into a 'consolidated liberal democracy' (1999: 272). These conflicting opinions of the nature of Korea's political characteristics reflect both the difficulty of assessing the legacy of the past – decades of authoritarian, developmentally oriented rule, underpinned by a Confucian acceptance of the importance of individual leaders over organizations – and a lack of clarity as to future political outcomes. Whether Korea retains its authoritarian characteristics or develops into a recognizably Western-style polity would seem to be linked not only to the ability of individual presidents to preside over necessary changes, but also the extent to which pro-democracy political actors in civil and political society can develop. It seems plausible that there is now state willingness in Korea to accept that political opposition is inherently legitimate, and confidence that the North Korean threat is evaporating.

Our analysis of Korea's gradual democratization points to the importance of both structure and agency factors in determining political outcomes, and illustrates 'how structural theories of democratization are incomplete without the inclusion of choice and action' by individual actors and factors (Potter 1997a: 237). The decision to strip large-scale landowners of their land, encouraged by the government of the US, and pass it to the landless five decades ago was an essential stage in the evolution of democracy. This is true even though clear signs of democratization did not happen until decades later. The point is that land reform measures destroyed the hitherto powerful landowning class which would have been expected – as in many Latin American countries – to be strong opponents of democratization. In other words, the inherited structural legacy of Confucianism was to an extent counterbalanced by contingent factors, including land reforms, international encouragement and the willingness of military leaders, encouraged by pro-democracy civil and political society actors, to agree to democratic reforms.

The Philippines

The colonial, political, economic and cultural backgrounds to attempts to democratize in the Philippines are very different from those in Korea. Unlike the latter, which saw a short period of Japanese colonial rule, the Philippines experienced nearly 400 years of foreign control: first under the Spanish (1564–1898), then under the Americans (1898–1946). This served to create a particular kind of authoritarian political system, built on the power of local oligarchs ('bosses') which was highly unconducive to democratization.

Second, at the time of independence in 1946, the Philippines economy, like that of Korea, was characterized by a largely unmodernized agricultural sector and underdeveloped industries. Large-scale landowners were an important political class in both countries but whereas land reforms in Korea followed independence, they did not in the Philippines.

Third, while South Korea developed an impressive economy under the *dirigiste* control of a highly focused state, in the Philippines both economic and political systems were deeply rooted in a patronage system that was not only a major source of serious inter-elite conflict but failed to develop a prosperous economy.

Fourth, whereas Korea had the legacy of Confucianism to inform post-colonial developments, the Philippines has a quite different cultural background rooted in Christianity. However, this did not prevent the emergence of a long-term dictator, Ferdinand Marcos, who ruled from 1965 to 1986.

Finally, by contrast with Korea's experience of a pacted transition, democratization in the Philippines occurred under the influence of popular pressure. Marcos had initially claimed that he wanted to undertake substantive political and economic reforms, but soon succumbed to the politics of patronage – for many observers, one of the Philippines' most important structural characteristics, eventually making it the central aspect of his government's operations. In short, the structural characteristics of the system soon overcame any true concerns with reform that Marcos may have had on coming to power.

The turn to democracy in 1986, delivered by 'popular power', reflected societal outrage at the incompetence and corruption of Marcos's regime. However, it might be argued that at this point the country did not face a clear choice between autocracy and democracy. Instead, the outcome would be determined by the extent to which inherited structural factors linked to authoritarianism would be overcome by contingent factors linked to democracy. Referring to the latter, observers note that the Philippines has a number of pro-democracy characteristics, including (1) an active civil society, with a high degree of associational activity; (2) a gradual strengthening of democratic institutions (despite serious economic setbacks in the late 1990s, the country's democratic institutions were said to have stood up 'robustly' (Putzel 1999: 214)); (3) flourishing, critical media, with dozens of Manila-published, as well as provincial, papers; and (4) most ordinary Filipinos claimed to be in favour of democracy – certainly, large percentages have regularly turned out to vote, averaging around 70 per cent in presidential and legislative polls since 1986 (IDEA 1998).

On the other hand, observers point out that democracy seems very fragile because it is not (yet) firmly institutionalized; that is, since 1986 successive elected governments have – like their authoritarian predecessors – ruled primarily for the benefit of a small civilian and military elite. Democracy after 1986 failed to lead to the development of a healthy party structure in the country's political system. Instead, it remained characterized by the importance of populism and clan politics, factors which had been central to political competition since the colonial period. This had four main, interrelated political characteristics: (1) clan alliances and 'bossism' (that is, control by powerful individuals, especially in the rural areas) dominated the political scene, penetrating the state and the bureaucracy so that they did not function as impersonal public authorities; (2) attempted political decentralization was ineffective as power remained in the hands of local 'bosses'; (3) government was beholden to the support of important political patrons; and (4) the judicial system was corrupted by the ability of powerful individuals and groups to influence outcomes. This led to sharp inequalities of treatment between rich and poor. In sum, the country's structural political characteristics made it highly unlikely that democratization from below would be characterized by fundamental political reforms.

Political culture and regime legitimacy

The legacy of US colonialism was an important structural factor inhibiting the development of representative institutions and democracy. While ostensibly democratic institutions had been introduced during American control (1898–1946), from the outset they were under the power of small numbers of oligarchs ('bosses'). Bosses were – and are – electoral and economic powerbrokers with virtually monopolistic control over entire localities to the extent that, after independence, patronage politics dominated the political system at national and local levels. The outcome was that the results of electoral contests were dependent on the ability of politicians to influence the voting process by buying votes. Often half-hearted attempts to create an effective party system failed, unable to overcome the legacy of irresponsible factionalism and landowner power.

The result, as Cammack, Pool and Tordoff note, was that the Philippines exhibits a 'blend of formally democratic institutions under oligarchic control', giving rise to 'an irresponsible political system' with three main characteristics (1993: 69). First, the country's factionalized political system was organized on the basis of patronage networks often financed by members of the political class sharing state funds among themselves. Second, unlike in Korea, the state declined to introduce land reform, thus ensuring that the social dominance of the landowning class continued. Third, there was a close relationship with the United States, the former colonial power. Marcos's big plus point for the US government was not only that he managed to stabilize the political system but also that he put much effort into defeating local communist insurgents. The US aided the regime by, *inter alia*, a free trade and aid agreement, which helped ensure that Marcos and his cronies were adequately – if corruptly – compensated for their endeavours. During Marcos's rule both he and his favoured friends benefited from control of important sectors of the economy, such as sugar and coconuts, while the Ministry of Human Settlements, run by Marcos's wife, Imelda, functioned primarily as a vast patronage machine.

In 1969, four years after his accession to power, and backed by the United States, Marcos 'bought himself reelection'. Three years later, in 1972, he declared martial law in order to avoid having to step down from power after two terms of office, as the constitution demanded. For the next decade and a half, Marcos ruled via a blend of 'corruption, manipulation, repression, and murder' (Cammack et al. 1993: 69). His hold on power was not only strengthened by US support but also by his close relationship with the country's armed forces, allies in fighting both communist and Muslim insurgents in some of the southern islands. Over time, the political influence of the armed forces grew to the extent that the military became a de facto partner of Marcos in government. However, the reputation of the military summarily dissolved in August 1983 when Benito Aquino, a popular opposition leader, was murdered, probably by military personnel. This act prompted the founding of the Reform the Armed Forces Movement, an organization that enjoyed the support of the United States government, anxious by this time to see the Marcos government 'clean up its act'.

In sum, the Philippines political culture was heavily rooted in factionalism, corruption and authoritarianism under Marcos. His regime, initially enjoying much support from the US, gradually lost its legitimacy, culminating in the murder of Benito Aquino in 1983, a trigger for the people's power movement.

Political participation and institutions

Democratic theory suggests that a robust, relatively unfragmented party structure is at the heart of a democratic political system. As already noted, in the Philippines parties have traditionally 'been weak in periods of democratic politics, and weaker still when used to mobilise support for authoritarian rule' (Cammack et al. 1993: 109). Between independence in 1946 and the imposition of martial law in 1972, political control oscillated between two weak parties, the Nacionalista Party and the Liberal Party. The result was that by the time of the overthrow of Marcos in 1986 and the landslide victory of Corazon (Cory) Aquino, wife of the late Benito Aquino, in May 1987, there was no articulated party structure in place to help determine political outcomes in a democratic direction.

Marcos's fall was facilitated by a burgeoning of civil society and political opposition which formed the core of the people's power movement, a direct result of several factors, including (1) widespread perceptions that the existing political system could not focus a fundamental attack on the authoritarian power; and (2) outrage at Marcos's electoral fraud in earlier elections, for example, that of 1978. Marcos, a neopatrimonial ruler wielding power primarily through his own personalist network, was never able to create a viable party to support his regime. However, as Luckham notes, the lack of a well articulated party structure meant that 'people's power' served only to 'usher in a formal democracy, *without guaranteeing it [would] remain democratic*', with Filipinos mobilized to support 'not democrats, but authoritarian populists' (1998: 310, emphasis added).

In 1987, despite pronouncements from the top, the coalition of interests that came to power behind Cory Aquino was determined not to build a democratic revolution but, if possible, to restore the Marcos-era *status quo ante*. Disappointing those who believed it would implement significant social and land reforms, the Aquino government conspicuously 'failed to advance the economic conditions for effective political participation by the lower-class majority'. On the other hand, *had* Cory Aquino sought to take such steps it was highly likely that 'she would not have survived' politically, as the armed forces would have stepped in to overthrow her government (Gills et al. 1993: 221). Presidents after Aquino, including the current leader, Joseph Estrada, made few attempts to solidify and strengthen the party system and other putatively democratic institutions. Despite frequently stated desires for fundamental political changes, post-Marcos political parties and other political institutions remained 'as weak nearly half a century on from independence as they had been at the outset' (Cammack et al. 1993: 112).

Economic and international factors

In the 1940s it would have been plausible to predict the long-term democratic consolidation and economic success of the Philippines, given its 'Americanist culture and political structures and a GNP per capita vastly ahead of Japan, South Korea, and Taiwan' (Pempel 1999: 155). But things turned out differently: by the end of the 1990s, Japan's GNP per capita was $32,380, South Korea's $7,970, and that of the Philippines $1,050 (World Bank 2000). This outcome made it plain just how poor the economic strategies and leadership of successive governments had been and that they had collectively mismanaged the economy to a considerable degree. While, as already noted, Marcos's regime was very successful in amassing wealth for the president, his family and his favoured cohorts, the country's economy did much less well during his rule, fatally affected by 'the political economy of patrimonialism' (Wurfel 1988: 258).

After Marcos the economy remained sickly, dependent to a considerable extent on external economic resources, which helped to perpetuate an environment of social polarization and extremes of poverty affecting millions of people. In the mid-1990s, the poorest 40 per cent of the country's households, over 30 million people, shared only one-sixth of the national income, with some families existing on the equivalent of US$1 a day or less. At this time, the perilous economic situation was exacerbated by the social conse- quences of the conditions of an IMF loan which hit the poorest hard (Elliot and Denny 1999). While the economy grew by an impressive 5.8 per cent in 1996–7, in the following year it shrank again, by 2.1 per cent (World Bank 2000: 231). Such circumstances would not be expected to be conducive to the consolidation of democracy.

Following Marcos's overthrow, the US government, determined 'to ensure the restoration of a liberal democratic regime friendly to Western interests', gained its objective with the election as president of Cory Aquino (Putzel 1997: 257). While US governments have claimed to encourage democratization in the Philippines, they have appeared to be content with highly limited democracy as long as it has sustained a stable political system. Certainly there has been little real encouragement in recent years to the country's rulers to deepen democratization beyond periodic elections. Reflecting such concerns, Gills, Rocamora and Wilson (1993) argue that recent democratic changes were little more than attempts to put a gloss on the con- tinuing hegemony of incumbent conservative elites aided by signifi- cant American governmental support.

Conclusion

The third round of post-Marcos elections, in 1998, demonstrated that, in a procedural sense, 'the democracy restored 12 years before was essentially stable and relatively healthy' (Putzel 1999: 198). That is, if the health of a democracy can be judged by the peaceful trans- fer of power through the electoral process, as Huntington (1991) claims, then the Philippines, in the midst of a regional economic crisis, appeared to pass the test. The question, however, is this: beyond the existence of certain procedural norms, what *kind* of democracy did the Philippines have? The first point to note is that it would be incor- rect to claim that there were *no* significant political changes after Marcos. One of the most obvious was that the old, albeit politically ineffectual, two-party structure broke down, replaced henceforward by a number of clan alliances which competed in elections as 'parties'. This meant that, in effect, there was a separate political party for each major contender for the presidency. But this development was not conducive to democratic consolidation.

Fifteen years after the overthrow of Marcos, democracy in the Philippines is both shallow and fragile, principally because of the mismatch between formal political institutions and the informal institutions that govern behaviour and influence the standards of legitimacy. The point is that informal institutions are slow to change, both because of the interests in society that they reflect – including 'bosses' – and because they govern mental models in and through which the great majority of people live their daily lives. For example, the extensive clan-based network of patronage produced a kind of social capital that may have been good for clan business interests, as well as the prosperity of the communities directly involved, but, on the debit side, the 'shared norms, values and networks produced by this system act as a barrier, rather than an aid, to the deepening of democracy and probably to the overall trajectory of economic development' (Putzel 1999: 216–17).

In sum, understanding the nature of the political system of the Philippines requires a focus on both structural and contingent factors. Structural issues include (1) the significance of historically determined configurations of power; (2) the role of external factors in determining democratic possibilities; (3) factors linked to the country's patchy modernization, including patterns of national integration linked to ethnic and religious identities which help to mould the political strategies of certain minority groups, such as the southern Muslims ('Moros') in opposition to the state. Contingent factors include what leading political actors do and why they do it. Crucial here are the perceptions of such individuals as to what political strategies and outcomes are appropriate for acquiring and retaining power.

5.5 Overall conclusions

We have noted in this chapter that, despite considerable political, cultural and other differences, polities in East and South East Asia have been characterized by long periods of authoritarian rule. In each case, authoritarian rule – whether it be the Confucian and military legacy in South Korea or that of 'bossism' in the Philippines – endowed post-authoritarian orders with highly significant autocratic and authoritarian circumstances. The result was that neither in South Korea nor the Philippines was the rule of law well developed, while governmental accountability was also lacking. Both countries retained strong memories of arbitrary exercises of power by unaccountable leaders and their military allies. These factors strongly inhibited the development of recognizably pro-democracy political cultures in South Korea and the Philippines, that is, what Lipset (1994) calls 'the effectiveness domain' of democratic culture.

The two countries examined in this chapter both passed a crucial first test for the embedding of recognizably democratic regimes – peaceful handing over of power following several elections. Yet neither has yet managed to transform itself into a polity with clearly representative institutions. Both remain hierarchically organized and politically fragmented. As Friedman notes, the lack of clearly and emphatically pro-democracy political cultures will affect legislative assemblies, political parties and other newly established democratic institutions, which, as a result, 'must consolidate themselves without yet benefiting from democratic culture and democratic socialization' (1994: 45). This goal has been elusive.

While the characteristics of post-transition governments in the region typically illustrate the importance of structural factors to recent political developments, they also emphasize that there are not one or two, but numerous, generic sets of 'Asian values' helping to mould political directions and outcomes. While South Korea appears to observers like Diamond to have made good democratic progress and to be well on the way to the development of a consolidated liberal democratic polity, others caution against undue optimism regarding progress towards *liberal* democracy. Shin suggests that, *pace* Diamond, Korea is 'likely to tread on a very unsteady and long march towards consolidation for many years, even decades to come' (1999: 262). Although Korea is relatively ethnically and religiously homogeneous – compared, for example, to many African and South Asian countries – the structural legacy of Confucianism appears to be a significant drawback to the development of liberal democracy. This is a way of saying that contingent factors, such as pro-democracy domestic and external actors, have not been able to outweigh inherited authoritarian factors of the political system. There is more of a consensus regarding the Philippines. While some observers see positive signs in the growth of pro-democracy civil society actors, it appears clear that the weight of inherited anti-democratic factors will be enough to prevent the development of a recognizably democratic polity in the short or medium term.

6
South Asia

6.1 Introduction

South Asian countries differ greatly in terms of size, geography, economic structures, political traditions, forms of rule, relations with
external powers, and cultures. The region has had a variable democratic history since its emergence from colonial rule in the late 1940s,
reflected in the region's political diversity: monarchical rule in Nepal,
long-running civil war in Sri Lanka between Tamils and Sinhalese,
alternating military and civilian regimes in Bangladesh and Pakistan,
and India's established democratic system. However, all regional
countries, with the exception of Pakistan, had democratically elected
governments in 2000.

During the 1980s and 1990s, South Asia became part of the third
wave of democracy. The consequence, Rizvi claims, was that the
'democratic transformation of South Asia in the aftermath of the
Cold War has been breathtaking' (1995: 84). Kumaraswamy notes
that the 'end of the cold war and the emerging new international
order' was important for democratization in the region (1999: 186).
In 1988, following pressure from the American government, Pakistan
shifted to democratic rule from military government (before revert-
ing again to military government in 1999). Both Bangladesh and
Nepal democratized in the early 1990s, from military and monarchical forms of rule respectively. Overall, regional democratic
progress was exemplified by the fact that during 1988–99, South Asia
witnessed over 20 governments, and, most unusually, *all* came to
power via democratic processes.

Table 6.1 Democracy in South Asia, 1989–1999

	Political rights (PR)		Civil liberties (CL)		PR + CL average	PR + CL average	Freedom rating
	1988–9	1998–9	1988–9	1998–9	1988–9	1998–9	1998–9
India	2	3	3	2	2.5	2.5	Free
Nepal	4	4	3	3	3.5	3.5	Partly free
Bangladesh	5	4	4	4	4.5	4	Partly free
Sri Lanka	3	4	4	4	3.5	4	Partly free
Pakistan	5	5	4	4	4.5	4.5	Partly free

Source: 'Annual survey of Freedom country scores, 1972–73 to 1998–99',
http://www.freedomhouse.org/survey99/method/

Freedom House data, reproduced in table 6.1, indicate that while India, Pakistan, Sri Lanka, Nepal and Bangladesh were all 'free' or 'partly free' states in 1999, only Bangladesh had seen an improvement in its political rights situation in the preceding decade. The civil liberties position showed a slight improvement in India, with things broadly the same in Bangladesh, Nepal, Pakistan and Sri Lanka. In short, while democratic institutions were commonly in place in South Asian countries in the 1990s, the progress of democracy across the region was slow and problematic.

We focus in the region's case studies on what many regard as its most politically interesting countries: India and Pakistan. While India is a long-term democracy and Pakistan has long alternated between military and civilian rule, both countries have recently had increasingly short-lived and tenuous governments. India, long noted for its democratic stability under the aegis of the hegemonic Congress Party, experienced a sharpening of political disputes, a general decline in political stability, and fragmentation of the party system, with numerous new parties claiming to represent formerly marginalized interests. This highlights how in India, whereas elections and party competition once focused on certain politically active castes and groups, previously politically marginal groups, often motivated by class, gender, ethnic or religious concerns, increasingly made their political preferences felt via the ballot box. In order to explain these developments, which some observers see as indicating democratic *de*consolidation, we focus on a range of structural and contingent factors.

In the 1990s the political situation in India's neighbour, Pakistan, was also characterized by political volatility. Short-lived elected governments followed each other rapidly, before the military stepped in in October 1999 to close down the democratic system. This was a generally popular move, indicative of declining popular belief in the efficacy of the country's democratic system. Despite the unconstitutional nature of the takeover, some prominent civilians called openly for a political system that gave the armed forces a permanent, institutionalized, 'supervisory' political role. Most ordinary people, disgusted at the inability of successive civilian governments to control the scale of corruption, were said to be 'disillusioned, apathetic, weary ... indifferent to the fate of the venal politicians ... so busy lining their own pockets that they had little time to ponder the welfare of the country and its people' (Ali 1999).

First, we turn our attention to the dissimilarities between India and Pakistan in order to highlight the importance of structural and contingent factors in explaining their political differences. Second, we focus upon (1) the declining political efficacy of structural factors in underpinning India's democratic system; and (2) the reasons for the difficulty Pakistan has had in establishing a viable democratic system.

6.2   Structural impediments to democracy in South Asia

The political histories of India and Pakistan reflect several *structural* factors of importance in explaining their differing democratic histories. They are:

- *Widespread religious and ethnic competition and conflicts*   Both countries have large numbers of different ethnic and religious groups which would, many democratic theorists would expect, make it difficult to develop an environment facilitating democratic sustainability.
- *The nature of the political relationship between the state and the armed forces*   Pakistan, but not India, has traditionally had a close relationship between state and military elites. In Pakistan, but not in India, the military has traditionally had a powerful political role.
- *Weak governmental legitimacy and accountability*   Following independence, for several decades successive Congress Party governments in India helped develop the country's political system rooted in democracy. Such an outcome did not occur in Pakistan, where neither a viable party system nor a hegemonic party like Congress developed. However, the increasing incidence of weak,

short-lived governments in both countries suggests that regimes
have struggled to build their legitimacy among increasingly
cynical populations, who see them as largely unaccountable and
unrepresentative.

Turning to *contingent* factors, India's democratic history is studded
with examples highlighting the importance of such factors. First,
pro-democracy nationalist leaders adeptly exploited the situation
immediately after World War II, when a much-weakened Britain
finally became willing to grant India freedom from colonial rule.
Second, incoming nationalist leaders, including the prime minister,
Jawaharlal Nehru, were personally strongly committed to democracy
and used their positions in power to help embed democratic institutions and norms of behaviour. Third, as the hegemony of the Congress Party waned in the wake of various corruption scandals – to
the extent that in the 1980s it lost its formerly tight grip on power –
new, populist leaders emerged who were able to exploit the situation
to further their own electoral fortunes.

The importance of contingency can also be seen in Pakistan's
political developments over time. First, there was the contingent
situation provided by the country's extraordinary emergence as an
independent nation in 1947, resulting in the creation of a dual
country – East and West Pakistan – separated by thousands of
kilometres of hostile Indian territory. Second, the breakdown of
democracy in 1999 was encouraged by the democratically malign
behaviour of senior politicians who, by their corruption and poor
rule, encouraged the army to take over.

6.3   Democratic consolidation in South Asia

We will now examine the comparative importance of the following
factors in order to compare outcomes in India and Pakistan:

1   political culture and regime legitimacy;
2   political participation and institutions;
3   economic and international factors.

Outcomes linked to the first two sets of factors – political culture
and regime legitimacy, and political participation and institutions –
primarily reflect the importance of structural characteristics, while the

latter, economic and international factors, are often informed more by contingent factors.

Political culture and regime legitimacy

Various factors, including the colonial legacy and the strategies of nationalist leaders, were important in accounting for the development of political cultures and perceptions of regime legitimacy in India and Pakistan.

First, a beneficial colonial political and administrative legacy is thought to bolster the chances of democracy and democratic consolidation (Rueschemeyer et al. 1992). While all South Asian countries, with the exception of the tiny Himalayan kingdom of Bhutan, were under British suzerainty for long periods until shortly after World War II, the colonial legacy in this regard was not uniform. While the supposedly beneficial legacy of British colonial structures is often said to be of particular importance in facilitating democracy and its survival in India, the influence of these structures was less clear in Pakistan. This indicates that colonial rule did not leave common political legacies, since among regional countries only India has managed to retain a democratic system over time. This suggests that we need to look beyond structural colonial legacies to explain divergent political outcomes in the two countries.

Since independence, Pakistan has tried various types of government – including civilian parliamentary and presidential rule, as well as military government – to achieve political stability, but without much democratic success. This can partly be explained by the fact that, whereas post-colonial governments in India inherited power in a large – yet politically and religiously relatively homogeneous country – Pakistan had different characteristics. While, like India, Pakistan faced independence with serious rural poverty, low and unstable agricultural yields and a weak economy prey to the vagaries of the annual monsoon, it also faced additional problems. First, there was a massive refugee flow from India in the late 1940s which complicated the political and social situation. Second, Pakistan developed a numerically large and unproductive military establishment which, fearing an attack from India, demanded – and received – a significant proportion of the country's wealth. This not only damaged the country's development chances but more generally led to the military having much political clout. Third, the two parts of the country – East and West Pakistan – were separated by thousands of kilometres of hostile

India. This circumstance not only seriously weakened production possibilities and trade links between them but also made it difficult to build national unity. In sum, while in India the colonial legacy broadly favoured the development of democracy, it did not in dismembered Pakistan.

Second, there was the role of nationalist leaders in helping develop national political cultures. In India, encouraged by the British colonial legacy and the strongly pro-democracy positions of leading nationalist politicians, there was a willingness on the part of political leaders, encouraged by a vibrant civil society, to try to make democracy work. Anxious to avoid a post-colonial political crisis, India's nationalist leaders collectively worked towards an accommodation of the country's different political forces. However, for democracy to thrive over time, as Rizvi points out, 'there has to be a continuing partnership between the elected leaders and the electorate' (1995: 85). Over time, in India, this partnership became strained. The problem, Kohli (1994) suggests, is that India's democratically elected governments failed to do enough to bolster citizens' belief that democracy had the ability to improve their circumstances. This is partly because popular access to government was constrained by layers of bureaucracy, and as a result citizen demands rarely filtered through to remote political leaders far from the concerns of most ordinary people.

The circumstances in Pakistan were initially similar, with nationalist leaders claiming to be strongly in favour of democracy. However, their inability to work together led to the first of Pakistan's many successful military coups in 1958 and, as we shall see below, subsequent problems with building a democratic system.

Political participation and institutions

Political society

A strong and independent political society can help facilitate democratization because it is a focus of interaction among political actors competing legitimately to exercise the right to control power and the state apparatus. While strong and cohesive party systems are thought fundamental to democracy, weak, fragmented party systems make democracy very difficult to achieve and consolidate.

Parties perform a variety of functions thought vital to the prospects of a stable democracy. First, an effective party system helps generally to build confidence in the democratic process by helping to moderate societal demands and to channel them into an institutionalized environment of conflict resolution. Second, it serves to lengthen the time horizons of actors as it periodically provides electoral losers with the means to mobilize resources for later rounds of political competition. Third, an effective party system helps prevent the grievances of disenchanted groups from spilling over into mass mobilization of the kind that takes to the streets to protest and that, as a result, is likely to antagonize the elites and may invite a return to authoritarian rule. In sum, effective political parties are important in helping democratically elected officials to govern, while offering a societally important form of representation.

What has been the impact of party systems in India and Pakistan on democratic outcomes? In India, the longevity of the democratic system has been linked to the unusual character of the Indian National Congress, later the Congress Party. Prior to decolonization, Congress had managed to develop relatively deep roots in rural society which, after the withdrawal of the British, helped the party both to gain and keep its hold on power for decades through electoral successes. Its ability to put down roots in society was reflected in the construction of a countrywide network of party branches and activists which for decades – from the late 1940s until the mid-1970s – helped to deliver continuous electoral victories for the party at the national level.

In Pakistan, the post-colonial political scene was initially dominated by the Muslim League led by the country's main nationalist leader, Mohammad Ali Jinnah. Jinnah's death in 1948 led to a period of great political turmoil, which culminated in a successful military coup and the imposition of martial law in 1958. Later, when the military was not in power, Pakistan had two main political parties – the Pakistan People's Party and the Pakistan Muslim League. But, like India, Pakistan saw increasing numbers of political parties and organizations, often based on sectional concerns. In both countries, such organizations, rooted in both political and civil society, sought to represent the interests of particularistic regional, ethnic or religious groups. This reflected rising demands from such groups for enhanced state recognition of group rights, a greater say in political outcomes, and/or a larger share of the national economic cake. Such issues, gathered together under the rubric of 'identity politics', highlight the difficulties in seeking solutions to the problem of how to construct post-colonial national unity and build democracy in both India and Pakistan (Vanhanen 1998: 73; Diamond 1999: 50–2).

Civil society

The literature on democratic consolidation is virtually unanimous in declaring that a vibrant civil society is normally rooted in a broad array of interest groups with a common purpose: to encourage the state to develop the strategic capacity to tackle various problems, including poverty and social insecurity. However, successive Pakistani and Indian governments, both military and civilian, relied on centralist and centralizing development strategies, modes of government from which most ordinary people felt excluded. In Pakistan, the weakness of civil society reflected the nature of the country's society, where 'loyalties to religious sects, clans, or ethnic groups tend to vitiate any incentive toward the individual initiative and choice necessary to the democratic process' (Dorr 1993: 132).

India's political history underlines the crucial role of a flourishing civil society for the institutionalization of democracy, while that of Pakistan indicates what can occur in the context of a weak, divided civil society. The sources of this situation are to be found in the colonial period. India had a relatively impressive range of interest groups and organizations under British rule which facilitated the emergence of a well-developed civil society at the time of independence in 1947. Sisson, in his account of the emergence of India's liberal democratic political culture, describes how in the nineteenth century the country witnessed the

> development of a rich associational life. These associations ranged from Westernized political discussion groups to reformist organizations that demanded the government use its resources to engineer social change; it included organizations of landed and commercial interests as well as cultural revivalist organizations and movements bent on resisting the encroachments of Western culture. Particularly after the Mutiny of 1857, numerous political associations were created for the purpose of petitioning government for reform. (1993: 40–1)

India's civil society was the product of two strands of development in the nineteenth and early twentieth centuries: first, facilitated by the relatively benign character of British rule, representative groups and organizations, building on traditional cultural attributes, were allowed to develop. Second, the growth and expansion of an indigenous business community under British rule aided the emergence and development of associated interest groups. Overall, the consequence of these developments was that, by the time of independence in 1947, India possessed a robust civil society which helped the development of the country's democracy.

Economic and international factors

While increasing national prosperity, relatively equitably distributed, is said to be crucial for democracy, lack of economic resources gives governments very little room for manoeuvre and makes effective governance very difficult to achieve. Thus, a country's wealth is said to be closely linked to the chances of democratization and, eventually, democratic consolidation. Judged by such a criterion neither India or Pakistan would have had a strong likelihood of developing democracy, as both are very poor, among the poorest countries in the world.

India emerged from colonial rule as 'a continental patchwork of colonial administrations and "princely states"' (Herring 1999: 312). Chances of economic growth were hardly encouraged by the fact that Indian capital had spread around the globe during the colonial period and was not, as a result, available to be used at home for development purposes. Given such an economic background it was a surprise to many that India managed to sustain democracy continuously from the first parliamentary elections in 1950–1, apart from the 1975–7 period of 'Emergency' when democratic institutions were suspended.

Turning to external factors, Pakistan's economic weakness gave the government of the United States an influential position because it could offer important financial assistance for development purposes. Fearful of the regional threat of the Soviet Union during the Cold War, successive American governments encouraged Pakistan's armed forces to have a major political role – which undermined the chances of democratic institutions developing. Washington judged that Pakistan's military would be the best guarantor of its interests in the South Asia region during the Cold War because Pakistan's 'natural' enemy, India, was strongly allied with the Soviet Union at this time. Pakistan's military governments – including those of General Ayub Khan (1958–68) and General Zia ul-Haq (1977–88) – were strongly backed by the US government because of their perceived ability to bring political stability at times of serious societal disruption and instability. Underlining the important American influence on Pakistan's politics, Ali (1999) suggests that the Zia government was 'spawned by the Pentagon . . . eager for a proxy to take on the Russians in Afghanistan'. In sum, during the Cold War, successive military regimes in Pakistan had considerable, if often tacit, support and approval from Washington in successfully pursuing non-democratic governance.

In sum, while both India and Pakistan shared a colonial background, the circumstances of their forced separation helped to explain differing political outcomes. Turning to external structural factors, while Pakistan was subject to strong US pressure to achieve stability at the expense of democracy, India was able to develop its political structures and processes without external interference. However, over time the efficacy of India's democratic system is said to have drained away. In the next section, we weigh up the evidence in this regard and also examine in more detail the structural attributes of Pakistan which have made a workable democratic system impossible to achieve.

6.4   Case studies: India and Pakistan

We have already referred to some of the ways in which the countries are politically different and it might be useful to summarize the distinctions between the countries before going any further. First, Pakistan has alternated between elected civilian governments and unelected military regimes, while India is a long-term democracy. Second, India has a politically disinterested military, unlike neighbouring Pakistan, with its long periods of military rule. Third, apart from a brief authoritarian period – the 1975–7 Emergency – India had periodic general elections supervised by an independent Electoral Commission. Defeated governments have bowed out (more or less) gracefully. Pakistan, by contrast, has never managed to embed democracy over a long period; it has never become the 'natural' system of government. Fourth, while India's media have long been fiercely independent – regularly covering stories of political wrongdoing and corruption – Pakistani newspapers, television and radio were traditionally less willing to expose such malignities. Fifth, India's courts have regularly convicted corrupt politicians and bureaucrats, handing out long prison sentences, with the judicial system an important conduit for an increasingly disillusioned public anxious to see corrupt public figures punished. Pakistan's courts are more politicized, with judicial outcomes often influenced by political pressures. Sixth, while Indians enjoy a robust set of constitutionally derived citizens' rights, largely defended by the courts, in Pakistan rights are less developed. Seventh, India's civil society is both vibrant and robust, with many civil rights organizations and local protest movements, while that of Pakistan is relatively underdeveloped. Finally, India's party system, evolving from the Congress-dominated system to the current multiparty system, has shown a great deal of flexibility in adapting to new challenges. The development of Pakistan's party system, on the other hand, has been stymied by long periods of military rule.

In sum, India has managed to embed political structures and processes that have facilitated the long-term survival of its democratic system, while in Pakistan comparable factors encouraging democracy have been lacking or underdeveloped. In the next section, we examine the nature of India's democracy, before turning to an assessment of the political scene in Pakistan and its failure to develop a workable democratic system.

India

India is a puzzle for the comparative study of democratic consolidation. Herring notes some of the problems the country had at the time of independence:

> India exited colonial rule with more than the usual obstacles: truly staggering rural poverty; low and unstable agricultural yields; dismemberment, which severed production and trade links and caused massive refugee flows when East and West Pakistan were hived off by Britain; and an economy that has often been described as a 'gamble on the monsoons' . . . [The end of] colonial rule . . . left India with a difficult geopolitical position in the region and eventually in the global cold war. Confrontation with Pakistan was a consequence of partition; costly wars with Pakistan . . . and unproductive military spending damaged development. (1999: 311–12)

The point is that, rather than a 'natural' democracy, India is a democratic anomaly: a very poor, ethnically and religiously diverse nation. How did it manage to embed democracy?

Political culture and regime legitimacy

Opinions about the health of democracy in India differ: some contend that, despite a failure to deal with poverty, India's democracy is actually in good health (Sisson 1993; Randall 1997). Others aver that the country's democracy is in trouble, and Diamond even suggests that India's democracy is *de*consolidating (1999: 72). Mitra and Enskat note that such a claim is not new, as 'the presumed collapse of India's institutions has been the staple of academic and journalistic discourse on Indian politics since the early 1980s' (1999: 145). There is some evidence, however, that in recent years pressures on India's democracy have been growing. Apart from the already mentioned institutional decay and economic disappointments, Randall points to (1) creeping authoritarianism, most clearly manifested in the mid-1970s resort to emergency rule; and (2) growing communal conflict (1997: 200). Kohli sees a 'recurring tendency . . . towards centralisation and powerlessness' and a diminution over time of state legitimacy, resulting in a weakening of India's democratic institutions (1994: 105). State legitimacy is said to have diminished because of the antics of politicians, who have, in many cases, lost the trust of the electorate. This is said to reflect the emergence of a class of politicians who seem most interested in furthering their own careers and opportunities, rather than in helping India's national progress. In short, declining state legitimacy has encouraged populist political leaders whose main concern is with power and how to get it, rather than with strengthening India's democratic institutions.

There are several points to make related to political culture (casting light on the importance of structural and contingent factors) as an explanatory factor in India's democratic trajectory. First, the nationalist leaders – of a social class and a generation that closely identified with the anti-colonial movement – were generally strongly in favour of democracy and the desirability of building democratic institutions. This encouraged the growth of a pro-democracy political culture which found its expression in the years of the leadership of Prime Minister Jawaharlal Nehru (1947–64). During this time, there were important institutional checks on the personal power of political leaders. However, over time, politicians of Nehru's generation were replaced by new, younger leaders predominantly 'from upwardly mobile, newly enfranchised, social classes' (Mitra and Enskat 1999: 127–8). Many among them lacked the clear commitment to democratic institutions that had characterized the post-colonial leaders and saw India's political system under Congress rule as a suitable environment for acquiring personal power and wealth.

India's political system was also structured by the dominance of the Congress Party: following independence, national structures of power were heavily linked to its commanding role. While its hold on power was linked to its national network of supporters, over time the need to mobilize the mass of ordinary Indians in an active way, especially in the rural areas, evaporated. Instead, the party ruled through a mutually beneficial relationship with sundry rural elites incorporated into the fold of the Congress Party via patronage links.

Such 'big men' – including large-scale landowners and members of dominant castes – could dictate to poor people in their domain how they should vote, and so had the power to deliver the vote to the Congress Party. In sum, India's political culture, while adhering to the norms of democratic competition encouraged by the British, developed to fit the country's highly unequal social and economic structure which privileged the interests of the elites over those of the mass of ordinary people. The resulting political system, while apparently consensual, was elite dominated.

The irony was that while the political elites professed a hope of actively incorporating India's masses into the political system, the system was actually geared to the opposite outcome. Central to elite dominance was a suitable mix of positive incentives, as well as persuasion and the selective use of laws – backed by the *threat* of coercion when necessary. State capacity to initiate and achieve major policy goals was rooted in the ability of political leaders to create and maintain majority coalitions in pursuit of their programmes. The difficulty was that to build and sustain the necessary consensus required that the link between rulers and supporters be embedded through the building of relationships and institutionalized primarily through political parties. Increasingly, however, this dimension was lacking.

Introducing democracy into India's highly inflexible and unequal social structure led to the emergence of distinct patterns of political activism, typically dominated by traditional elites, especially in the rural areas. But as India modernized, political leaders experienced increasing difficulty in forging even moderate levels of consensual authority. One consequence was that, over time, political society became increasingly fragmented. It became harder to maintain a democratically constituted, coherent centre of power which, in turn, served to encourage the growth of personalistic populism. As democratic politics and competitive mobilization diminished the corporate cohesiveness of India's traditional social structure, the Congress 'system', dominated by 'big men' in the rural areas, gradually lost the ability to mobilize India's rural voters. The result, as democratic politics undermined the traditional relationship between traditional 'superiors' and 'inferiors', was that social conflict became interwoven with political conflict to challenge the authority of democratic institutions and leaders.

Political participation and institutions

Political society   The democratic consolidation literature highlights the importance of (1) institutionalized, relatively unfragmented party systems; and (2) democratically elected leaders whose authority is rooted in well-organized parties, compared with leaders with diffuse and populist support bases. Observers have noted that post-independence India seemed for decades to reflect both of these democratically desirable features under the structural dominance of the Congress Party. As already noted, the long-term electoral power of Congress had its roots in the colonial period when the party managed to develop deep roots in rural society and construct a countrywide network of activists forming the core of the nationalist movement. For decades after independence, the party's countrywide presence was highly important in delivering Congress successive electoral victories. Later, however, Congress experienced electoral decline, with its hegemony eclipsed by the rise of identity-based parties. Overall, the number of political parties rose from a handful in the immediate post-independence period to around 450 in the mid-1990s (Kohli 1994: 89).

Many of the new parties based their electoral appeal on factors to do with identity issues, including religion, ethnicity, class and caste, while pursuing political agendas claiming to protect the disadvantaged, especially in the rural areas, from rapid economic change and agitating for the lower castes in demanding higher quotas for university places and government jobs. Such bread and butter issues gave such parties a ready constituency especially among the poor and helped them acquire electoral attractiveness. As Goldenberg (1999a) notes, while such party leaders may be 'boorish and corrupt, and have only a passing acquaintance with parliamentary niceties, they are seen as authentic by their supporters'. This can be seen in their growing electoral appeal: the absolute figure of just over 60 per cent of the voting age population voting in the 1998 election masks a significant increase in the rise in political participation of groups supporting such parties. The result was that 'India . . . is perhaps the only functioning democracy where the participation of people at the lower orders, in absolute terms, is higher than that of the elite.' But 'it is only in the last two or three decades that voters became conscious of their power. The vote has become a weapon of the weak' (Goldenberg 1999a).

In sum, Congress was once seen as the party of the poor and the disadvantaged but it failed to deliver enough tangible benefits to this constituency. This focused attention on the loss of its ability to channel the aspirations of the poor through its once highly effective networks, controlled from Delhi by its urban-based, upper-caste leadership. Growing numbers of parties emerged, reflecting the shift in popular political allegiances and increasing political involvement by previously underrepresented groups. Previously marginal social groups discovered the negotiable value of the vote and became eager players in the political arena.

With the old Congress network fast dissolving in the 1970s, a new strategy to win political power emerged: populism. Populist politicians, exploiting the changing political landscape through the skilful use of symbols and gestures, grasped the opportunity offered by the structural demise of Congress to proclaim identification with the aspirations of the mass of ordinary people. But populism turned out to be a two-edged sword: on the one hand, it proved an efficacious strategy in constructing national-level majority coalitions; on the other, it was deinstitutionalizing, unable to provide viable solutions to the problem of rebuilding democratic authority in an increasingly fragmented political society. In office, typically without viable parties or programmes, populist leaders promised much while achieving little, especially in relation to the poor and disadvantaged, the very constituencies that these leaders professed to represent.

Two points have emerged from the recent rise of populism in India. First, the structural decline of the once hegemonic Congress Party facilitated the rise of sundry populist leaders. However, these people, while exploiting the contingent factors associated with the decline of Congress, were unable or unwilling to build strong party structures to underpin their positions. The result was a swift turnaround of such leaders, which served to render India's political system both fragile and unstable.

The point is that the failure to build viable political institutions was ultimately self-defeating for populists: without viable parties, links between such leaders and their supporters were likely to remain both weak and underdeveloped. And because elections were won on general, non-programmatic promises, victors found it very difficult to translate a general mandate into specific policies and programmes. Lacking sufficient discussion and consensus, major policy pronouncements frequently garnered considerable opposition, even from erstwhile supporters. The consequence was that governmental initiatives regularly faltered, as, for example, in April 1999 when a coalition government, headed by the Hindu-chauvinist Bharatiya Janata Party (BJP), fell apart after just one year. The result was another general election, a further event in a cycle of centralization, powerlessness, and policy failures paving the way for other populist challengers.

In sum, India's party system became both complex and fragmented over time, a situation characterized by (1) the electoral decline of the Congress Party; (2) the emergence of hundreds of new parties, including particularistic parties claiming to be the champions of the poor or other identifiable groups; and (3) weak, unstable coalition governments.

Civil society Recent opinion surveys in India suggest that while most voters value the country's democratic system, many are highly suspicious of the people who run it. Many ordinary Indians have a 'negative evaluation of government officials and the police', the result of the 'plethora of corruption and other scandals involving political leaders' (Mitra and Enskat 1999: 147). Widespread mistrust of the members of the political class has been linked to the lack of a feeling of political efficacy in some parts of the country, providing 'a breeding space for the "rebels" familiar to students of civic culture' (Mitra and Enskat 1999: 123). On the other hand, in terms of aggregate indicators of political participation, India does reasonably well. Consistent voting turnouts in post-Emergency national level elections of around 60 per cent or more of the voting age population suggest that a majority of citizens believe it worthwhile to cast their ballots in elections.

But voting may not be enough for some people: while the majority of citizens choose to express their political preferences via the ballot box this does not stop many people – especially among women, the poor and other disadvantaged groups – from also being active in civil society groups. For example, grassroots activists have had a significant political impact on environmental issues, such as the anti-Narmada dam campaign (Haynes 1997). In sum, India has a massive number of political activists at the grassroots level organized in millions of civil society groups. But until recently their activities were ignored by both the national media and many of the party establishments, which were both uninformed and uninterested (Chakravartty 1997: 90).

The rise in civil society groups is not necessarily good news for India's democratic institutions, as the kinds of interests they often reflect, such as ethnic and religious concerns, tend to be suspicious of extant democratic mechanisms. India experienced serious politicization of communal tensions from the early 1980s, spreading from the urban into the rural areas, where they had hitherto been largely unknown. They became pronounced in various southern parts of the country, such as Tamil Nadu, as well as in the north, including Punjab and Jammu-Kashmir. Increasingly, with demands for separation or autonomy accompanied by growing communal violence, political violence came increasingly to characterize relations between, on the one hand, Sikhs and Hindus, and, on the other, Hindus and Muslims.

The conflict between Sikhs and Hindus, rooted in the demand of the former for their own state in Punjab, was catalysed by various terrorist acts perpetuated by militant Sikhs, including, in 1984, the assassination of the then prime minister, Indira Gandhi. This was followed, in several northern Indian cities, by the widespread destruction of Sikh-owned property and the murders of Sikhs by Hindu gangs.

At the time of independence, the Congress Party had reluctantly accepted partition, but decisively rejected the two-nation – Hindu/Muslim – theory. In the 1980s, however, India saw tensions rise between Muslims and Hindus, a situation that facilitated the rise of the BJP. The BJP emerged as a major force in the Indian political arena, through its emphasis on Hindutva ('Hindu-ness'), a serious challenge to traditional Indian understandings of, and commitment to, secularism (Chiriyankandath 1996). Intercommunal relations between Hindus and Muslims reached a nadir in December 1992 when a historic mosque at Ayodhya was destroyed by Hindu extremists. Widespread communal riots followed, with a huge loss of human life and destruction of property. But this seemed to do little to undermine the BJP's growing attractiveness as it rose to be the most popular party in national elections in the late 1990s. Following the 1998 and 1999 elections, the BJP's leader, Atal Bihari Vajpayee, emerged as national prime minister, a reflection of the ability of the party to accrue significant numbers of votes nationally. However, while the BJP is an openly Hindu-chauvinist party, it has shown a willingness to dilute or side-step controversial and contentious issues when necessary in order to help the party leaders forge post-election coalitions with smaller, often regional, parties.

Economic and international factors

Because India has been a democracy for decades it has not come under pressure from foreign governments to democratize; nor did it become part of the third wave of democracy like several of its regional neighbours. But India's democratic continuity raises major doubts about at least one important conventional assumption relating to democratization and democratic consolidation: the need for growing national wealth, relatively equitably distributed (Przeworski et al. 1996). What is India's record in this regard? While poverty reduction was laid down as a central aspiration by the country's nationalist leaders at the time of independence, progress has been slow. Half a century after independence in 1947, India was one of the poorest countries in the world (165th out of 210). It had a GNP per capita of only US$430 and more than half of Indians were judged to live on less than $1 a day (World Bank 2000: 230). A consequence of the failure to develop faster economic prosperity, Chakravartty argues, was that there was growing concern in the country about the fate of the poor, linked to 'a lot of disillusionment . . . about [democracy's] decline' and its ability to tackle the problem of poverty (1997: 89–90).

Conclusion

India presents a paradox: on the one hand, it maintained its democratic system for decades while most other poor countries did not. However, we saw that over time the structural factors that facilitated democracy – the colonial legacy, the personal commitment of the first generation of nationalist leaders to democracy, a countrywide network of activists linked into the Congress Party – were overtaken by the rise of populism, identity politics, and an array of activist civil society organizations. These developments reflected the fact that many ordinary people, while still turning out to cast their ballots in elections, regarded the extant political system as one that had failed to lead to the changes they desired. This was because successive Indian governments found it impossible to solve people's economic and political problems, amidst declining popular legitimacy of the political class and serious communal clashes and tensions in various parts of the country. On the other hand, India's democracy has a great deal of resilience and there seems little real doubt at the current time about the ability of its democratic political system to survive. This is because there are regular, keenly fought, relatively free and fair elections, with relatively high turnouts of voters; a politically disinterested military and judiciary; a vibrant civil society; free media; popular faith in the country's political institutions; and a state that is 'relatively strong and institutionalized' (Moore 1998: 89).

Pakistan

Pakistan is an entirely artificial creation. It was created as the homeland for India's tens of millions of Muslims following serious communal conflict in the late 1940s that left an estimated 1 million people dead. Carved out of India, initially in two territories (East and West Pakistan) separated from each other by thousands of kilometres, the country became independent in August 1947. A republic was established in 1956. Fifteen years later Pakistan's national territory was confined to the former West Pakistan following the de facto independence of Bangladesh (formerly East Pakistan). After a military coup in July 1977, martial law was in operation until 1985, when a partial democracy emerged. Constitutional democracy followed in 1988, surviving until October 1999.

Pakistan started its life with a number of inauspicious domestic structural characteristics that militated against the establishment of a workable democratic system. In addition, there was no sustained external encouragement to democratize. This was largely because Pakistan was a key regional ally of the US during the Cold War, a time when American governments preferred their allies to be stable rather than necessarily democratic. In other words, the long-term support of US governments for 'stable' – that is, military – governments was an important structural characteristic that helped undermine chances of democratization in Pakistan.

Political culture and regime legitimacy

The difficulty of developing a national political culture supportive of democracy was clear from the outset. Pakistan was founded on the idea that the Muslims of India formed a secular nation and, as a result, were entitled to a territorial homeland of their own, in much the same way that the Jews (and especially Zionists) in the diaspora considered that they could only flourish within their own nation-state. Pakistan was initially in two halves: East and West, separated by India, and with practically no history of shared national unity. The consequence was that the members of the Pakistani 'nation' did not speak a common language, have a homogeneous culture, or even share a common geographical or economic unit. Thus Pakistan was emphatically not a nation in the traditional Western sense of a group of people living in a contiguous territory who believe they have the same ethnic origins, and share linguistic, religious and other cultural attributes. Over time, lack of shared characteristics proved fatal to putative national unity: following a civil war, the independent state of Bangladesh (neé East Pakistan) was created in 1971 with India's help.

At the time of the establishment of East and West Pakistan, the main problem for the country's rulers was twofold: first, how to create a national identity to suit the reality of the new boundaries and, second, how to devise a workable system of government for a populace divided by huge geographical distances, as well as ethnic, cultural, regional, economic, linguistic, ideological and religious differences. Initially, it was assumed that the umbrella of Muslim identity would take care of these differences. Consequently, the new political leaders espoused an Islamic form of nationalism as the country's unifying symbol. The appeal to their heterogeneous people's shared Muslim heritage was enough to overcome the immediate differences but not enough to suppress the contradictions of Muslim religious feeling, regional nationalisms and class antagonisms within the new state. As Lapidus put it: 'Pakistan was born as an Islamic state to differentiate it from the rest of the [Indian] subcontinent, but Muslim identity [did] not prove adequate to unite the country internally' (1988: 742). In sum, the founding structural circumstances of Pakistan were not conducive to long-term national unity or to democracy.

Fifty years after independence, Diamond characterized Pakistan as being at 'the edge of political chaos, with massive political corruption and heavy-handed presidential intervention forcing out one elected government after another' (1999: 29). At this time, many Pakistanis were very condemnatory of their political leaders, a position explained in part by recent corruption scandals involving senior politicians (Robinson 1999b; Diamond 1999: 92). Sizeable majorities of the Pakistani public considered that the country lacked an impartial judiciary (62 per cent), freedom of the press (56 per cent), or a government free of corruption (64 per cent). As Diamond put it: 'The bottom line: nine years into civilian government, half do *not* consider Pakistan a democratic state (about a quarter do)' (1999: 50). The consequence, for Diamond, was that Pakistan was a 'hollow democracy, rife with semiloyal and disloyal behavior on the part of important political actors. No one should confuse its persistence with consolidation or with liberal democracy' (1999: 73).

Political participation and institutions

Political society Initially, after the break from India, Pakistan's leaders enjoyed a high degree of popular 'inverse legitimation'. That is, the new government was widely regarded as legitimate because it was the regime established after what many Pakistanis saw as unconscionable and incomprehensible Indian aggression. But the benefits of the honeymoon period soon disappeared. Governmental legitimacy declined due to poor economic performances, the use of political repression to stifle opposition forces, and serious state-level corruption. Democracy did not become institutionalized in the early years of independence and, as a result, it became impossible to establish a workable democratic system.

Pakistan's political system became notable for personalistic rather than institutional wielding of power, facilitated by three developments. First, Pakistan's federal system was designed to provide provincial legislatures and governments to check the power of the state at the national level. However, these important checks and balance soon became filled with cronies of figures at the centre, and as a result the ability to check the power of the national government diminished. Second, religious, ethnic and regional divisions helped make Pakistan's politics both volatile and violent. Third, when the Muslim League government gained power after partition it was at the cost of abandoning its political hinterland in northern India, a development which served, more generally, to blight the growth of a competitive party system. Instead, political leaders, both civilian and military, presided over a political system rooted in populism, with power heavily personalized and frequently abused.

Pakistan failed to develop a viable party system. Political parties were banned in the late 1950s, and normally heavily controlled by the state when they were allowed to function. Following a brief period of freedom for parties in the 1970s and the first half of 1980s, the military dictator, General Zia, banned them again, claiming that the very concept of pluralistic parties was 'non-Islamic'. When they were allowed to operate, parties were essentially sectional in character, largely ineffectual at mobilizing citizens and prone to enter – and quickly leave – unstable multiparty alignments. In sum, the characteristics of Pakistan's political system, reflecting the characteristics of its inauspicious founding, and alternating between military and civilian rule, were not encouraging for the development of democracy.

Following General Zia's death in a mysterious plane crash in 1988, large numbers of political parties and groups emerged or re-emerged. The main contenders for political power at this time were broad-based coalitions. One was the Pakistan Democratic Alliance (PDA), dominated by the left-of-centre Pakistan People's Party, led by Benazir Bhutto, allied to several smaller parties. Its opponent was the Islam-e-Jamhoori Itthad (IJI), a coalition whose main components were the Pakistan Muslim League and the Jamaat-i-Islami (Pakistan Islamic Assembly). Other significant parties at this time included Altaf Hussain's MQM, representing the *mohajir* community in Sind, that is, Muslim refugees from India who entered Pakistan in the late 1940s, and the regionally based Awami National Party, with roots in the

North-West Frontier Province and northern Baluchistan. The point
is that these coalitions comprised parties representing a variety of
sectional interests, including ethnic, religious and regional interests.
However, their very diversity meant that the winning coalition would
comprise a conglomerate of competing groups whose main aim would
be to acquire as much power as possible and to deny it to their rivals.

The armed forces   No discussion of the problems of democracy in
Pakistan can avoid the structural political role of the armed forces.
The military has maintained a political high profile for decades,
after gaining significant political clout soon after independence. This
situation was not only facilitated by the violent circumstances of
Pakistan's founding, but also by the country's serious political
instability over the years. In short, in contrast to India, the military
in Pakistan has had an important political position for decades, with
the country's political vicissitudes rooted in struggles for power
between competing sets of civilian and military elites.

The roots of the military's political involvement go back to the
immediate post-independence period, a time characterized by significant political instability. Following growing political chaos, the
military eventually stepped in to try to resolve the situation in 1958.
Field Marshall Mohammad Ayub Khan, supreme commander of the
armed forces and chief martial law administrator, took over the
presidency. Constitutional government, under a presidential system
based on indirect elections, was restored four years later, in 1962.
However, the political significance of the military remained high, bolstered by Pakistan's war with India in 1965. In addition, student disturbances and growing political and economic discontent, focused in
but not restricted to East Pakistan, plunged the nation back into crisis
and led to the military forming another government in 1969 under
the army commander-in-chief General Agha Mohammad Yahya Khan.
The constitution was suspended and the national and provincial
assemblies were dismissed. During General Zia's period in government (1977–88), the structural political position of the military was
underpinned by a controversial amendment which gave the armed
forces a permanent say in political decision-making. However, the
amendment was overturned following the death of General Zia in a
plane crash in 1988.

The death of Zia highlighted the importance of contingency in
Pakistan's recent political outcomes. With the armed forces temporarily weakened, civilian elites – themselves divided into two main
factions – were temporarily able to gain the upper hand and take
power following a general election in late 1988. Over time, however,
the military reasserted its political power, and a new policy-making

body formalized a political role for the military in January 1997.
President Leghari announced the formation of a Council for Defence
and National Security (CDNS), comprising himself, the prime minister, several cabinet ministers, and the heads of the branches of the
armed forces. The earlier collapse of a civilian government, that of
Benazir Bhutto, in 1990, and also those of Nawaz Sharif in 1993 and
1999 – all engineered by factions within the armed forces – served
further to emphasize the military's continued political clout. In sum,
the almost continuous political involvement of Pakistan's armed
forces for decades – sometimes in power, sometimes merely in an
'advisory' role – was key to the failure of democracy to take root.

Civil Society For several reasons, unlike India, Pakistan has not
managed to develop a vibrant civil society. It is sometimes suggested
that Muslim societies have certain structural characteristics making
the formation of a robust civil society unlikely, including a rigid societal hierarchy, assumptions of unquestioning obedience, and an often
lowly structural position for women (Dorr 1993). In Pakistan, unlike
in India, relatively few women's organizations have emerged in recent
years. In sum, sociocultural conditions in Pakistan may have
restricted the development of the organization of civil society.

Islam was also of importance in another way in undermining the
development of civil society in Pakistan, While the country emerged
as a homeland for India's Muslims, this did not mean that there was
only one concept of the idea of a Muslim state; in fact, there were at
least two. On the one hand, the secularized political elite considered
Islam a communal, political and national identity that could be
stripped of its religious content. On the other hand, a sizeable
segment of the populace, led by Muslim religious leaders, expected –
and later, when it was not forthcoming, demanded – a state whose
constitution, institutions and routines of daily life would be emphatically governed by Islamic law and Islamic norms. The importance of
the struggles – both that over the role of Islam and the ethnic and
regional rivalries between West and East Pakistan – can be gauged
by the fact that no constitution could be devised until 1956, a decade
after the founding of the state. The constitution declared Pakistan to
be an 'Islamic state', and made all parliamentary legislation subject
to review by an Islamic Research Institute.

Following the military coup in 1958, the constitution was abol-
ished and the Republic of Pakistan was declared. The aim was to try
to curb the power of the religious leaders. Over the next 40 years,
however, the issue of the nature of the state in Pakistan was not
resolved, with various rulers, such as General Zia ul-Haq seeking to
Islamicize the state further, while secular civilian political leaders,

such as Zulfikar Ali Bhutto (prime minister, 1972–7) tried to reduce religion's political influence. Later, attempting to increase support from the conservative Islamic establishment, the government of Nawaz Sharif (1988–93) achieved the passage of an Islamic law in 1991. While for many religious Muslims the law did not go far enough in seeking to Islamicize the country, many secular-minded Pakistanis feared that a theocracy was being established. In sum, the difficulty of establishing a sociopolitical position for Islam undermined the chances of developing a flourishing civil society in Pakistan.

A third factor linked to a weak civil society was suspicion and competition between ethnic groups which frequently erupted into violence. Muslim refugees from India, *mohajirs*, were at the centre of some outbreaks of ethnic conflict. Fleeing from India at the time of partition, most *mohajir* migrants settled in Sind but found they were not welcomed by local people. Initial suspicion between the communities erupted into violence in the 1980s. The main *mohajir* political movement, the Mohajir Quami Movement (the MQM: National Front of Refugees), was formed in 1984. It became a highly significant political factor, especially in Karachi, where *mohajirs* account for more than 60 per cent of the population of more than 12 million. During the latter half of the 1980s the MQM took part in elections, helping to form both provincial and national governments. The movement briefly entered into an alliance with Benazir Bhutto's Pakistan People's Party for the 1988 elections, before later shifting into opposition. But the MQM's entry into conventional politics did nothing to end the political violence. So serious did the situation become that the army was dispatched to Karachi in June 1992 to restore order, a move which alienated the *mohajirs* still further. On coming to power, Benazir Bhutto initiated a political dialogue with the MQM, a body she had once labelled a terrorist organization. While talks with Bhutto served to legitimize the MQM and to enhance the position of its leader, Altaf Hussain, ultimately they led nowhere in terms of a political settlement. In sum, three main factors – a lowly position for women, conflict over the role of religion in politics, and ethnic conflict, especially between refugees from India and local people in Sind – helped ensure that civil society in Pakistan remained underdeveloped.

Economic and international factors

Pakistan is one of the poorest countries in the world, with a GNP per capita in 1998 of $480. The country's poverty made it open to external influences, especially from foreign governments, such as that of the US, which emerged as an important aid donor during the Cold War, a time when Pakistan's regional enemy, India, enjoyed backing and some largesse from the Soviet Union. Over time, the United States government was a profound influence on political outcomes in Pakistan, encouraging the armed forces – not democratic institutions – to adopt and develop their political position. As Kumaraswamy has noted, 'in successfully pursuing . . . non-democratic governance, Islamabad enjoyed the tacit support and approval of Washington' (1999: 187). This was because the US government saw the military as the best guarantor of American interests in South Asia, a region on which the Soviet Union was thought to have designs. As a consequence, military governments (including those of General Ayub Khan, between 1958 and 1968, and that of General Zia ul-Haq, 1977–88) were heavily backed by the US government.

The often unconditional backing of the United States for Pakistan's military regimes came to an end in the late 1980s when the Cold War ceased. From this time, the US government discarded its prolonged association with dictatorial rule in Pakistan, instead publicly endorsing the re-establishment of democracy. While a new democratically elected government came to power in 1988, this did not usher in a period of democratic stability. Instead, as Woollacott (1999) notes, such an outcome was highly implausible. This could be seen from a 'glance at Pakistan's past. [This] suggests the problem may lie . . . in the repeated attempts, by leaders in and out of uniform, to dominate the whole political structure of the country by placing their own people in every position.'

The overall point is that, as a consequence of various structural factors, the differences between military rulers like General Zia and civilian leaders such as Benazir Bhutto and Nawaz Sharif was not great. The characteristics of Pakistan's power attributes led to an impulse on the part of all recent rulers to achieve total control. Such attempts eventually led to the formation of anti-regime coalitions to seek their removal; and then the process began all over again. The point is that it did not need the United States government to create the conditions where military government was a feasible alternative to weak, lacklustre civilian rule. These were supplied by the structural conditions of Pakistan's founding.

Conclusion

The problems Pakistan experienced in trying unsuccessfully to develop workable democratic institutions indicate that structural

conditions leading to authoritarian rule were more politically significant than contingent factors that might encourage democratization.
While Pakistan has had recent examples of multiparty elections, consistently low turnouts of voters (in the 30–45 per cent range) suggested that voters set no great store by the idea that democracy would
be a fundamental improvement on military rule. Under the last civilian government, that of Nawaz Sharif (1996–9), there were clear
signs of the development of a personalistic democracy, characterized
by weak political institutions and feeble developmental powers, with
a centralization of power at the apex of the political system but with
little in the way of developmental power. The armed forces kept a
close eye on the civilian regimes and soon found reasons to oust them.
The consequence was that, prior to the most recent military takeover
in October 1999, each of the elected governments since 1988 had
been dismissed under military pressure. However, the democratization process had lost momentum long before the military resumed
government.

6.5   Overall conclusions

Given several unpropitious sets of circumstances, including widespread poverty, religious and ethnic divisions, and the fact that
democratic institutions were increasingly bypassed by power-hungry
populist politicians who promised the voters much while delivering
little, how can we account for the survival of India's democracy? Certainly there have been signs of growing popular disenchantment with
the established political system, reflected in a loss of confidence in
the political class, the growth of hundreds of mostly particularistic
parties, and coalition governments being the rule rather than the
exception in recent years. But such coalitions tended to be tenuous,
tentative and volatile. Having such a large number of often disparate
interests in government together meant that it was almost impossible
to devise policies which would garner enough support to get measures passed by the national legislature.

Following independence, certain structural characteristics were
instrumental in the development of the country's pro-democracy
political culture. These included the generally beneficial legacy of
political institutions inherited from British colonialism, important in
bringing together the country's numerous cultures, religions and
ethnic groups under the aegis of democratically elected governments.

The significance of structural factors was also reflected in the fact that, for three decades after independence, India held regular, free and fair elections and the Congress Party was elected to power at the national level.

Later, in the 1980s, this arrangement gave way to an increasingly volatile political terrain, characterized by the electoral decline of Congress, increasingly short-lived, coalition governments, and a plethora of new parties. These developments provided contingent factors for change, reflected in the fact that many ordinary people, especially in rural areas, were much less influenced than before by the powerful figures who had formerly influenced the way that many would vote. Increasingly, ordinary people preferred to cast their votes for populist leaders who exploited the conditions provided by the post-Emergency situation to achieve power at the expense of the formerly hegemonic Congress Party. However, presiding over short-lived unstable governments, such leaders found it very difficult to achieve their objectives. In sum, the survival of democracy is linked to a number of structural characteristics of the country's political system – which, however, were gradually, but not fatally, undermined by contingent factors.

Why has it proved impossible to institutionalize democracy in Pakistan? In part the answer is linked to the fact that the inauspicious structural circumstance of the country's founding were not conducive to this outcome. The armed forces, encouraged during the Cold War by the government of the US, became powerful political actors, an institution highly suspicious of civilian-led governments and of democracy itself. Difficulties were also added to by a third malign structural characteristic: serious ethnic and religious tensions, with groups divided, on the one hand, over the public and political role of religion and, on the other, over the respective political importance of the country's constituent ethnic groups. A contingent factor – the entry into Pakistan of a large number of politically active refugees from India (*mohajirs*) – did not help the situation in a country already politically divided among indigenous ethnic groups. The result was that in Pakistan democracy is a distant goal, its chances seriously undermined by the poisonous rivalry between, on the one hand, the chief political party factions and their leaders and, on the other, the entrenched conflict between military and civilian leaders for power.

7
Africa

7.1 Introduction

Sub-Saharan Africa (henceforward in this chapter, Africa) is a culturally and religiously diverse, politically complex region of more than 40 countries. The background to Africa's democratic transitions – typically in the late 1980s or early 1990s – was an array of apparently unpropitious structural characteristics which, according to many observers, made it unlikely that the region would democratize along with other 'third wave' regions. In other words, despite the diversity one would expect from such a large number of countries, most African countries shared characteristics that made the likelihood of democratization, much less democratic consolidation, seem remote. On the other hand, the impetus for reform was the result of a combination of domestic and international factors linked to the region's endemic economic and political problems. That is, beset by economic problems and growing societal strife, Africa seemed in crisis at the end of the 1980s. As Villalón put it, African countries seemed 'somehow [to have] "gone wrong" since independence' (1998: 3). Fundamental reforms of state structures and institutions were widely deemed necessary, both at home and abroad, to correct things.

As a result of such pressures, a regional wave of democratic transitions took place from the late 1980s, with changes of regime by the ballot box in a large number of countries. Among them were Benin, Cape Verde, the Central African Republic, Ghana, Guinea-Bissau, Lesotho, Madagascar, Malawi, Mali, Namibia, Sao Tomé e Principe, Sierra Leone, South Africa and Zambia. However, not all political changes at this time were in a democratic direction: some regional countries – including Burundi, Liberia, Rwanda, Somalia and Sudan – collapsed into novel or renewed civil conflict. Others experienced a turn or return to military rule – occurring, for example, in Côte d'Ivoire, Burundi, Niger, and Congo-Brazzaville. Finally, in a handful of African countries incumbent governments stayed put, at least initially, and simply refused to allow any meaningful test of public opinion – for example, in Nigeria (until 1999), Togo, and the Democratic Republic of the Congo (formerly Zaire). In sum, Africa experienced various kinds of political changes, including democratization, from the late 1980s. In some cases, this resulted in a democratically elected regime staking power for the first time in decades.

Unlike in the other regions we have looked at so far in the book, many African democratic transitions often began with popular uprisings against unelected leaders which gradually developed into demands for multiparty elections and democratic governments. However, such protest-led, reformist-oriented actions 'did not necessarily lay a firm foundation for the subsequent institutionalisation of democratic regimes' (Bratton and van de Walle 1997: 278). African countries experienced various modes of democratic transition, and then introduced rather similar sets of constitutional reforms, often in quick succession. The characteristic sequence was (re)legalization of political parties; constitutional separation of powers; date set for elections. Some transitions were via the transformation mode (explained in chapter 2), that is, directed by incumbent governments, typically non-competitive – military or single-party – regimes. These were administrations where state office holders were appointed rather than elected. Examples include Cape Verde, Lesotho, Sao Tomé, Seychelles and Mozambique. The outcome, typically, was that incumbent rulers were able to exploit the advantages of incumbency to win elections and retain power.

Pacted transitions, common in Latin America, were rare in Africa. Only South Africa provides a clear example in this regard. South Africa's transition involved concerted negotiation and bargaining between the white-dominated government and the black opposition, led by Nelson Mandela. More common were two further transition modes, unique to Africa: (1) 'rapid elections'; and (2) 'national conferences'. 'Rapid elections' were conducted by competitive one-party regimes, and contenders for state jobs had to put themselves up for popular election, for example, in Tanzania and Kenya. Governments in those countries summarily decreed the nature and characteristics of transition and, giving fragmented oppositions little time to organize or campaign, easily won the ensuing elections.

The 'national conference' has been described as an 'indigenously generated African contribution to political institution building and regime transition' (Bratton and van de Walle 1997: 111–12). This mode was associated with plebiscitary one-party regimes in francophone countries, including Benin, Mali and Zaire (now the Democratic Republic of the Congo). In this transition mode, both government and opposition forces, along with representatives of societal groupings, were represented in a national conference. Following often prolonged debate about the appropriate way forward, political outcomes of the national conferences were variable: in Benin and Mali they led to the rejection of incumbent governments at the polls, while in Zaire there was seemingly endless prevarication by the government which led to stalemate between it and the opposition. This only ended when the incumbent national leader – President Mobutu, who had ruled since 1965 following a civil war – precipitously fled the country. His place was taken by a victorious guerrilla leader, Laurent Kabila. However, this did not lead to political progress: no elections had taken place by the end of 2000, as the country relapsed into inconclusive civil war following Kabila's assassination. In sum, while Africa experienced various modes of political transitions from authoritarian rule, political outcomes were variable.

The overall outcome of Africa's political transitions is shown in table 7.1. At the end of the 1990s, that is, a decade after the transition from authoritarian rule, six African countries were judged by Freedom House to have 'free' political systems, 16 were perceived as 'partly free' (that is, they were limited democracies according to the terminology introduced in chapter 1), and more than 20 African countries were judged to have 'not free' regimes. Two points emerge from this: first, there were improvements in the position of political rights and civil liberties in some – but not all – regional countries. Second, despite regional democratization, some post-transition governments seemed to rule much as their authoritarian predecessors had, that is, with scant concern for citizens' political rights and civil liberties. It would seem that anti-democracy structural and institutional logics – such as patronage and clientelism – remained at the heart of political competition in some post-transition regimes in Africa. This suggests that, in some cases, Africa's democratic transitions did not lead to regimes qualitatively different from their antecedents because institutional structures, deeply ingrained in the societies and politics of most African countries, could not be changed in a fundamental way simply because there had been relatively free and fair elections.

Given widespread structural impediments to democracy – such as weak, unrepresentative state institutions, less-than-robust civil

Table 7.1 New democracies in Africa, 1989–1999

	Political rights (PR)		Civil liberties (CL)		PR + CL average	PR + CL average	Freedom rating
	1988–9	1998–9	1988–9	1998–9	1988–9	1998–9	1998–9
Cape Verde	5	1	6	2	5.5	1.5	Free
Sao Tomé	7	1	7	2	7	1.5	Free
South Africa	5	1	6	2	5.5	1.5	Free
Benin	7	2	7	2	7	2	Free
Malawi	6	2	7	3	6.5	2.5	Free
Namibia	–	2	–	3	–	2.5	Free
Madagascar	5	2	5	4	5	3	Partly free
Mali	7	3	6	3	6.5	3	Partly free
Seychelles	6	3	6	3	6	3	Partly free
Ghana	7	3	6	4	6.5	3.5	Partly free
Guinea-Bissau	6	3	7	4	6.5	3.5	Partly free
Mozambique	6	3	7	4	6.5	3.5	Partly free
Central African Rep.	6	3	6	5	6	4	Partly free
Comoros	6	4	6	4	6	4	Partly free
Lesotho	5	4	6	4	5.5	4	Partly free
Uganda	5	4	4	4	4.5	4	Partly free
Burkina Faso	7	5	6	4	6.5	4.5	Partly free
Ethiopia	6	4	7	5	6.5	4.5	Partly free
Gabon	6	5	6	4	6	4.5	Partly free
Zambia	5	5	5	4	5	4.5	Partly free
Tanzania	6	5	6	5	6	5	Partly free
Zimbabwe	5	5	6	5	5.5	5	Partly free

Source: 'Annual survey of Freedom country scores, 1972–73 to 1998–99',
http://www.freedomhouse.org/survey99/method/

societies, fragile economies and often pronounced ethnic and/or religious competition or conflict – then Africa's democratic progress was likely to be highly problematic. It would be necessary to erect and embed democratically accountable institutions with such an inauspicious background, often more or less from scratch. As a result, many observers assessed the chances of democratization and democratic sustainability in Africa to be poor.

This pessimism seemed to be confirmed by the slow pace of democratization in many African countries in the 1990s. By the end of the decade, there had typically been two rounds of elections in African countries where democracy had been introduced. Outcomes were generally ambivalent, with 'a mixed bag of evidence related to assessing prospects for [democratic] consolidation' (Wiseman 1999: 141). Generally, democratic transitions had failed to produce 'adequate political frameworks for the reforms which need to be implemented to increase political accountability and spur sustainable economic development' (Chabal 1998: 300). On the other hand, there was more optimism regarding a few countries, including South Africa and Ghana, where it appeared that democracy might be taking root. In such cases, the significance of contingent factors to democratic outcomes, including the importance of individual agency, was highlighted. In such circumstances, it appeared that if there was sufficient political will on the part of political leaders to build democracy then, despite the obstacles, it could be developed in even the most unpropitious surroundings. This was confirmation that, as Sisk notes, 'crafting a "conflict-mitigating democratic system" in plural societies' . . . 'depend[s] largely on *the major social actors choosing to work together to that end*' (1995: 40, emphasis added).

In the next part of the chapter we shall examine the structural impediments to democracy and democratic sustainability in Africa and see why they were collectively seen as major problems for democracy and democratic sustainability. In the second part of the chapter we turn to the case studies: South Africa and Ghana. In both countries, democratic outcomes were closely linked not only to the determination of their national leaders – Nelson Mandela and Jerry Rawlings, respectively – but also to a range of complementary domestic and international pressures. From a large array of potential countries, the case studies have been chosen to illustrate the relative significance to democracy and democratic consolidation of structural and contingent factors. However, they represent very different trajectories: Ghana is typical of Africa, with its long periods of military rule and economic weakness. The case of South Africa is, on the other hand, both regionally unique and too important to omit from a survey of African democratization and the problems of democratic consolidation. What they have in common is that each country engendered – at least qualified – optimism for its chances of democracy and democratic sustainability. This was largely because in the face of unfavourable structural characteristics – in South Africa, the legacy of apartheid was a huge impediment to overcome, while in Ghana two decades of authoritarian rule and relative economic weakness were not conducive to easy or swift democratization – state leaders did extremely well to preside over a fair measure of democratic consolidation. In each case, encouraged by both internal and external actors, democratically elected leaders showed their commitment to democracy and put much effort into trying to develop it. More generally, the case studies highlight the importance of contingent factors in developing democracy in what might initially seem to be unpropitious surroundings.

7.2   Structural impediments to democracy in Africa

Among the regions we have examined so far in this book, Africa stands out as the one with the most impediments to democracy. Numerous, panregional *structural* characteristics make democracy an unlikely outcome of political changes. They include:

- *Long periods of personalistic rule prior to democratization, resulting in few, if any, extant democratically accountable institutions*   Many African countries have legacies of personalistic rule, making the building of democratic institutions problematic because there are few foundations to build on. Bratton and van de Walle suggest that trying to build stable democracy in countries with little or no heritage of political competition is likely to result in experiments that are 'fragile, possibly transitory and constantly threatened by reversal' (1997: 278).
- *Political cultures that do not value democracy above other kinds of political systems*   To build democracy requires not only that democratic institutions are built, but also that they are 'valued'. That is, political culture must develop to the extent that democracy is regarded by the vast majority of political actors as the best, most viable political system available. Both elites and the mass of ordinary people must see the value of democracy and demonstrate that they are willing to stand up for it.
- *Widespread religious and ethnic competition and conflicts*   Many regional countries have large numbers of different ethnic and religious groups which would, many democratic theorists would expect, make it difficult to develop an environment facilitating democratic sustainability.
- *Weak, fragmented civil societies*   Africa has long been noted for its weak, fragmented civil societies that failed for decades to encourage authoritarian governments to democratize.
- *Close political relationships between the state and the military*   Many regional countries have traditionally seen close relationships between state and military elites. This typically led to the military developing a powerful political role.
- *Weak governmental legitimacy and accountability*   The increasing incidence of weak, short-lived governments in Africa suggests that regimes have struggled to build their legitimacy among increasingly cynical populations who see them as largely unaccountable and unrepresentative.

If political actors and the mass of ordinary people genuinely value democracy, and strive to do all they can to create or rejuvenate democratic institutions, then democratic consolidation, even under objectively inauspicious conditions, might be achievable. Africa provides several recent examples to illustrate the importance of contingency to political outcomes. One is the well-known role of the former president of South Africa, Nelson Mandela, whose decision to enter into political negotiations with the apartheid government following his release from prison was widely judged as a pivotal event in the shift to democracy. Another, less well-known example is from the East African country of Uganda. There, the government introduced democracy, albeit an unconventional 'no-party' variation, known as the 'movement system', in 1986 (Hansen and Twaddle 1995). The interesting question is why the regime didn't decree a multiparty route like most others in Africa. The issue gains piquancy when we note that there was little doubt that the regime would have won elections had it chosen to allow a multiparty system. One interpretation is that the country's powerful leader, Yoweri Museveni, sincerely believed that multipartyism was the root cause of the evils of tribalism and religious prejudice which had led to two decades of conflict in Uganda prior to his rule. The point is that Museveni's personal decision to pursue an unconventional form of democracy highlights the importance of both structure and contingency to Uganda's political outcomes from the mid-1980s.

In sum, the weight of structural impediments and the legacy of institutional precedents help shape the realm of what is possible regarding democracy and its sustainability in Africa. In order to facilitate democracy under such adverse circumstances, the role of contingent factors – including that of human agency – would be crucial in securing clear democratic progress.

7.3   Democratic consolidation in Africa

Next we examine the comparative importance in Africa of the factors we have examined earlier to other areas, in order to illustrate the problems of democracy and democratic consolidation in this region:

1   political culture and regime legitimacy;
2   political participation and institutions;
3   economic and international factors.

Political culture and regime legitimacy

Most African countries decolonized in the 1960s after decades of colonial rule. While styles of European rule differed from country to country, they were all built on authoritarian systems of government. Unlike in India, there were rarely any attempts to develop political systems prior to independence that would be conducive to post-colonial democratization. This was because, unlike Indians, Africans were not thought by their colonial rulers 'to be ready' for taking part in democratic politics. However, following World War II, the weaknesses of the region's main colonial powers (Britain and France) led them to quit their African possessions much more quickly than they had originally planned. The colonial powers began to leave in the mid-1950s – Sudan (1956) and Ghana (1957) were the first countries to experience decolonization – and inaugurated democratic systems via multiparty elections. But in nearly all cases these systems, with few if any indigenous roots, lasted only a few years before various kinds of authoritarian governments – typically, personal or military regimes or one-party dictatorships – took over. Under their rule, citizens were routinely denied many political rights and civil liberties. The result was that, by the 1970s, very few African governments were democratically elected.

In sum, following independence from colonial rule Africa was soon replete with military, one-party and other non-democratic governments, systems which lasted, in many cases, for around two decades prior to democratization from the late 1980s. During the authoritarian era there was an absence of democratically accountable institutions, with the result that there was a lack of democratically appropriate institutions for political competition to build on after democratic transitions. In short, very few African countries had managed to develop pro-democracy political cultures at the time of their democratic transitions.

Political participation and institutions

Political society

The consequence of years of authoritarianism, as Robert McNamara, a former president of the World Bank, observed, was that 'Africa faces problems of governance . . . far more severe than those of other regions' (Harsch 1996: 24). Despite apparently significant changes to the formal architecture and institutions of political regimes – including new, democratically orientated constitutions – it was the *continuities* in African politics, straddling both authoritarian and democratic eras, that many observers noted. Three were notable in terms of the difficulties of developing democratically accountable regimes after transitions:

- *presidentialism*, involving the systematic concentration of political power in the hands of one individual leader;
- *clientelism*, a system of personal favours and patronage in return for loyalty and support between patrons and clients;
- the use of *state resources* for political legitimization.

Intimately connected to these three aspects of African political life is the concept of *personalistic rule*. A regime is characterized by personalistic rule when the national leader possesses a monopoly over patronage and uses this power to strengthen and perpetuate his or her rule. During the authoritarian era the task was facilitated by the fact that in very few of the region's countries were there political rules or institutions sufficiently robust to check the power of personalistic rulers. This might seem paradoxical when it is understood that, during the first three decades of African independence, there was a strong focus on what was known as 'state-led development', with three generic types of regime prevailing: 'Afro-Marxist' (for example, Benin, Ethiopia, Angola, Mozambique); 'African socialist' (for example, Ghana (until 1966), Tanzania, Guinea); and 'capitalist' (for example, Kenya, Nigeria, Côte d'Ivoire) (Young 1982).

While they differed in their proclaimed ideological orientations, these regimes all highlighted the importance of a 'strong' state to spearhead the drive for national unity and economic development. African leaders in these types of regimes all argued that 'strong' rule was necessary to prevent their countries from violently disintegrating under the weight of ethnic, religious and/or regional pressures. To forestall such an outcome, leaders alleged, it was generally necessary to keep tight control over the political environment and, in particular, the development of political society. Consequently, open political competition and multipartyism – deemed likely to emphasize ethnic and/or religious cleavages – were not allowed.

It is the case that when multipartyism has been allowed in Africa then political parties have frequently couched their electoral appeals in ethnic or religious terms. The consequence was that majority rule was often fraught with hazards because it often led to domination by powerful ethnic or religious groups to the detriment of others. Recent examples include electoral outcomes in Malawi, Côte d'Ivoire, Congo-Brazzaville, and Kenya, where, according to Lawson, 'voting patterns since 1990 have followed ethno-regional boundaries to a remarkable degree' (1999: 13–14). This reflects the fact that, historically, political violence in Africa organized around ethnic or religious themes has been common. A consequence was that in most cases it was exceedingly difficult for governments to develop a strong sense of national identity among their diverse people. Often, prevailing religious and ethnic divisions helped fuel rulers' personalistic tendencies, since when they were in power rulers had to satisfy ethnic or religious supporters in order to ensure their own positions. In sum, political participation and the institutionalization of democracy was made difficult by the widespread existence of ethnic and religious divisions in many African countries.

Concerns about religious and ethnic fragmentation were central components of the 'strong' state argument articulated by African rulers such as Julius Nyerere (Tanzania) and Samora Machel (Mozambique). When such rulers seemed capable of improving their countries' political and economic situations – without conventionally democratizing – their arguments tended to be accepted. However, authoritarian attempts at developmental authoritarianism eventually failed across the region, an outcome that helped to focus societal demands for political changes and democracy.

In sum, 'politicized ethnicity' and 'politicized religion' have been constructed in country after country in Africa. Yet this outcome was rarely the result of 'primordial' bonds among fellow members of ethnic or religious groups, that is, the outcome of *ancient* hatreds. Instead, it was often strategic, self-serving actions of politicians that were crucial in encouraging the politicization of ethnicity or religion. Whipping up such sentiments was a convenient, often electorally successful way of garnering political support. The instrumental use of ethnic identity is a frequently adopted tactic to achieve the narrow ends of individual politicians, who, in striving to create or retain support for their bids for power, help to perpetuate the notion that ethnically or religiously divided African states cannot easily develop recognizably democratic political systems. However, skilful political leaders – such as Tanzania's former leader, Julius Nyerere, South Africa's former president, Nelson Mandela, Jerry Rawlings of Ghana and Yoweri Museveni of Uganda – were able significantly to defuse such issues, pursuing a commitment to rule for all ethnic and religious groups, rather than just one or two.

Civil society

Many conceptions of civil society emphasize the importance to democracy of free associations of autonomous individuals who organize themselves into an array of organizations with broadly political outlooks and goals. We have noted in earlier chapters the importance of what Risse-Kappen calls 'sturdy' civil societies that, typically, emerge from 'relatively "strong" societies, that is, those without profound ideological, ethnic, religious or class cleavages'. Sturdy civil societies also tend to be 'rather "politicized" civil societies, easily mobilized for political causes [by] centralized social organizations such as business, labor or churches' (1995: 282). In other words, sturdy civil societies can form effective counterweights to the state, fighting its (over)dominance, by both limiting and legitimating its power and, as a result, keeping the state within substantive and procedural confinement. In short, sturdy civil societies are crucial factors in helping undermine or prevent the arbitrary logic of personal power. This is so because they can help bolster the rule of law and facilitate the establishment and embedding of unbiased bureaucratic processes.

However, in many African countries the failure or inability of civil society organizations 'to organize in such a way as to defend and promote their interests has often crippled their ability to counter the state's hegemonic drives' (Villalón 1995: 24). But this is not to suggest that African civil societies have invariably been weak and ineffective in seeking to control the state and what it tries to do. In fact, in many cases, civil societies became fragmented and frail during the decades of authoritarian rule but had earlier been much more effective in standing up for societal interests. For example, various civil society organizations – including Christian churches, trade unions and civic associations – were often important sources of opposition to colonial rule in many African countries in the late 1950s and 1960s. However, over the next quarter century – when authoritarian rule became endemic throughout Africa – the efficacy of civil society faded away nearly everywhere. However, there were a few exceptions – for example, in South Africa, Ghana, Uganda, Zimbabwe and Nigeria. In these countries, civil societies were able consistently to resist and frustrate 'efforts to perpetuate authoritarian rule' (Diamond 1988: 23). As we shall see below in our case studies, opposition from civil society to authoritarian rule was an important factor in democratization. More generally, often galvanized by worsening economic conditions and by events in Eastern Europe which saw the widespread overthrow of unelected regimes, many African countries saw a resurgence of civil society in the 1980s, when 'diverse urban groups join[ed] forces in loose protest coalitions' (Bratton and van de Walle 1997: 102).

In sum, demands for fundamental change began with a resurgence of civil society in many African countries. This amounted to a rediscovery of a political voice, often catalysed by economic disappointments and by international developments, such as contemporaneous political reforms in Eastern Europe which saw the political demise of entrenched, authoritarian regimes. However, although a variety of mostly urban-based civil society organizations – including churches, trade unions and business and human rights groups – were in the forefront of initial demands for change, their voices tended to fade away once transition got under way, replaced by professional politicians who, along with the parties they led, became the main symbols of democracy.

Economic and international factors

Many African countries – including Angola, Benin, Democratic Republic of the Congo (formerly Zaire), Ethiopia, Ghana, Guinea, Kenya, Liberia, Mali, Mozambique, Niger, Sierra Leone, Somalia, Uganda and Zambia – are among the world's poorest states (World Bank 2000: 230–1). Reflecting this dire position, Africa's quality of life indicators are generally poor: each year more than 4 million children die before they reach the age of five years, a third of Africa's children are malnourished, one in eight disabled, and more than 30 per cent receive no primary education (UNDP 1996). The extent of the economic problems afflicting Africa can be gauged from the fact that, starting from a low base, between 1980 and the mid-1990s there was an *average regional decline annually* in per capita GNP of 0.8 per cent, at a time when populations were growing at an average of around 3 per cent a year. This implies a real annual fall in GNP per capita of around 4 per cent. The consequence was that Africa had the second worst regional record in the world in the 1980s and early 1990s: only the Middle East, hit hard by sharp falls in global oil prices, showed a greater percentage drop.

The region's endemic economic weakness was one of the key reasons for the eruption of demands for wide-ranging reforms from the 1980s. Across the region at this time, economic reform programmes were instituted at the behest of the International Monetary

Fund and the World Bank. Driven by the understanding that one of the prime causes for Africa's economic weaknesses and political instability was the lack of democratic governments, external pressure was also applied to authoritarian regimes – vulnerable to such external pressures because of their countries' economic weaknesses – to allow meaningful democratization. The economic results of external pressure, however, were generally disappointing. Occasionally, as in Ghana and Uganda, the programmes achieved some macroeconomic stability and economic growth. More typically, however, the failure of economic reforms to lead to sustained economic growth helped to catalyse further popular anti-state protests, directed at, for example, apparent regime incapacity in Zambia, state corruption in Kenya, and Tanzania's governmental impotence.

The point is that, reflecting the difficulties of reforming inherited political and economic structures, post-transition African governments rarely found it an easy task to deal with two pressing concerns simultaneously, on the one hand, significant economic reforms and, on the other, fundamental political changes. For example, Frederick Chiluba, elected as Zambia's president in November 1991, found it impossible to turn round the country's economy, heavily dependent on flagging copper exports, or to control state-level corruption. Rises in prices, partly a result of drought, brought widespread strikes and popular discontent that reflected a drop in popular support not only for Chiluba's government but for the very concept of multiparty democracy (Burnell 2000). The general point is that Africa's dire economic position made the task of democratization exceedingly difficult even with substantial external encouragement.

Against the background of continued economic weaknesses, many African governments were vulnerable not only to domestic calls for reform but also to calls from foreign governments to allow more political reforms. Foreign aid donors made it clear that they believed that what was needed was better *governance*, that is, more democracy coupled with fundamental economic reforms. African regimes that chose to disallow democracy and to deny their citizens' human and civil rights could expect to be refused aid. Africa's economic failures, it was believed, were to a large degree the consequence of a lack of democracy and political accountability. Without significant political changes, economic reforms would inevitably lack impact.

In the late 1980s and early 1990s the United States Agency for International Development shifted from a traditionally single-minded concern with economic development, to inaugurate 'governance and democratization' programmes across Africa (Green 1999). More generally, many bilateral aid donors began to attach political conditions to foreign aid programmes. However, over time, observers noted that Western support for democratization became increasingly rhetorical rather than substantial (Lawson 1999). This was because re-emerging strategic concerns for regional order and security and the deepening of market-based reforms began to take precedence over democracy and democratic consolidation in Africa. 'Presentability became the effective criterion' for African governments to acquire 'the stamp of international approval. Both African regimes and their foreign sponsors engaged in "democracy as illusion"' (Joseph 1997: 11). Successive French governments supported decidedly undemocratic political friends, such as President Eyadema in Togo, because France wished to retain its traditional influence in the country (Cumming 1999). However, in Uganda, there was strong Western support for a regime that, while not conventionally democratic, could nevertheless point to increased national integrity, social stability, regular, relatively free and fair elections, and economic progress. In sum, foreign aid donors were important in encouraging authoritarian governments to commence democratic transitions. Later, however, they generally became more concerned with strategic rather than democratic goals in the region, and, as a result, sustained pressure to democratize diminished.

We have seen in this section that Africa had an array of structural impediments to democratic sustainability. Not only were there problems linked to long-term authoritarian regimes and the personalization of political power, but also endemic economic weaknesses. While domestic pressures – principally from civil society – and external encouragement – primarily from foreign governments and international financial institutions – helped lead to democratic transitions, there was no guarantee that they would be sufficient to institutionalize democratic regimes in the post-transition period.

7.4 Case studies: South Africa and Ghana

The case studies of South Africa and Ghana have been chosen to illustrate the relative significance to democracy and democratic consolidation of structural and contingent factors. They represent very different trajectories and while Ghana is more typical of Africa, the South Africa case is too important to omit from a survey of African democratization and the problems of democratic consolidation. Both countries stimulated a degree of optimism for chances of both democrracy and democratic sustainability. South Africa, with unfavourable structural characteristics, including the legacy of apartheid, had a huge impediment to overcome. On the other hand, Ghana had had two decades of authoritarian rule and relative economic weakness. Such factors were not conducive to easy or swift democratization. The point is that state leaders in both countries did extremely well to preside over a fair measure of democratization. Encouraged by both internal and external actors, democratically elected leaders in Ghana and South Africa showed much commitment to democracy. The case studies highlight the importance of contingent factors in developing democracy in what might initially seem to be unpropitious surroundings.

South Africa

South Africa is a country of more than 40 million people. About 12 per cent are white of European origin, and a similar proportion are people of mixed white European and black African characteristics. The remainder, over 30 million, are black Africans. This unusual mix is one of the reasons why South Africa is not a 'typical' African country. Another is that the country is very wealthy in African terms: a GNP per capita of $2,880 in 1998 makes it the richest regional nation. However, there has traditionally been a sharp polarization in wealth between black South Africans and most whites (World Bank 2000: 231, table 1).

Rather than narrowing the gap between the majority of poor South Africans and the minority rich elite, democratization actually led to a widening wealth imbalance in the country. This was most clearly seen in the polarization between a new black elite and the poor black majority: by the end of the 1990s, that is, half a decade after democratization in 1994, the richest 20 per cent of blacks accounted for nearly two-thirds of all the income brought in by black workers. This led to growing concern, especially among trade union activists, that the government had done too little to redress the legacies of apartheid rule. The government responded, however, that to increase the size of the economic cake so that all South Africans would benefit necessitated a strategy which looked to the global picture: to compete South Africa had to offer an attractive economic context to potential and current foreign investors.

We examine two main issues in this section. First, we look at a crucial contingent factor in the context of South Africa's democratization, that is, the willingness of Nelson Mandela, leader of the main opposition party, the African National Congress (ANC), and that of the head of the then ruling National Party (NP), President de Klerk, to embark on a democratization programme which culminated in the landslide victory of the ANC in 1994. The second issue is to highlight the temporary nature of the importance of contingent factors to South Africa's longer term political outcome. Once the democratic transition was over, then structural characteristics reasserted themselves to the extent that some opposition groups began to question to what extent democracy had actually changed things in South Africa.

Political culture and regime legitimacy

South Africa was ruled by exclusively white governments for decades prior to a shift to democracy in 1994. The change to democracy came in three swift stages: collapse of apartheid rule; a pacted democratic transition; attempts to consolidate democracy. The collapse of the apartheid system and the democratic transition were encouraged by both domestic and international factors.

Collapse of apartheid rule Domestically, apartheid had long been embraced by many white South Africans as a way, they believed, to ensure their domination in a context of political order. This justification began to evaporate following a serious black insurrection in the mid-1980s. This suggested that the apartheid system, rather than providing order, was leading instead to serious opposition and unrest, including civil disobedience, strikes and riots. Second, pressure from civil society organizations encouraged democratization; while, third, the declining economic situation also encouraged demands for change. Adding to the pressure were various external factors, including direct (governmental, non-governmental, moral, economic, diplomatic, military) pressures, the indirect influence of global economic relations, and diffusion and demonstration effects – especially the collapse of communist rule in Eastern Europe.

McGarry suggests that democratic transition occurred not because the dominant white group 'came to [its] senses, but because it became sensible for [it], because of the changing environments [it] faced, to reach agreement' (1998: 855). Guelke (1999) argues that President de Klerk's National Party government calculated that Mandela's African National Congress was seriously weakened by the demise of the USSR and the associated loss of support to the extent that it would be anxious to negotiate a settlement to the political conflict. Another interpretation is that the government reached a settlement in 1994 not so much because it became persuaded by the activities of liberal civil society activists (President de Klerk consistently refused to apologize for apartheid), but principally because of changing circumstances at home and abroad. That is, interrelated external and internal pressures were pivotal in persuading the de Klerk government to seek and secure a negotiated settlement.

De Klerk was well aware that the proportion of whites among South Africa's population, which held steady at around 20 per cent between 1910 and 1960, had dropped to 15 per cent by 1985, and was projected to fall to 11 per cent by 2010. The belief was that this waning demographic presence would ultimately endanger the ability of the white minority to occupy strategic positions in the state apparatus and economy, and to run and staff the institutions of apartheid. McGarry suggests that the looming demographic crisis was an important factor encouraging President de Klerk to put forward the prospect of a negotiated settlement that would be 'indispensable for the survival of the whites as a shrinking minority' (1998: 863). In sum, 'South African whites were brought together to negotiate because of a range of domestic crises and diffuse international pressures' (McGarry 1998: 855).

Democratic transition   It was a surprise to many that South Africa's turn to democracy was not accompanied by the feared racial conflagration threatened by dissident groups, such as Eugene Terre Blanche's Afrikaner Resistance Movement or Chief Buthelezi's Inkatha Freedom Party. The threat was dissipated, it is suggested, in part because of the strong desire of mainstream politicians, both black and white, to make the new democracy work.

Democratic reforms were, unusually for Africa, the result of a pacted transition. South Africa's transition could be described as a textbook example of the situation outlined by Huntington: conflicting political groupings 'can neither do without each other nor unilaterally impose their preferred solution on each other if they are to satisfy their respective divergent interests' (1991: 141–2). The terms of the pact between the two sides – black and white – involved, at least in the short term, not a majoritarian democracy but a power-sharing agreement preserving many of the institutions of the former regime and, critics allege, avoiding a meaningful redistribution of economic resources. In addition, transition theory suggests that a precondition for elite-pacted democratization is the preservation of capitalist institutions through the public suppression of 'extremists' and radicals and the incorporation and cooption of political leaders who, if left outside the negotiations, might disturb the balance of the agreement 'moderates' are attempting to construct (Przeworski 1991). Once agreement on the political way forward was reached, however, it proved impossible for the ANC and the NP together to impose their terms on the other interest groups which had been involved in the negotiations. As Kiloh remarks, 'for a pact to be successful it is necessary for the parties to it to guarantee the support of their followers by buying off or disciplining extremist wings. In South Africa this was not possible as opposition to the agreement came from those excluded by it who had already spun out of control of the two main protagonists' (1997a: 318).

Contingency was important for the democratic transition in South Africa and, surely central to this, was the almost unparalleled statesmanship of Nelson Mandela, a man incarcerated for nearly three decades in one of the country's most notorious jails until his release in 1990. The moderate stance of the most important opposition group – Mandela's ANC – was crucial to the government's willingness to negotiate. Although Mandela had suspended the ANC's 'armed struggle' only *after* the start of negotiations, this struggle had actually been rather tame, hardly ever directed against the white population *per se*. And, unlike the more radical Pan-African Congress, leading ANC figures went out of their way to assuage white fears, reassuring the white community that South Africa belonged to *all* of its citizens. Mandela's moderation also encouraged the development of a desire for limited change among many whites: not only was he a supremely important, although ageing politician; there were also fears that his anointed successor, Thabo Mbeki, would be distinctly less accommodating to the white constituency. And, while the ANC insisted on, and ultimately achieved, majority rule, it reassured many whites, including even some among the most conservative Afrikaners, that their culture would be accommodated in the new order. Finally, the ANC's movement away from socialist economics in the late 1980s helped to reassure whites that they could retain private power while releasing their grip on the public variety.

In sum, the pacted transition to democracy in South Africa assuaged fears among many whites that a Mandela-led regime would be 'too radical'; the settlement with the ANC posed little or no threat to their continued existence and identity, whether physically or culturally. Taylor argues that white and black elites cooperated in helping create a political climate wherein radical changes were impossible (n.d.: 9).

Political participation and institutions

We have already noted the positive role of a consolidated party system for democratic progress, providing as it does a forum for political actors to compete legitimately to exercise the right to control power and the state apparatus (Linz and Stepan 1996). In addition, autonomous political parties can help keep power-holders in check. It is for this reason that political parties are sometimes seen as *the* crucial key to consolidation, especially when, as in South Africa, a pervasive legitimacy has not prevailed during the process of democratization. The point is that the more rapidly the party spectrum forms during transition, then the more likely is progress towards democratic consolidation. In inchoate party systems voters tend to respond to personalistic appeals rather than party affiliation, favouring populist leaders who govern without attempting to establish solid institutional foundations for their rule.

Following transition, South Africa quickly consolidated its party system under the hegemony of the ANC. The ANC won an emphatic electoral victory in the 1994 elections, gaining nearly 63 per cent of the vote on a massive turnout: more than 85 per cent of the population of voting age cast their ballots. Mandela was voted president by a unanimous vote of the new Assembly. The ANC underlined its dominance five years later, when, in the 1999 elections, it gained just under two-thirds (66.4 per cent) of the vote. Its dominance was made clear when no other party could muster even 10 per cent of the vote: the leading opposition party, the Democratic Party, achieved slightly more than 9 per cent; the Inkatha Freedom Party managed 8.6 per cent; and the erstwhile governing party, the National Party, gained under 6 per cent. While the result of the second elections appeared to confirm that South Africa had a party system conducive to democratic consolidation, there were also fears that the dominance of the ANC might lead it to rewrite the constitution – which it could do if it gained two-thirds of the popular vote – and proceed to rule in a manner unconducive to the well-being of the white minority.

Economic and international factors

Apartheid's collapse was facilitated by an increasingly serious economic position. Strong economic growth in the 1960s and 1970s had given way, in the 1980s and early 1990s, to stagnation and then decline. The declining economic situation was reflected in an average annual *negative* GNP growth during the 1985–95 decade of 1.1

per cent (World Bank 1997: 215). Economic decline, which many believed was linked to the continuation of the apartheid system, which discouraged international and domestic investors from investing in South Africa, threatened the material privileges of whites while narrowing governmental options. It not only affected the state's ability to buy off the emerging black middle class but also, given the rising cost of defence expenditures, threw into increasing question the state's ability to defend itself. Finally, international economic sanctions, reinforced by cultural, academic and sporting boycotts, effectively cut whites off from the Western community with which they identified, making them feel very isolated.

Once in power, ANC plans for large-scale nationalization and the redistribution of resources were abandoned and a more moderate liberalization of the highly protected South African economy was substituted instead. It soon became clear that, following the democratic transition and the installation of the ANC government, many leading figures within the government, including President Mandela, were strongly in favour of a mixed economy. Some observers argue that this strategy was chosen because within the ANC the 'pro-capitalism' strand had become dominant, the spearhead of an emerging black bourgeoisie. Enthusiastically accepting the basic tenets of economic neoliberalism, the main goal of such people was to acquire a larger slice of the economic cake. However, while a capitalist development strategy suited a powerful group in and close to the ANC who materially benefited from the strategy, it was less clear that many poor black South Africans benefited economically under the arrangements. Sceptics argued that the government's economic policies, with their emphasis on business and the free market, encouraged both corruption and a culture of acquisitiveness at the apex of the government. Such a development, it was feared, was unlikely to be conducive to democratic consolidation, not only reliant on a perception that economic gains were being shared relatively equitably but also on the institutionalization of a representative political system able to channel and regulate societal demands.

The concern was that, nearly a decade after apartheid rule came to an end, the enormous hopes generated by the country's political transition had given way for many poor South Africans to the disappointing realities of frustrated change. The government's response was that little was to be gained by radical policies of wealth redistribution that would frighten off potential foreign investors. Mandela's successor as president, Thabo Mbeki, also pointed out that, whatever government was in power, the nature of the country's involvement in the world economy would severely constrain governmental ability to bring about a significant shift in economic resources from the rich minority to the poor majority. South Africa had to compete in a global economy, a situation that meant that the economy had to be competitive. It was recognized that the problem for political stability was that although South Africa was the richest country in Africa, at least a quarter of the population lived below the poverty line. But to provide the necessary conditions for the large increases in wages and employment which the influential trade union confederation, COSATU, demanded, it would have been necessary for the economy to grow substantially year on year; and this, the government argued, could only be accomplished if businesses and investors remained in the country, and new ones came in. If the government had quickly moved to deal with the economic imbalances through an aggressive redistribution of wealth then it is likely that many foreign investors would have been frightened off.

As already noted, the democratic transition was strongly encouraged by various foreign governments. Since then, the importance of the global economy – and South Africa's place within it – has been an important factor in government policies. But to compete within the global economy it has been necessary to put in place what are widely perceived as conservative economic policies which have not sought strongly to redistribute wealth. Given the skewed nature of the South African economy – with whites receiving the lion's share of available resources – the government's failure to redress the situation led to a growing collapse in support for the ANC regime from its crucially important trade union ally, which claimed in mid-2000 that its conservative policies risked creating a major political crisis.

Conclusion

We noted in chapter 2 that the transplacement mode of transition is rooted in elite pacts. Under such a regime, democracy is perceived less as a model set of political ideals than a second-best compromise. The key to a successful transition is in the ability of political players to arrive at negotiated agreements where they get some of what they want, via a process of what Di Palma (1990) calls political 'crafting' that produces democratically orientated rules and institutions that all politically significant parties agree to support. The inference is that it is conceivable that, given sufficient political will among leading actors, that democracy can be inaugurated and then consolidated. And this even in countries whose position looks, on the surface, not to be favourable, for example, where there is a low level of economic development and/or serious ethnic or religious divisions. In short,

political outcomes consistent with democratization can be suscep-
tible to political 'crafting', that is, the actions of human agency.

South Africa is good example of a pacted transition which resulted
in a democracy which retained many of the features of the old regime,
with one important distinction. That is, what had formerly been the
political and economic domination of a small *white* elite changed to
control by a numerically small group of powerful *blacks* linked to
the ANC. However, following the democratic transition, South Africa
had to deal with structural continuities which, some argued, would
bedevil the achievement of the fundamental political and economic
transformations that would be necessary to make a new political and
economic start (Lane and Ersson 1997). At the end of the 1990s,
despite the huge achievement of black majority rule, several problems
for democratic consolidation remained: (1) how to consolidate
democracy in a climate of major economic gains for an emerging
black middle class while the majority of poor blacks were failing to
receive the benefits they wanted to see; (2) how to institutionalize a
strong and representative political system to ensure broad political
participation by channelling and regulating societal demands; and (3)
the development of a national political culture valuing democracy
more than other, undemocratic political forms. This would be dependent on building trust between the state and dissident groups, such
as radical Afrikaners and a suspicious Zulu constituency principally
represented by Chief Buthelezi's Inkatha Freedom Party.

Resolving these problems would be dependent on a continuing
strong commitment to democracy on the part of the government,
which itself would depend on the ability to construct a national consensus about the way forward. In broad outline, this process took the
form of an ANC-led bid after 1994 to forge a new, inclusive South
African nation constructed on the principles of a non-racial democracy. The ANC's nation-building project extended beyond the juridi-
cal and geographical spheres to a provisional bid for unity (or, at
least, a kind of truce) at the cultural, social and political levels. But,
to the critics of the post-1994 status quo, the fundamental problematic of the nation-building project was that it could only be accomplished by utilizing an unacceptable compromise constructed on the
continuity and the perpetuation of values, institutions, systems and
practices identified with the past.

Ghana

Ghana is a West African country with a population of around 17
million people and a chequered post-colonial political history. Its

neighbours are Côte d'Ivoire, Togo and Burkina Faso. After independence from British rule in 1957, a decade of initially democratic
latterly dictatorial rule by Kwame Nkrumah and his Convention
People's Party government ended in 1966 with a joint police/military
coup d'état. Handing over power to elected civilians in 1969, the
military struck again in 1972. Seven years later, in early 1979, a
junior ranks coup brought Flight-Lieutenant Jerry Rawlings to power
for the first time. An elected civilian government took charge
following elections in September of the same year. Two years of
conspicuously unsuccessful rule followed and Rawlings returned to
power through a further coup in late 1981. Two decades later,
Rawlings was still in power, the elected head of state presiding over
a multiparty political system, a situation, most observers concur, that
was primarily due to the personal efforts of Rawlings.

Political culture and regime legitimacy

Rawlings rejected 'Western-style' multiparty democracy for many
years. This was because, he claimed, it was 'unsuitable for Ghanaian
realities' because it would be likely to lead to a situation where
multipartyism became a focus for ethnic division. However, over
time, encouraged by a combination of domestic and external pressures, Rawlings became a convert to multiparty democracy. As table
7.1 above showed (p. 137), during the 1990s things improved considerably in relation to political rights and civil liberties, Ghana's
'score' moving from an average of 6.5 to 3.5. The result was that in
1999, according to Freedom House, Ghana was a 'partly free' state
or, in our terminology, a limited democracy. During the 1990s, Rawlings and his elected government managed not only to rebuild the confidence of many Ghanaians in the state but also to gain for the
country impressive amounts of foreign aid necessary to rebuild the
shattered economy.

To understand the nature of Ghana's current political system, and
to gauge the chances of democracy being consolidated, it is necessary
to begin the analysis with the historical past. It is both convenient
and analytically appropriate to divide Ghana's post-colonial political
history into two phases, 1957 to 1981 and post-1981. The first period
saw a common enough saga in post-colonial Africa of democratic
aspirations and visions increasingly sacrificed to the day-to-day exi-
gencies of governmental rule. During this time it was very difficult
for successive governments to establish their legitimacy – a legacy
important for later regimes, which found that they were widely

regarded with suspicion by many ordinary people. Governmental failures helped to create a political culture of cynicism and a deep distrust of the political class among many ordinary Ghanaians which continues into the current time.

The roots are to be found in President Nkrumah's populist-nationalist regime (1957–66), which greatly disappointed various constituencies of interest during its decade in power to the extent that the joint police-military coup that seized power was welcomed by many ordinary people. However, the junta which replaced Nkrumah's government found that running a state was rather more complex than they had bargained for. Consequently, it soon handed over power to a civilian government, which failed to turn round the ailing economy or to establish a democratic system of rule. Re-enter the military, this time with very few real pretensions to rule wisely or well. Power became a means to an end, with state resources stolen with impunity by senior, and not so senior, governmental figures, to the extent that by the mid-1970s Ghana seemed not only close to economic collapse but also characterized by 'political enfeeblement [and] social fragmentation' (Chazan 1991: 22). In 1979, Rawlings led an unsuccessful military coup. Two years later he led a successful one.

Rawlings's accession to power in 1981 marks the start of the second phase of Ghana's post-colonial history. It is a story of evolving political stability and increased economic steadiness, and, since 1992, a democratically elected regime and signs of democratic consolidation. However, the 20-year period is intensely controversial, centring on the figure of Rawlings: nothing divides Ghanaians more than their opinions regarding their ruler of the last two decades. All would agree that he was a pivotal, absolutely central figure in the country's political and economic fortunes: a hate figure for some, a hero for others. But even his greatest critics might well agree that his initially chaotic, then authoritarian, latterly increasingly democratic rule managed to guide Ghana through the uncertainties of the late 1970s to democracy and comparative economic equilibrium.

The country entered a chaotic phase in its politics that lasted from 1982 to 1983–4, when a series of populist political and economic strategies were tried without much success. From 1983–4 to the early 1990s the government attempted to manage the economy and engineer desired political changes through a mix of often clumsily applied administrative controls and popular mobilization; over time the regime became more authoritarian, increasingly unwilling to listen to alternative suggestions to deal with the country's problems. Until 1992, and a democratic transition, Rawlings's economic and political policies remained insulated by his authoritarian style and wide powers of coercion. Decisions were made by a small, strongly centralized coterie around, and including, Rawlings; and it seemed to many that populist rhetoric took the place of building state institutions. During the 1980s and 1990s, when coup attempts were regularly made, a key to the regime's continued survival was tight control of a large, loyal security apparatus. Originally designed to mobilize the population in defence of what Rawlings persisted in calling a 'revolution', over time it evolved into an oppressive machine to smash dissent. By the early 1990s the rough tactics of the regime's militants and security personnel had imposed acquiescence on the country's once vocal political opposition to the extent that many Ghanaians claimed a 'culture of silence' existed; that is, people were simply too afraid to criticize the government openly. This climate, some argued, made it very difficult – if not impossible – to develop a pro-democracy political culture, or for the regime to appear to be legitimate.

Political participation and institutions

Ghana's post-1992 political system has a president at its apex, along with a unicameral, 200-seat legislature. Jerry Rawlings was voted president by impressive margins over his nearest challenger in relatively free and fair elections in 1992 and 1996. His party, the National Democratic Congress, also managed to achieve substantial majorities in parliamentary elections in the same years. Some observers suggest that there were only limited signs of the development of political institutions in Ghana during the 1990s, although there were also no clear signs of a reversion to authoritarianism. However, the legacy of the past was that the societal consensus necessary to hasten democratic consolidation was hard to develop. Put another way, there was little apparent recognition that government and opposition had a vested interest in building democratic institutions. However, despite this, many procedural criteria for democracy *were* respected, including multiple political parties, independent interest associations, and a free press (Jeffries 1998).

The 1996 polls and their aftermath provide a convenient reference point to assess the progress of democratic consolidation in Ghana. On the one hand, it is noteworthy that in 1996, unlike 1992, the opposition parties were prepared to accept the results of the elections and play a conventional opposition role in the new parliament. This appeared to signify, at least to some degree, that there was some agreement regarding the rules of the political game. On the other hand, there was little evidence that such political actors were able to agree on all the basic principles of cooperation and competition necessary for democratic consolidation. Each competing party appeared to consider itself uniquely qualified to govern, and the Rawlings regime sought to use an array of mechanisms to perpetuate itself in power. There was little apparent sign that either government or opposition acted other than in furtherance of their own immediate interests; there was an underdeveloped sense of working together in pursuit of national aims. While formal rules of political engagement and competition were enunciated, principally in the new constitution, they nevertheless seemed to be treated by the government as rather pliable arrangements to be moulded or avoided as and when necessary. In short, Ghana's democracy did not show clear signs of consolidation in the 1990s, primarily because rules of fair play, acceptable to all significant political and social actors, were not obviously operational at all times.

Economic and international factors

The importance of foreign aid for Ghana's economy makes it particularly necessary to look at economic and international aspects together. Ghana experienced serious, prolonged economic decline in the 1970s and 1980s when the economy – built on the export of cocoa and minerals – collapsed. This outcome was largely the result of governmental mismanagement, and the result was that the living standards of most Ghanaians fell rapidly. However, by the late 1980s, several years into an economic structural adjustment programme (SAP), Ghana had become the star pupil of the International Monetary Fund (IMF) in Africa, held up as a staunch exponent and regional showcase example of successful economic reform. As a reward, Ghana received more than US$9 billion in foreign loans over the next decade, principally from the IMF and the World Bank. The consequence was that Ghana achieved significant economic growth – an annual average of around 5 per cent – between the mid-1980s and the mid-1990s, a situation which undoubtedly helped the electoral chances of Rawlings and his party in 1992. With annual population growth nearly 3 per cent a year, the resulting real growth of over 2 per cent a year was a commendable achievement, one of the best in Africa at the time (Bentsi-Enchill 1998: 8). However, the country remained very poor – ranked 171st in global terms, at US$390 annual per capita income in 1998. Progress towards reducing poverty was painfully slow, with the poorest 20 per cent of the population receiving just 8.4 per cent of total income (World Bank 2000: 238, table 5).

The IMF and the World Bank, along with the important aid donors, including the governments of Britain and the United States, made it plain that aid and loan flows could be reduced, held up or even halted unless there were moves towards a recognizably democratic system (Boafo-Arthur 1998: 170–3). Consequently, the shift to democracy in 1992 needs to be seen in the context of external pressures which augmented pressures from domestic sources, such as the opposition political parties. Once democracy was installed, both Rawlings and his party performed electorally better in the rural than the urban areas in both sets of elections. The main reason for the division in the votes is that economic structural adjustment produced evident benefits for many rural dwellers and clear costs for their urban counterparts. Thus there was a clear policy to increase the welfare of deprived rural dwellers which facilitated the retention of power by Rawlings.

Conclusion

By 2000, the fact of having a vocal, reasonably effective opposition was gradually affecting Ghanaian politics: for the first time in 20 years a regime led by Rawlings regularly had to answer publicly for its programmes and policies. The presence of a 66-member opposition bloc in the 200-seat legislature helped facilitate relatively open debate and, taken as a whole, served as a real check on what the NDC government could do. The leading opposition party, the National People's Party (NPP), with 60 seats, nearly a third of the total, was one of the strongest legal opposition parties in Africa, with a reasonable expectation of gaining power at the polls in the next elections due in late 2000. These polls did in fact lead to a victory for Rawlings's rival, J. Kufnor. These developments help suggest that the framework for representative democracy was being created in Ghana in the 1990s.

Some institutions were undoubtedly strengthened over time. For example, the country's Supreme Court showed its independence by making a series of judgements supporting opposition claims of undue government influence on various constitutional issues. In addition, in the 1990s, independent newspapers either commenced or resumed publication, and most seemed quite unafraid to criticize the government, especially over corruption issues, which regularly appeared in the press. Finally, opposition parties held frequent, sometimes well-attended, public rallies and press conferences to criticize government policies and programmes, a strategy which usefully augmented their increased voice and stature in parliament.

7.5 Overall conclusions

The evidence of this chapter confirms that South Africa and Ghana are important democratic case studies. This is because their political stories in the 1990s help shed light on an issue of wider significance to democratic consolidation: the role of contingency in helping to bring about democratic transformations. However, both case study areas, and more generally African countries, do not necessarily have the structural basis for sustaining democracy. While in South Africa and Ghana political reforms, developing from both external and internal encouragement and catalysed by the commitment of individual political leaders, culminated in democratic transitions, there was no certainty that this background would be sufficient for democratic sustainability.

In both South Africa and Ghana national leaders were for years firmly against multiparty elections. Then, in the early 1990s, they changed their minds. It seems likely that Ghana's president, Jerry Rawlings, was happy to go along the multiparty route not only because he reckoned that he and his somewhat hastily constructed political party would win elections, but also that he would win Western favour for doing so. Turning to South Africa, most observers would acknowledge the crucial personal role of Nelson Mandela in the country's democratic transition. And, for the first few years after the country's transition, Mandela was the national president – an absolutely pivotal figure, centrally involved in deciding the country's political direction. However, over time, Mandela's personal role was of less significance to democratic outcomes than was the country's inauspicious structural basis for sustaining democratic consolidation.

Some observers were surprised that the entrenched system – based on white political and economic dominance – was not demolished by the new ANC government when it came to power in 1994 (Taylor n.d.: 9). That is, radicals believed that both capitalism and parliamentary government were essential aspects of the apartheid system and that, once in power, a black-led government would reform the system root and branch. When this failed to happen, critics alleged that the Westminster model had been chosen not to facilitate 'real' democracy but rather to perpetuate the apartheid system – under a different guise, with white domination replaced by the primacy of a new black elite, connected to the ANC government. Instead of the existing system, what many radicals wanted to see was a 'direct democracy', that is, a bottom-up system. This would be built on the

foundations of the rudimentary organs of people's power which had
emerged in the 1980s during the popular struggle against apartheid.
Such political institutions stressed the accountability of leaders to the
rank and file (Marais 1998).

There is an important strand of analysis that, while focusing on
South Africa, is of more general relevance to Africa in that it highlights the problems of democratization arising from the general lack
of a regional structural basis for democratic sustainability. Lane
and Ersson (1997) point to the following difficulties for democratic
sustainability:

1   inauspicious social conditions;
2   fragile economies and high population growth;
3   semi-presidentialism with parliamentarism, often in the context
    of informal one-party dominance;
4   lack of developed democratically accountable institutions, includ-
    ing robust opposition parties.

It is ironic that Lane and Ersson raise these drawbacks in the
context of South Africa, often seen as the region's pre-eminent case
of successful democratization. This is very much a situation of
whether the glass is half empty or half full. As Southall points out,
there is clear evidence that South Africa has made 'very significant
strides towards the consolidation of democracy since 1994', not only
exemplified by the second successful election in 1999 but also by the
fact that there is a lively debate about the appropriate political way
forward (2000: 168). In sum, for South Africa's 'democratic opti-
mists' democracy appears to be doing better than merely surviving,
an apparent confirmation of the efficacy of elite-pacted transitions for
democratic consolidation. However, growing cynicism and a belief
that things are not improving quickly enough for the mass of impoverished South Africans could threaten the long-term consolidation of
democracy, as the 'democratic pessimists' fear. In sum, it is difficult
not to conclude that the democratic prognosis in South Africa will
become progressively less optimistic *unless* the government can see a
way to deal both with the country's economic polarization and with
the growing numbers of radicals – focused in the country's powerful
trade union movement – who appear to be increasingly disenchanted
with the form of post-apartheid democracy.

8
The Middle East

8.1   Introduction

It is often suggested not only that the Middle East region is filled with countries that have few structural characteristics conducive to democracy, but also that things have been that way for a long time. Others assert that, in fact, the countries of the region do not comprise an unchanging, undemocratic monolith and point to three periods of profound political changes in the region during the late nineteenth and early twentieth centuries. The first major political change occurred while regional countries were under Ottoman (Turkish) colonial rule, when national assemblies were created in North Africa and the Arabian peninsular between the 1860s and the 1930s. The second took place after Ottoman rule collapsed around the time of World War I: parliamentary regimes were created in a number of regional countries, for example, in Egypt (during 1924–58), Iraq (1936–58) and Lebanon (1946–75).

A third period of political change occurred in the late 1950s and early 1960s, when governments in Egypt, Iraq, Libya and Syria, perceived as overly conservative, were overthrown by radical, often youthful, army officers. Their goal was to get rid of their countries' traditionalist political systems, manifested by unrepresentative governments regarded as unforgivably subservient to the West. However, over time, it appeared that the new rulers had no real intention of conventionally democratizing their political systems. Instead, they installed a variety of authoritarian regimes, including facade democracies, whose characteristics were explained in chapter 1. We noted that facade democracies typically have few conventional attributes of democracy beyond regular, albeit heavily controlled, elections. By virtue of their positions, rulers in such systems regularly win presidential elections with a huge proportion – typically, over 90 per cent – of the popular vote. The overall point is that there is a variety of kinds of regime in the Middle East region which developed in the wake of three periods of political upheaval over the last hundred years or so. Significantly, the extant types of regime – whether monarchical or dominated by the military or a single party – are characterized by a lack of democracy: they tend to be both authoritarian and unrepresentative, closely supported by the armed forces, often buoyed up by significant oil revenues.

Apart from Turkey – a democracy since 1983 – and a few (hesitantly) democratizing countries, including Kuwait, Jordan, Morocco and Algeria, democratic systems are lacking in the region. Waterbury contends that 'the Arab Middle East is exceptional in its resistance to political liberalisation, respect for human rights, and formal democratic practice' (1994: 23). However, while various kinds of authoritarian regimes are the norm this should not imply that this is the result of characteristics rooted in history. Instead, the nature of such regimes is explicable by reference to their structural characteristics, which are rarely conducive to democratization. Why is the Middle East, a region of nearly 20 countries (see table 8.1 below), apparently so uncongenial towards democracy? Karl suggests that Middle Eastern countries are characterized by 'a culture of repression and passivity that is antithetical to democratic citizenship' (1995: 79). On the other hand, Ibrahim asserts that significant political changes are beginning to take place in the region, resulting in political elites in a number of regional countries 'beginning a march from which ultimately there may be no retreat' (1995: 43). To what extent can Middle Eastern countries reconcile what some see as their citizens' growing desire for democracy with their own largely undemocratic political backgrounds?

Ibrahim appears to be suggesting that in fact the Middle East region is not entirely different from the other democratizing regions, as he detects some movement towards democracy. But Karl and Waterbury see things differently: they highlight what they see as the structural drawbacks to regional democratization. As we have seen in earlier chapters, if a polity has more anti-democracy than pro-democracy structures, then this will be a powerful inhibitory factor for chances of democracy and democratic consolidation. But we have also noted that the importance of contingent factors – including the personal preferences of powerful political leaders and a range of external factors –

Table 8.1 Democracy in the Middle East, 1989–1999

	Political rights (PR)		Civil liberties (CL)		PR + CL average	PR + CL average	Freedom rating
	1988–9	1998–9	1988–9	1998–9	1988–9	1998–9	1998–9
Jordan	6	4	5	5	5.5	4.5	Partly free
Morocco	4	5	5	4	4.5	4.5	Partly free
Turkey	2	4	4	5	3	4.5	Partly free
Kuwait	6	5	5	5	5.5	5	Partly free
Algeria	5	6	6	5	5.5	5.5	Not free
Lebanon	6	6	5	5	5.5	5.5	Not free
Tunisia	6	6	4	5	5	5.5	Not free
UAE	5	6	5	5	5	5.5	Not free
Yemen:							
North/South	5/7	5	5/7	6	6	5.5	Not free
Egypt	5	6	4	6	4.5	6	Not free
Iran	5	6	6	6	5.5	6	Not free
Oman	6	6	6	6	6	6	Not free
Bahrain	5	7	5	6	5	6.5	Not free
Qatar	5	7	5	6	5	6.5	Not free
Libya	6	7	6	7	6	7	Not free
Saudi Arabia	6	7	7	7	6.5	7	Not free
Syria	6	7	7	7	6.5	7	Not free

Source: 'Annual survey of Freedom country scores, 1972–73 to 1998–99',
http://www.freedomhouse.org/survey99/method/

should not be overlooked in this regard. However, in the Middle East, unlike in Africa, external factors did not clearly encourage democracy in the late 1980s and 1990s. The collapse of the Soviet Union and the regional fallout from the Gulf War of 1991 led to tentative moves towards democracy in some countries of the region, but greater repression in others. It is also difficult to detect in the recent political histories of Middle Eastern countries the kind of pro-democracy figures – such as Nelson Mandela and Jerry Rawlings – who were so important to democratic progress in South Africa and Ghana.

The region's countries can be divided politically into three distinct groups. The first comprises just one country – Turkey – where democratization has made significant, albeit patchy, progress since its most recent inauguration in 1983 (see table 8.2 below, p. 185). The second category is made up of four countries – Jordan, Kuwait, Morocco, Algeria – that, according to Freedom House data, have made some democratic progress in recent years. The third category is a residual one: it is characterized by a dozen authoritarian regimes where there seems to have been little or no progress towards democracy in recent years. The Freedom House picture for 1988–9 to 1998–9 is depicted in table 8.1.

In this chapter we begin by focusing on the structural characteristics of the region's political and social systems which are often said to be unconducive to democratization. After that we turn to our case studies: Kuwait and Turkey. We focus on these countries for the following reasons. First, Kuwait was selected because its recent democratic progress reflects the importance of an important contingent factor: the political impact of the Gulf War of 1990–1, when Kuwait was invaded and occupied by its neighbour, Iraq. Kuwait is a small, oil-rich and wealthy country which gained independence from Britain in 1961. Until recently dominated by an autocratic ruler and his family, Kuwait had little in the way of other formal political institutions over the years. In short, the country's structural characteristics were not initially beneficial to democratization. However, democratic progress was encouraged by the Gulf War, which damaged the legitimacy of the country's ruler. Encouraged both by foreign governments and domestic pressures from civil society to allow more political freedoms, the emir responded by tentatively embarking on a democratization programme.

Founded on the collapsed Ottoman empire in 1923, Turkey is a very different example. A populous country of more than 65 million people – 80 per cent are Turkish, with a number of minority peoples, including Kurds – straddling the divide between Europe and Asia, its political history reflects not only the political importance of a centralizing state but also that of the military. Ninety-eight per cent of the population are Muslims, and Islam maintains a strong social and political position despite the secular emphasis of state policy since the founding of the Turkish republic. But Turkey is actually a second wave, rather than a third wave democracy, having first democratized in 1950. However, the country was taken over by the military three times over the next few decades – in 1960, 1971 and 1980 – before the latest round of democracy which began in 1983. Focusing on Turkey will highlight the importance of both structural and contingent factors in this country's tentative, long drawn-out democratization.

8.2 Structural impediments to democracy in the Middle East

Middle East countries have the following *structural* characteristics said to make the creation of recognizably democratic political systems very difficult:

- *Political systems headed by personalistic leaders* Such rulers preside over strong, centralized states and are often unwilling to devolve any real power to other political institutions.
- *Politically significant militaries* Typically, leaders of the armed forces see it as their job to protect the state from attack from within and without. Among the internal attacks are numerous challenges from groups wishing to change the political status quo.
- *Weak and fragmented civil societies* Civil societies in the region's countries are often weak and fragmented and do not present much of a challenge to governments to encourage them to amend undemocratic behaviour.
- *The cultural and religious hegemony of Islam*   Islam is often said to be a religious system which, like Confucianism (examined in chapter 5), is not beneficial to democratization. The regional ubiquity and sociopolitical significance of Islam is said not only to help explain the authoritarian nature of most governing regimes, but also to account for what Karl has referred to as a 'culture of repression and passivity that is antithetical to democratic citizenship' (1995: 79).

Where recognizably democratic regimes have been installed, we can note the importance of *contingent* factors. For example, Turkey's democratization in 1983 and democratic progress since then was encouraged by certain external actors, including the US government and the European Union (EU). (Turkey is keen to gain EU membership.) However, the example of Turkey also illustrates the importance of structural legacies for democratic outcomes: from the early 1920s the country has been dominated politically by the military. Since the early 1980s, Turkey's most recent democratic experiment has failed to lead to democratic consolidation; and this was not because it was a Muslim country, but because the military, like its counterpart in Algeria, kept a close hold on political developments, strongly discouraging what they saw as extremist parties from taking part in open political competition. In Kuwait, too, as already noted, recent political outcomes were also affected by contingent events, especially the invasion by Iraq in 1990, which turned out to be a catalyst for tentative democratization.

8.3   Democratization in the Middle East

Political culture and regime legitimacy

Two factors are perceived as particularly important in relation
to political culture and regime legitimacy in the Middle East: the
colonial legacy and the role of Islam.

The colonial legacy

The Middle East region has no tradition of conventional democracy
and no beneficial colonial legacy which, as in India, can be seen
as an important contributory factor in the development of a pro-
democracy political culture. Instead, like Africa, the Middle East was
long controlled by colonial rulers intent on governing as cheaply and
as expeditiously as possible, with little or no concern to build democratic political systems.

The Middle East region was colonized for hundreds of years by
the Turkish (Ottoman) empire, prior to its collapse around the time
of World War I. Ottoman control was followed by brief European
domination in many of the region's countries, via mandates and protectorates awarded to various countries, including Britain and France,
by the League of Nations. As a result, under the overall auspices of
the League of Nations, Aden (now part of Yemen) was under British
control, Algeria was administered by France, and Libya was ruled by
Italy. There were also communities of European settlers: the French
in Algeria, Jews in Palestine. Elsewhere there were independent
monarchies, for example, in Saudi Arabia.

Despite differences in governing style, it is nevertheless useful to
focus on a particular pattern of control that I shall call the 'colonial-
style state', characterized by authoritarian systems of rule. Such states
definitively shaped the exercise of power and defined the political
arena in most of the region's countries, whose borders were created
or dominated by the Europeans between the world wars. Throughout the region, it was generally the dominant colonial power –
whether Ottoman, British, French or other – that first created the
essential features of a state, giving the new country a capital city, a
state bureaucracy, a legal system, a flag and internationally recognized boundaries. Collectively, these developments led to the breakdown of 'traditional' social units like the tribe or the extended family,

and the modernization of polities under central governments. Sometimes these processes were undertaken on the basis of a pre-existing administrative entity, as in Algeria; by detaching a part of a former Ottoman province (for example, TransJordan); or by linking together several erstwhile Ottoman-run provinces (for example, Syria and Iraq). The important point is that, despite diversity, single centres of authority were crucial to the new post-Ottoman polities. The new regimes focused on and encompassed 'standard rules and regulations . . . supposed to be applied equally to all those who lived within [their] boundaries as citizens' (Owen 1992: 15). However, the new post-Ottoman governments, some of which were briefly under European control, were collectively characterized not only by their authoritarian styles of government but also by the lack of pressures to democratize.

European rule in the region gradually dissolved in the 1930s and 1940s as various regional countries – including Iraq, Syria and Lebanon – demanded, and received, their independence. However, the strongly centralized states created under Ottoman or European rule were retained, with the justification that they were the best vehicle to promote and preside over the planned large-scale projects of economic development and social welfare. State control of development was justified for two main reasons: first, private sectors had failed to meet the challenge of development in the early independence period; and, second, the sudden exodus of hundreds of thousands of foreign officials, businessmen and agriculturists – affecting Egypt during the Suez crisis of 1956, and French North Africa immediately after the end of colonialism in the early 1960s – left many regional countries lacking in skilled people to run the new states. After World War II, in order to embed themselves in power, modernizing regimes embarked on the implementation of land reform programmes, both to break the power of large-scale landowners and to pass agricultural land to landless labourers (Bromley 1994). In sum, decolonization in the 1930s and 1940s was followed by a general expansion in the power and pervasiveness of the institutions of the state: the bureaucracy, the police, the army, and the number of public enterprises. This built on and strengthened the incumbent authoritarian structures of power bequeathed by colonial rule.

One of the most important structures of power was the armed forces. The new rulers perceived the need to bolster security after the departure of the colonial power in order to affirm control over the whole of their new territories. The *quid pro quo* was that the armed forces expected to receive an impressive proportion of available economic resources. While the Middle East was no different from other

post-colonial regions, such as Africa, in this regard, what differenti-
ated it from other regions where the military had a political role has
been 'the quantity of [economic] resources devoted to the military
and the power of incumbent elites the armed forces underpin'
(Bromley 1994: 114). Reflecting the huge growth in revenues from
oil in the 1970s, the military's share of GNP expenditure 'in the
Middle East was nearly twice that of the next most militarized region
(the Warsaw pact) and over three times the world average' (Picard
1990: 190).

In sum, Middle Eastern states emerged after colonialism with
structural characteristics conducive to authoritarian rule: centralized
polities, with personalistic rulers underpinned by large bureaucracies
and powerful military establishments. These factors were singularly
unconducive to the establishment of democratic regimes in the region.

Islam

What was the role of Islam in the perpetuation of regional authoritarianism after colonial rule? The Middle East is distinctive in that,
with the exception of Israel, all its countries are predominantly
Muslim – typically around 90 per cent or more of populations (Beeley
1992: 296–7). It is often suggested that Islam is more than 'just' a
religion: it is also a cultural, social and political system of immense
importance. The rules of conduct fundamental to Islam were laid
down by God via the Prophet Muhammad 1,400 years ago, and as
a consequence Muslims must serve God through obedience to these
designated rules. True freedom in Islam is said to be achieved not by
individual efforts but by 'surrendering to the Divine will rather than
in some artificial separation from the community of God . . . Rights
remain subordinate to and determined by duties' (Vincent 1986: 42).
As a result, the 'language of duty' – in the context of the importance
of community – is said to be more natural than the 'language of individual rights' in Islam. This is said to restrict or deny the importance
of the individual while highlighting collective over individual rights.
As Vincent explains, the Muslim community – the *umma* – is seen as
a 'compact wall whose bricks support each other' and 'provide for
the integration of human personality . . . through self-abnegation and
action for the good of the collectivity' (1986: 42). In sum, Islam
affirms the importance of the community over that of the individual.
It also emphasizes that rulers are placed in their positions by God
and, as a result, their wisdom is boundless and not to be challenged
by ordinary people.

Many Middle Eastern governments have claimed divine sanction for their rule: that is, they claim to be in power because it is God's will; everything they do is sanctioned by God. Of course, this is a potential justification for harsh or arbitrary government, and can be used to justify the denial of democracy and freedom of speech, and harsh treatment of minorities. On the other hand, other regimes, such as Iran before its revolution, Egypt, Algeria, Syria, Turkey and Iraq, have sought to build nation-states along Western lines, often with little public role acknowledged for Islam (Haynes 1998). In such countries, the status of Islam was downplayed, and religious professionals were coopted into the state structure or neutralized.

In sum, the political culture and regime legitimacy of many Middle Eastern countries is said to be strongly linked to the hegemony of Islam, the ubiquitous regional religion. The characteristics of Islam are said fundamentally to influence the political culture of the region's states to the extent that Western-style democracy would be very difficult to introduce in most of them.

Political participation and institutions

The state

Various kinds of state emerged in the Middle East region after colonial rule. Apart from Turkey, a democracy since 1983 whose political characteristics will be examined below, Kamrava (1998) notes the contemporary existence of three other systems in the region: (1) 'exclusionary' ; (2) 'inclusionary'; and (3) 'sultanistic'. Exclusionary governments are found in Algeria, Syria, Sudan and Tunisia, and are subdivided into two kinds of regimes: 'military'; and '*mukhaberat*' (non-military, non-monarchical). What they have in common is that the mass of ordinary people have traditionally been denied a say in how they are governed. The regimes typically rely on the intelligence services and/or the armed forces to enforce a depoliticization of society, principally through repression and fear. Among states in this category, only Algeria has allowed relatively free elections in recent years after a decade-long civil war accompanied by popular demands for change, a situation Sadiki describes as a popular 'cry for justice, equality and emancipation' (1997: 139).

Second, there are the inclusionary regimes which, despite the name, are not conventionally democratic. They can be based either on single-party or 'no-party' systems and are found in Iran, Libya and

Iraq. These are polities, Sadiki observes, where governments seek to deflect any demands for change that surface by turning 'streets and neighbourhoods into political theatres ... successfully divert[ing] popular political energies into projects that actually sustain the very basis of the regime' (1997: 133).

Third, there are the 'sultanistic' states, subdivided into 'oil monarchies' and 'civil myth' regimes. Among the former are Kuwait, Bahrain, Qatar, Oman, Saudi Arabia and the United Arab Emirates. Characteristically, they are regimes that are dominated by personalistic rulers, and have substantial oil wealth and relatively small populations. Governments of the oil monarchies have often been little concerned to accommodate the intermittent demands for greater political participation and accountability that have surfaced in recent years. Only one country in this category, Kuwait, has a recent history of tentative democratization bolstered by the Gulf War of 1991, which led to strong demands for greater democracy.

Civil myth regimes have rulers whose power is derived from their personal religious or secular attributes. They are found in Jordan and Morocco. Neither country has large oil reserves and associated wealth, and they have experienced economic problems in recent years. They were also affected by the global trend towards democracy associated with the third wave and the demise of the Soviet Union. Both countries, particularly the former, have seen a trend towards political liberalization and perhaps democratization in recent years.

In sum, the three kinds of regimes noted here – exclusionary, inclusionary and sultanistic – are all notable for denying their citizens democracy. However, in recent years several have seen either political liberalization – Jordan, Morocco – or even tentative democratization. In such cases, the importance of contingent factors can be noted, including economic problems leading to political reforms; the demonstration effect provided by the collapse of authoritarian regimes in Eastern Europe, which led in some cases to growing political demands for change; or, in the case of Kuwait, the Gulf War of 1990–1 which helped kick-start democratization.

Political society

Political parties have been a feature of the region since soon after World War I. They were often in the vanguard of anti-colonial struggles against, successively, the Ottomans and then the British and French. Anti-colonial struggles reached a high point in the 1930s and 1940s when a number of states – Iraq (1932), Lebanon (1945), Syria

(1944), Jordan (1946), Palestine (1947) – achieved independence. However, political parties that do not overtly support the government have always been viewed with extreme suspicion and have usually been banned. This is because political parties were often perceived by rulers as socially divisive, actual or putative champions of 'harmful' ideologies – such as socialism – and as conduits for unwelcome foreign political penetration. Multiparty competition was associated with division, waste and inefficiency, a handicap to nation-building and development. There were two general results: (1) competitive party systems withered; and (2), when competitive elections were permitted, candidates for office would be compelled to stand as independents, not as party representatives.

Single-party regimes have traditionally been common in the region, judged by governments to be the best means of directing a planned economy and of supervising countrywide systems of mobilization and control. Single parties were created after colonial rule either by the organization that led the struggle for independence or by whichever group of civilians or military personnel managed later to grab power. Single-party regimes were established in about a third of Middle Eastern countries – including Tunisia, Algeria, Syria, Iraq, Egypt and Sudan. Such parties tended to call themselves 'socialist', yet what often seemed of most importance was the goal of monopolizing the state's official ideology to dominate political discourse and, more generally, to control their country's political terrain. They had very few clear – if any – aims to democratize the political scene.

Recently, however, there has been a resurgence of political parties in the region, associated with political liberalization or democratization. For example, in each of Jordan, Morocco and Turkey there have been more than 20 parties, Algeria has had around 40, while Lebanon has had about 100 (Banks and Muller 1998: 20–1). Even in Kuwait, where political parties were banned in the 1960s and are still officially illegal, five distinct political 'tendencies' have recently been allowed to operate, with ideological orientations ranging from the secular left to radical Islamic groups. Because such political parties are often more the creation of individual politicians than the reflection of an institutionalized party structure, their contribution to building a political scene helpful to democracy is difficult to judge. Certainly, as Abukhalil (1997) notes, the new parties rarely seem to have broad and reliable ties with the mass of the people. In fact, many seem incapable of arriving at policy positions contrasting with those of the government to the extent of offering viable alternatives in democratic governance. In addition, many of the region's new parties have rigid organizations, undemocratic party regulations and proce-

dures and personalistic leaders: 'Collective leadership is rarely practised' and rank-and-file participation in decision-making is often
absent (Abukhalil 1997: 154). The consequence is that it is unclear
to what extent the development of parties reflects growing democracy. In sum, because of the paucity of their democratic characteristics, it is unclear if the recent increase in the number of regional
political parties will encourage democratic progress.

Civil society

Said (1996) suggests that politically effective civil societies are lacking
in the region, while Bromley predicts that 'weakness[es] of and divisions within civil society seem likely to be a major problem in the
future process of democratisation' (1994: 166). Such authors perceive
the region's weak, fragmented civil societies as the result of ethnic
and religious divisions; low levels of industrialization; and underdeveloped class forces. On the other hand, some observers now claim
that this situation is changing, with an expanding role for civil society
in countries where 'autocratic rule has been entrenched for long
periods' (Sadiki 1997: 149). In such views, popular political involvement is said to mean that people are increasingly willing to confront
the state to demand greater political and economic freedoms (Kramer
1992; El-Kenz 1991). In short, rulers are increasingly challenged to
allow democracy and more human and civil rights in traditionally
authoritarian regional regimes.

The roots of such opposition, it is suggested, can be seen in a per-
vading sense of anomie among certain sections of the population,
especially in the burgeoning numbers of the young, the under-
employed and unemployed, and the religiously orientated. Demands
surface from across the political spectrum, from the nationalist and
secularist left, at one extreme, to the broad Islamist movement, at the
other. Leftwich notes, however, that 'the strongest supporters of
[liberal] democratic processes come from the more secular sections
of the societies, as in Turkey, Egypt and Algeria' (1997: 531). Such
people are committed to secularism and Western-style modernization,
with a 'scramble for their market shares', to 'learn how to compete
in a merciless world economy', secure jobs and move out of poverty
(Ajami 1993: 5).

Many governments see the various Islamist groups as their biggest
threat, because they have grown in political significance in most
regional countries since the late 1970s. The example of Iran's
revolution – a massive outburst of people's power that accomplished

the removal of an unpopular ruler, the Shah – spurred Islamists across the Middle East region to try to emulate their success. The consequence was that in the 1980s the Islamists widely emerged as the most significant oppositional voice in intellectual, social and political life (Haynes 1998: 125–47). For example, the Front Islamic de Salut (FIS) in Algeria and Hamas in the Palestinian Authority emerged at this time as powerful organizations with ready constituencies among the poor, the young and the alienated. More generally, the rise of political Islam was facilitated because the authorities generally felt it expedient to leave the mosque alone, and it was from there that the Islamist groups emanated.

In sum, gradually more vociferous political and civil societies across the region reflect growing societal concerns with diminishing state legitimacy and authority. This is the result, on the one hand, of increasing numbers of people experiencing economic hardship and unemployment and, on the other, growing fear of the impact of Westernization on traditional cultures (Haynes 1995b; Esposito and Piscatori 1991). Some manifestations of opposition are expressed through conventional political parties, while others are focused in and through the Islamist groups.

Economic and international factors

We saw in earlier chapters that changes associated with the third wave of democracy showed little respect for income distinctions between countries: it engulfed Asian countries with mounting incomes and robust economies, as well as Latin American and African countries undergoing economic crisis. What impact did economic issues have on progress towards democracy in the Middle East? While it seems clear that the region acquired greater economic prosperity as a result of its possession of significant oil reserves than it would have done without it, there is little clear evidence of a simple relationship between socioeconomic modernization and the development of democracy.

This suggests that other factors have to be taken into account to explain political outcomes in the region. For example, Turkey has a democratically elected government with a relatively low per capita GNP ($3,160 in 1998), while oil-rich Gulf states, such as the United Arab Emirates ($18,220, not far short of that of Britain, $21,400), Saudi Arabia ($6,790, nearly double that of democratic Poland, $3,900) and Oman ($4,950, higher than democratic Hungary,

$4,510) have greater per capita economic prosperity *but* less democracy (World Bank 1999: 190–1, table 1; World Bank 2000: 272, table 1a). In the past, when oil prices were high, authoritarian rulers could hope to buy off sociopolitical discontent through the assiduous use of oil wealth.

But not all regional countries are oil rich: Saudi Arabia, Algeria, the United Arab Emirates, Libya, Qatar, Oman, Kuwait, Iran, Iraq and a few others have significant oil reserves; others – such as Yemen, Syria and Jordan – have few or none. However, oil wealth has to an extent been spread around the region – for example, when Egyptian workers in Saudi Arabia send a portion of their wages home. In short, it is clear that the key to the region's economic prosperity is to be found in its possession of significant oil reserves. But this has been a two-edged sword: on the one hand, oil wealth has helped insulate some states from demands for increased political participation. This was particularly the case when oil prices rose swiftly, as they did in the 1970s. On the other hand, when they dropped sharply, as they did in the mid-1980s, regimes found it much more difficult to buy off discontent. The consequence of falling oil prices was that most Middle Eastern governments were compelled to inaugurate economic reform programmes in the 1980s or 1990s. But attempts at economic reform – typically involving deregulation, privatization of state-owned resources, and a dismantling of state bureaucracies – led to increasing hardship as many ordinary people lost their state jobs and experienced a reduction or the elimination of long-standing price subsidies on basic goods.

In many countries, the economic privations associated with recent economic reform programmes served to undermine the traditional bargain – known as *khubz* – between rulers and ruled. *Khubz* was an informal pact between rulers and ruled: the former would provide the mass of ordinary people with most of their material needs, while, in return, the latter – implicitly – agreed to be politically passive (Sadiki 1997: 133). But growing economic hardship led to 'bread uprisings': people took to the streets, and such protests sometimes developed into demonstrations with a wider focus: against 'social inequality, corruption, nepotism, authoritarianism and regime incompetence' (Sadiki 1997: 138–9). In sum, across the region demands for fundamental political and economic changes increasingly surfaced in the 1980s and 1990s. The key cause was that economic reform programmes failed to lead to beneficial changes but rather hit the poor hardest. The latter responded by taking to the streets in protest at what they saw as economic mismanagement.

Domestic pressures for change dovetailed with international developments at this time. The pivotal position of the Middle East in global oil production, the importance of the area to the Soviet Union and the US during the Cold War, and the volatility of intrastate and interstate relations combined to produce a combustible combination of geological, geographical and historical circumstances which were instrumental in shaping the region's political development. To analyse the external context of the region's politics and to note the influence of structural and contingent factors, we focus on three interrelated levels of analysis: (1) interstate and intrastate politics which led to the involvement of external powers in the region; (2) struggles by the superpowers for a regional hegemony of influence during the Cold War; and (3) the international politics of oil.

First, the region's perennial Arab–Israeli conflict and the associated Palestinian problem, coupled with tension between conservative monarchical and radical republican regimes and between radical Islamist and conservative-secular ones, resulted in regional states relying on the superpowers for arms deliveries and security. Western governments perceived the Islamist groups to be anti-democratic. Consequently, if more 'open politics' in the region meant politics with a more Islamic flavour, then democracy would not be supported. Instead, Western governments supported anti-Islamist incumbent regimes, almost irrespective of regime character. For this reason the US under the Clinton presidency said little about alleged electoral fraud in Egypt's 1995 general elections, from which the mainstream, non-violent Muslim Brotherhood was excluded. In addition, after a brief flowering of political freedom in Algeria in the late 1980s and early 1990s, Western powers, including the US and France, fearful of influxes of refugees, managed to accommodate themselves to the military junta's annulment of parliamentary elections in 1992. During the subsequent civil war – with serious human rights violations related to it carried out by the military and security forces against ordinary people – up to 100,000 people died. In short, if it appeared to Western governments that democratization would let the Islamists take positions of power then they preferred to support incumbent non-democratic regimes.

Second, policies of regional states were intimately connected with the strategic goals of the US and the Soviet Union during the Cold War, but the alignments with the superpowers were a perennial source of interstate tensions. Later, the demise of the Soviet Union and the Eastern European regional communist bloc encouraged oppositional activity in many Middle Eastern countries, with secular and Islamic activists attacking incumbent governments, using the language of political liberalization and democracy. Richard Murphy, a former American Assistant Secretary of State for the Near East, affirmed that the US government had no serious problems in dealing with incum-

bent regimes as long as they were not Islamist ones. Murphy suggested that the problem was not that Muslims were not 'ready' for
democracy, but that Washington was 'not ready for the choices that
most would probably make' (Murphy quoted in Hirst 1999). That
is, the US government feared that Islamist regimes would be hostile
to American and other Western regional interests.

Third, the importance of the region's oil for the well-being of
Western economies was such that, in order to ensure continued access
to oil supplies, the American government established a Rapid Deploy-
ment Force (now 'US Central Command'), the core of the United
Nations coalition force which drove Iraq from Kuwait in 1991. The
importance of an ensured oil supply for Western economies meant
that their governments were much more concerned with the region's
political stability than helping advance democracy. Richard Murphy,
quoted above, affirmed that democracy was, theoretically, one of the
'good things' the United States wanted to see in the region. In practice, however, regional security concerns, including an assured oil
supply and advancing the Arab–Israeli peace process, 'rank[ed] far
ahead of participatory politics in the list of America's real goals'.
More open politics might not only endanger oil supplies but also the
Arab–Israeli peace process.

Murphy's comments highlight that Western governments do not
necessarily support pro-democracy movements in the region, but
often prefer the status quo. For Western governments, democracy can
raise 'the prospect of old and reliable friends . . . being transformed
into more independent and less predictable nations. This prospect
generates a fear that such nations could make western access to oil
less secure. Thus global order and stability [in the region] have often
been defined in terms of preservation of the *status quo*' (Esposito
2000: 122). The issue was put into sharp focus by the Gulf War of
1991, which not only highlighted Iraq's aggression but also led to a
renewed focus on regional political reforms and democracy.

In this section we have highlighted a number of points relating to
structure and contingency in relation to democracy in the Middle
East. First, we noted that the structural domination of some authoritarian governments was facilitated by the possession of oil reserves
which enabled them to buy off political discontent by the use of oil
wealth. Second, the contingent factor of falls in oil prices from the
mid-1980s, leading to the adoption of economic reform programmes
which hurt the poor, encouraged the emergence of more vocal political and civil societies. They were concerned not only with economic
hardships but also with sociopolitical concerns, such as diminishing
state legitimacy and authority, unemployment, fears of secularization

and perceived western cultural hegemony. Third, Western support for democratization – a general feature of the third wave of democracy – was very tentative in the Middle East. This was not only because some authoritarian regimes – such as Kuwait, Saudi Arabia and Egypt – were staunch friends, but also because democratization would in many cases encourage Islamist groups to try to achieve political power via the ballot box.

8.4 Case studies: Kuwait and Turkey

The importance of such factors can be seen in the accounts of democratization in Kuwait and Turkey, the case studies in this section of the chapter. First, we will examine democratization in Kuwait, an 'oil monarchy' which tentatively democratized during the 1990s as a result primarily of the impact of the Gulf War of 1990–1. Our second case study is Turkey, the region's only clear-cut democracy. The purpose of selecting these countries is to show that moves towards democracy were linked to the influence of a range of contingent and structural factors. Overcoming structural impediments to democracy required that governments, and especially key leaders, could follow through with a process of democracy which, while satisfying popular aspirations, would not fundamentally threaten the stability of their country. Whether rulers could successfully pursue a policy of controlled democratization was linked to the following factors:

1 support, or at least an absence of overt opposition, from the armed forces;
2 'moderate' political and civil societies that would not attempt to force the pace of democratization beyond what rulers saw as suitable;
3 encouragement from Western governments to democratize but without undermining regional stability.

Kuwait

We noted earlier that there are a number of sultanistic states in the region, subdivided into 'oil monarchies' and 'civil myth' regimes. Kuwait – along with Bahrain, Qatar, Oman, Saudi Arabia and the

United Arab Emirates – is an oil monarchy. Kuwait shares the characteristics of such regimes: dominated by personalistic rulers, typically with little in the way of other formal political institutions, they
have relatively small populations and enjoy substantial oil wealth.
The latter long enabled the oil monarchies, including Kuwait, to 'buy
off' political opposition through relatively lavish social welfare
systems. Over time, this was an effective mechanism in dealing with
any demands for greater political participation and accountability.
While in Kuwait non-party elections began in the 1960s, democratization was significantly bolstered by the Gulf War of 1991, which led
to strong demands for greater democracy. In other words, the contingent factor of the Gulf War – during which Kuwait was invaded
and occupied for months by its neighbour, Iraq – was a significant
event in the development of democracy in Kuwait.

Political culture and regime legitimacy

The country of Kuwait was created in 1961, following the country's
independence from British colonial rule. The new country's political
system was initially rooted in the near-absolute power of the country's
ruler, the emir. He was strongly supported not only by Kuwait's armed
forces but also by the former colonial power, Britain, who saw the emir
as a close ally, an invaluable friend in a strategically important region.
The country's political culture reflected the emir's personal political
domination; and he was not minded to develop a democratic system,
although he did sanction the introduction of non-party elections in the
1960s to the country's national advisory body.
   As a result of the unwillingness to introduce and develop a democratic system, for 30 years after independence, that is, until the Gulf
War of 1990–1, Kuwait's political culture and the legitimacy of the
ruling regime were intimately linked to the family rule of the al Sabah
family. The emir's claim to power and societal legitimacy was
based on his traditional authority, a common characteristic of other
sultanistic regimes, including the other Gulf Emirates and Saudi
Arabia.

Political participation and institutions

While the basis of Kuwait's political system was not in autonomous
political parties competing for power at periodic elections but in the
person of the emir himself, the emir indicated that he was willing to
institutionalize its political system. As a result, he introduced, soon

after independence, a 'national charter' which would set out the form of rule he had chosen. Under its terms representatives of a variety of political and social groups would periodically meet to advise the emir as to the characteristics of the rules for Kuwait's future political life and direction. This system had a major appeal for the emir, who was worried about the danger of opening up the political system to multiparty competition.

Under the auspices of the national charter, a consultative assembly was formed which produced a constitution in 1962. This provided for the election of a national assembly, for which elections were held the following year. Competing for 50 seats, over 200 men – including members of the ruling al Sabah family as well merchants, intellectuals and Bedouin – stood for election, exclusively as independents; political parties were not allowed and women were not permitted to stand or to vote. In addition, the number of men allowed to participate was governed by a stringent residence qualification. As a result, the electorate was restricted to just 17,000 men, comprising male members of families that were deemed to have lived continuously in Kuwait since 1920. Further elections were held on the same basis in 1967 and 1975. However, in 1976, the national assembly was suddenly dissolved by the emir, who was concerned that the very existence of the national assembly might exacerbate tensions between rival communities as the Lebanese civil war began to escalate. Earlier, problems had arisen from the efforts of a small group of opposition politicians who wanted to curb some of the powers of the al Sabah family. They alleged that the family had interfered in the elections to prevent the election of some of its main critics.

After a gap of five years, the emir agreed to allow new elections in 1981. As before, state meddling and the formation of tiny constituencies made it difficult for members of the unofficial opposition to project themselves as candidates for office. However, new groups – including men who stressed their religious credentials as members of one of the two strands of Islam, Sunnis or Shi'ites – managed to win election to the national assembly; however, political parties stayed banned, as they were for the next election in 1985. On the latter occasion, despite the attempt to prevent the formation of recognized groups representing various societal interests, voting delivered an assembly including four 'unofficial groupings' of two or three deputies backed by 'readily identifiable organizations' with 'established platforms', including pro-democracy groups and Arab nationalists (Owen 1992 quoting Peterson). However, it appears that this assembly was too radical for the liking of the emir: it lasted only a year, until 1986, before being dissolved.

This time the period without an assembly was four years, during which pressures for a return to democratic life surfaced. Eventually the government proposed the founding of a national council, whose main purpose would be to work out a way for the confrontations of the past between the government and the national assembly to be minimized. Two-thirds of 75 seats were put up for direct election and voting was held in June of 1986, but the turnout was low compared to 1985. This was partly the result of a boycott by a substantial number of former members of parliament. Discussions were then held with the intention of further constitutional amendments and the promulgation of a Kuwaiti national charter that would have detailed the nature of politics in the country. However, this process was interrupted by Iraq's invasion of Kuwait in August 1990. The Iraqi invasion greatly affected the status quo in Kuwait and resulted in loud demands for a democratic political system rather than the quasi-democracy which had been practised intermittently since the 1960s.

In sum, the legitimacy of al Sabah family rule was seriously called into question as a result of the Iraqi invasion in 1990. Many ordinary Kuwaitis believed that the regime had shown itself to be incompetent when trying to deal with invading Iraqis, and a demand for democracy followed. In addition, after the expulsion of the Iraqis by United Nations forces the regime showed itself to be incapable again, this time in its failure to rebuild the shattered political and social structures along lines satisfactory to the majority of its citizens. Overall, the contingent factors provided by the circumstances of the Iraqi invasion turned out to be more important than the structural position of absolutist rule: as a consequence, Kuwait tentatively democratized.

Parliamentary life was resumed with a heated and spirited electoral campaign in the summer of 1992. Elections were held in October – with few complaints about voting irregularities – and with an 85 per cent turnout of the electorate. Opposition forces won a clear majority in the national assembly, with competing – Sunni and Shi'i – religious groups winning at least a third of the 50 seats. The new parliament represented a victory for democratic forces that had neither accepted the 1986 suspension of the legislature nor the regime's lacklustre performance during the 1990–1 crisis with Iraq (Ibrahim 1995: 46). Further elections were held in 1996 and again in July 1999, 18 months ahead of schedule. The latter ensued due to a governmental mistake which caused 120,000 copies of the Qur'an to be printed with errors, with verses missing, repeated or misplaced. Following a call from 20 MPs – two-fifths of the total – criticizing the Islamic Affairs minister, the emir dissolved parliament as he was constitutionally bound to do. The result of the July 1999 elections was that only 16 (32 per cent) of the 50 seats went to known government supporters. Consequently, the emir accepted the resignation of the government and invited opposition members of the legislature to form the next government. In sum, there was evidence of gradual, if intermittent, progress towards more representative political institutions in Kuwait. The process was facilitated by the contingent factor of the Gulf War, which produced strong demands from Kuwaitis for greater democracy, a request to which the emir acceded.

Economic and international factors

As already noted, Kuwait has substantial oil wealth and a relatively small population, which enabled the state to deal with many of the citizenry's economic wants for long periods. Kuwait's oil reserves were estimated at 100 billion barrels in 1986, the third largest reserves in the world. As a result of its huge oil income, Kuwait became, prior to the events of 1990–1, by regional standards a highly developed welfare state. The government provided citizens with medical, educational and other services, without the payment of personal income tax. However, between 1986 and 1988, when oil prices declined, per capita income declined by 12 per cent from $16,600 to $14,630, before rising again slightly in 1989. However, the systematic destruction of the country's oil extraction facilities by the Iraqi forces in 1991 led to a virtual cessation of output for a time, before virtually full production was resumed in 1993. Despite the resumption of oil extraction, the economy remained affected by lingering problems from the Gulf War, including the accumulation of substantial debts and growing budget deficits. In sum, the decline of Kuwait's wealth and welfare system as a result of falling oil prices and the Iraqi invasion helped to fuel demands for democracy.

Conclusion

From slow, tentative beginnings in the early 1960s, the overall position of democracy in Kuwait improved over time, and especially during the 1990s following the Gulf War. Since that time, the emir has seen his personal power gradually decline while that of other political institutions, notably the national assembly, has perceptibly grown. While the emir may well have had residual fears about opening up the political systems to multiparty competition, the development of such a system in all but name implies that he was willing to countenance democratic expansion as long as the outcome was not the assumption of a leading role by groups that were inherently opposed to his continued rule. The economic prosperity and the developed welfare system established in Kuwait, and their destruction by the Iraqi forces in 1991, were important contributory factors to democratic progress.

Turkey

Turkey has a population of more than 65 million people, of which more than 80 per cent are Turkish. There are also a number of minority peoples, including Kurds, and this has periodically informed the nature of the country's politics. In addition, 98 per cent of the population are Muslims, and Islam maintains a strong social and political position despite the secular emphasis of state policy since the founding of the Turkish republic in the 1920s, following the demise of the Ottoman empire. In recent years, demands for more Islam in public life have conflicted with the country's strongly pro-secular orientation laid down by the founder of the Turkish republic, Kemal Atatürk.

Political culture and regime legitimacy

First becoming a democracy in 1950, Turkey has been taken over by the military on three occasions, in 1960, 1971 and 1980. Its latest round of democracy dates from 1983. Between the early 1970s and the late 1990s, as table 8.2 shows, Turkey fluctuated between being a 'free' and a 'partly free' country. Under democratic rule since 1983, the position of both political rights and civil liberties improved then declined. This situation is linked to the traditionally important political role of the armed forces which, for decades, have sought to control the country's political development in a strongly secular direction. Overall, the armed forces are the country's most important political institution, eclipsing underdeveloped political institutions, such as the increasingly fragmented party system, and this has been the case since the formation of the Turkish republic in 1923. The political importance of the armed forces can be seen in the fact that none of Turkey's three democratic transitions (1946, 1961, 1983) involved an elite settlement, often seen as facilitating democratization, but were carried out under the aegis of the military and according to its terms.

Table 8.2 Turkey's democratic position, 1973–1999

	Political rights + civil liberties average	Freedom rating
1973	3.5	Partly free
1977	2.5	Free
1983	4.5	Partly free
1987	3	Partly free
1991	3	Partly free
1995	5	Partly free
1999	4.5	Partly free

Source: Ozbudun 1996; 'Annual survey of Freedom country scores, 1972–73 to 1998–99', http://www.freedomhouse.org/survey99/method/

The most recent transition from military rule in 1983 exemplified the degree to which the outgoing military regime in Turkey set the terms of its departure from power. These included restrictions on which parties could compete in elections. Post-1983 constitutional amendments eradicated some of the legacies of military rule, including the ban on political activity by former politicians, and on cooperation between political parties and civil society organizations, including trade unions and professional organizations. In addition, other constitutional exit guarantees, such as the president's power to block constitutional amendments, automatically expired in 1989. On the other hand, the progress of civilianization – and hence democratic consolidation after 1983 – arguably had less to do with formal constitutional change than with informal practice and adaptation. The point is that nearly two decades after democratization, the military retains a political salience in Turkey which puts in doubt the country's commitment to democracy. In sum, the long-term structural effect of military domination has influenced the country's political culture and has made it difficult to develop an emphatically democratic regime.

While the roots of the military's political involvement can be traced back to the time of the Ottoman empire, the founding of the modern state of Turkey in 1923 inaugurated three-quarters of a century of aggressive modernization and secularization, initially under the leadership of a military hero, Mustafa Kemal 'Atatürk' ('Father of the Turks'), who imposed Western-style civil law. The Turkish Republic inherited from the Ottoman empire a strong, centralized and highly bureaucratic state which Atatürk proceeded to mould to his own vision. Believing that Turkey's indigenous traditions were expressions of backwardness, Atatürk judged that progress would come by emulating the institutions and absorbing the values of the European powers. This ideological perspective was firmly embedded in state policy, defended by the politically powerful armed forces.

Over the decades, the armed forces had control over its own processes of recruitment, training and promotion, resulting in the creation of a particular military culture facilitating the development of a specific role within Turkish society: as *the* defender of Atatürk's revolution. The institutional autonomy of the armed forces made it very difficult to manipulate the military for political purposes from outside its ranks. In recent years it has demonstrated a profound ability to maintain its cohesion and organizational integrity – during a period when Turkish society itself became increasingly fragmented into competing classes, ethnic and religious groups, and factions. The political clout of the military was demonstrated by the fact that the armed forces could – and did – close down political parties which it believed to be 'extremist': that is, either too religiously oriented or too ideologically radical. In addition, the military top brass has in recent years annually purged the officer corps to root out those suspected of sympathizing with Islamic groups or Kurdish rebels.

In sum, supported by the military, national leaders have shown little concern for the wishes of the national legislature, which has resulted in a lack of horizontal accountability between the leader and the legislature. In addition, civilian political leaders have sometimes sought to make policy by decree following discussions with senior military figures. Finally, Turkey's political culture and the legitimacy of successive regimes has been strongly moulded by the heavily politicized armed forces. As a result, Turkey is a limited democracy which has failed in recent years to make clear democratic progress.

Political participation and institutions

A choate political party system is often associated with democratic sustainability. Turkey offers an example of a party system that began with just two parties for the first contested election in 1950, with numbers of parties growing, over time, as a consequence of increasing political polarization and ideological division. The consequence was that by the end of the 1990s there were more than 30 parties, with ideological concerns ranging from those represented by secular, ultranationalist parties, through Islamic groups, to those of the extreme left.

By the 1970s, Turkey's party system was characterized by volatility, fragmentation and ideological polarization (Ozbudun 1996: 126). Volatility took the form of sudden and significant changes in the shares of the votes gained by the main parties from one election to the next. Fragmentation was reflected in increasing numbers of parties appearing in parliament, while ideological polarization was represented by parties such as the Islamic National Salvation Party and the ultranationalist National Action Party. The appearance of ideologically polarized parties was symptomatic of wider divisions appearing in society at this time: including inside the bureaucracy, the universities, schools, the media and the police. This was a symptom of an important transformation in the Turkish system as a whole, a sharpening left–right ideological dimension that encouraged the military to return to power in 1980, leading to the temporary cessation of democracy.

How to explain Turkey's sharpening ideological divisions in the 1970s? It seems certain that the loss of political efficacy of centre parties was exacerbated by the country's serious fiscal, social and economic difficulties and pervasive state-level political corruption from the 1970s, which appeared to encourage some people to look to extremist solutions. Economic problems placed new limits on the largesse that parties were able to distribute among their supporters. This was a serious blow to their chances of picking up votes (Ozbudun 1996). The drift from the moderate parties was also encouraged by the fact that most of Turkey's political parties were organized as strongly centralized organizations, highly dependent on access to government patronage, dominated by their top leaders who were rarely challenged from below. The consequence was that Turkey's parties did not develop as electoral vehicles to represent various societal interests but as clientelist networks through which government resources could be channelled to supporters. Moderate parties tended to neglect essential organizational work, concentrating instead on media appeals and image-building with the help of professional public relations experts. The result was that their local party organizations were often dominated by small groups of activists whose power came from the fact that they could control access to the senior leadership. At this level organization tended to be loose, membership records were not well kept and branches only really sprang to life at election times. The point is that such parties did not fulfil the necessary role of choate parties and were not, as a result, conducive to democratic consolidation.

The military government tried to overhaul the party system by manipulating electoral laws. In 1983 it introduced a statute proclaiming that a 10 per cent national threshold – and even higher constituency thresholds – were necessary for parties to take seats in parliament. The hope was that this would lead to the elimination of the most intensely ideological parties, leading instead to a 'manageable' system of two or three parties. However, there continued to be a weakening of the politically moderate centre-right and centre-left, with a rise in popularity both of nationalist and religious parties. For example, in the 1995 elections Refah, the main Islamic grouping, achieved 21.4 per cent of the vote, the ultranationalist NAP gained 8.2 per cent, and the Kurdish nationalist HADEP garnered 4.2 per cent. This result was enough for Refah to become the largest party in terms of their share of the vote. While this result 'boost[ed] the combined extremist vote share to one-third and raised the possibility that Turkish democracy [was] facing a systemic challenge' (Ozbudun 1996: 126), it also reflected the fact that parties such as Refah put in much care and attention to grassroots organization, a strategy which paid off in electoral successes (Haynes 1999b: 141–6).

Turning to civil society, a lack of consultation by government and a resulting lack of consensus meant that governmental policies often faced heavy societal resistance and remained unimplemented. Opposition was not only focused among the burgeoning numbers of political parties, but also in Turkey's relatively robust civil society. Groups within civil society, many of which were concentrated in the country's powerful trade union movement, tended to be characterized by a relatively high degree of organizational independence, and to be supported in their clashes with the state by the relatively strong and independent judiciary.

In sum, Turkey's party system was not conducive to democratic consolidation as it became increasingly fragmented, volatile and ideologically polarized. Parties were very often the personal vehicles of senior leaders, which did not encourage the development of essential representational roles among supporters. Those parties that did seek to recruit supporters energetically at the grassroots were often those labelled extremist. Civil society organizations, especially those connected to the trade union movement, served as an important focus of anti-state opposition.

Economic and international factors

Since the 1970s, Turkey has experienced often serious economic problems which have had an impact on political developments. Turkey enjoyed sustained economic growth during the 1960s, but it declined in the 1970s. Turkey, not an oil producer, felt the impact of rising oil prices, leading to severe balance of payments problems and high price inflation. By 1975 two-thirds of export earnings were spent on buying oil products and inflation had soared to over 100 per cent a year; in 1980 an economic austerity programme was introduced to try to deal with the problems. While this led to substantial macro-economic improvements, including better export performance and falling price inflation, the improvements did not last. By the late 1980s inflation had risen again to over 70 per cent a year. Encouraged by the IMF, the government introduced new, forceful measures to try to deal with inflation. However, it remained high – around 80 per cent in the mid-1990s, before rising to about 100 per cent in 1997. To attempt to deal with the situation, the government introduced a three-year economic stabilization programme, which cut state jobs and led to increased hardship among millions of ordinary people.

The problem for Turkish governments has been that economic problems have tended to stimulate the rise of 'extremist' parties which have called for radical solutions – such as fundamental political reforms – to deal with the situation. But radical solutions are often seen as potentially destabilizing and therefore anathema to the self-appointed guardians of the status quo: the military. Whereas in the past the armed forces would deal with perceived instability by, if necessary, taking over government for a time, increasingly this option is unavailable. This is largely because Turkey is anxious to gain membership of the European Union, an organization only open to democracies with good human rights records. Although Turkey became an associate member of the European Economic Community in 1964, its relations with the EEC's successor, the EU, have deteriorated, especially in the wake of the 1980 military coup, not only because it dissolved democracy but also because some armed forces personnel were accused of serious human rights violations.

The resumption of democracy in 1983 led to a rebuilding of Turkey's links with the EU and the Council of Europe. In 1989, the EC Commission laid down a number of stringent conditions for admission to the Community, including a better human rights record and progress towards improved relations with Greece. But Turkey could not fulfil these conditions and remained outside the EU. In 1995 Turkey and the EU signed a customs union, but the country was again passed over for membership, as it was again in mid-1997 when in principle five Eastern European states were allowed to join. It seems likely that Turkey's recent military actions against rebellious Kurds have been a factor in the decision to deny it EU membership. In sum, Turkey's desire for EU membership may have encouraged the army not to attempt to take power since 1980, but its inability to deal with various human rights problems and the issue of the Kurds have meant that it was denied its goal as an EU member.

Conclusion

After nearly two decades of democracy, Turkey seemed at a democratic impasse at the end of the 1990s. On the one hand, there was said to be a strong 'commitment to democracy at both elite and mass levels' (Ozbudun 1996) while, on the other hand, it had proved impossible to institutionalize democracy in a manner commensurate with democratic consolidation. While a high proportion of citizens vote in elections – over 80 per cent on average in the five national-level elections since 1983 – the choices they make have not necessarily helped the cause of democratization, as they tend increasingly to vote for extremist parties, a course of action viewed with disfavour by the armed forces (Günes-Ayata 1994). Yet it seems unlikely that overtly authoritarian government will return to Turkey in the short term, not least because this would make the possibility of EU membership recede still further.

However, as Diamond notes, democratic *persistence* is not the same thing as 'the genuine stability that flows from consolidation ... Stability requires not merely a passive acceptance of the system, because there is no better alternative at the moment, but a positive belief in the moral value of democracy in principle' (1996: 77). This state of affairs is lacking in Turkey. The situation reflects the respective importance of structural and contingent factors. Regarding the former, the long-term political control of the armed forces has been an impediment to democratization since the military has taken on itself the role of political guardian. The result has been that democratic progress has been circumscribed by the willingness of the military to intervene politically, if necessary to circumvent political outcomes sanctioned by the ballot box, such as the electoral victory of Refah in 1995. The importance of contingency can also be noted in Turkey's recent political history: in particular, both economic downturns and the continuing desire for EU membership have helped to shape political developments over time.

8.5   Overall conclusions

While in the Muslim Middle East democracy has made some progress in recent years, evidence presented in this chapter confirms Diamond's view that 'culturally and historically, this has been the most difficult terrain in the world for political freedom and democracy' (1999: 270). Attempts to explain why this should be the case are often linked to the political importance of Islam; strong, centralized states, often led by personalistic leaders, bequeathed by colonialism; and strongly politicized militaries anxious to maintain the political status quo. On the one hand, we have noted the importance of contingency factors in relation to political outcomes in the region. Kuwait's ruler, encouraged by events associated with the Gulf War, was willing to oversee a significant measure of democratic progress, rather than cracking down on opposition in an attempt to quell pro-democracy demands.

On the other hand, as we have seen, democratic reforms significantly failed to progress in Turkey, largely because of the stultifying effect of continued military meddling in political issues, for example, in relation to the perceived legitimacy of certain political parties, such as Refah. This reflected the long-term structural position of the military, a self-appointed guardian of the status quo. Not only over Turkey, but more generally over the region, there hangs the real or imagined spectre of what the Turkish military probably most fears: the Islamists. Regional governments, along with their foreign allies, often seem convinced that any government dominated by Islamists would be one which would deny fundamental freedoms. In this context, the brief flowering of liberalization in Iran, followed by a later crackdown, is offered as proof. However, the array of opposition trends that the Islamists often represent will not go away: unless rulers and their military allies allow greater democracy. Consequently, there is a good chance that support for radical religious groups will remain an important feature of the political scene across the region.

Gradual political reforms and increasing democracy in Kuwait offer evidence for the view of Bernard Lewis, noted by Diamond: that is, to be most effective, democratic progress should be 'gradual and unforced', proceeding in 'slow stages' through reforming autocratic regimes towards more open and competitive political systems (Lewis quoted in Diamond 1999: 270). This is because, Diamond suggests: 'an abrupt democratic opening could trigger either a neo-authoritarian reaction from a faction of the ruling elite or a breakthrough to an Islamic fundamentalist regime that would have no use for democracy or liberalism' (1999: 270). However, while this may be an accurate enough assessment in some of the countries in the region, the chequered history of democracy in Turkey would suggest that it does not require 'an abrupt democratic opening' to trigger the scenario Diamond suggests. Over the last decades, Turkish regimes, both unelected and elected, have given short shrift to societal criticism and political dissent, as well as independent associations and parties, when they appeared to those in power to threaten the continuity of Turkish political life and the social fabric of the country. Despite the singularity of its own political experiences, the Turkish example also suggests a conclusion of wider relevance to the Middle East region: structural factors – including politically active militaries and state intolerance of criticism – have made democratic progress difficult.

9
Conclusions

This book has sought to examine the problematic issue of democratic consolidation in new democracies in Latin America, Asia, Africa and the Middle East. In this, the final chapter, I discuss the general arguments and comparative implications of the material presented in earlier chapters, consider the implications for a wider understanding of political change, and make predictions as to the future for democracy in these regions.

Twenty-five years after the commencement of the third wave of democracy, how best to characterize the democratic position in Africa, Asia, Latin America and the Middle East? The short answer is that it is highly variable, with major differences between individual countries. While numbers of democratically elected governments in these regions increased greatly over the last two decades, significant numbers of non-democratic regimes – such as personalist dictatorships, single-party and communist states, and military regimes – remained. While forms of authoritarian rule differed from regime to regime, what they had in common was a denial of political rights and civil liberties to their citizens: human rights were often ignored, women's demands belittled, environmental safeguards – if they existed – bypassed, and ethnic and religious minorities were denied freedom of expression.

How were things different in the new democracies? While they exhibited sometimes profound political variations, most had several factors in common. First, all had some form of regular, relatively free and fair electoral competition. Second, once democratically elected governments were in power they were – at least in theory – more democratically accountable than authoritarian regimes. This was because, third, under such governments a range of issues could now become contested ground; that is, they could appear on the political agenda; and differing viewpoints could – at least theoretically – be expressed, debated and contested. None of this is to imply that democratic consolidation was a straightforward process. We saw in chapter 1 that clear, sustained progress towards democratic consolidation has been difficult – but not impossible – to achieve: one in three of the new democracies in Latin America, Asia and Africa managed to gain the Freedom House designation of 'free' state by the end of the 1990s.

This statistic appears to confirm what many observers have noted: despite the high degree of optimism relating to the hoped-for progress towards democratic consolidation in the late 1980s and early 1990s, in relatively few cases were there clear signs of democratic consolidation within a few years of the end of transition. Moreover, it does not seem simply a matter of time before democratic consolidation is widely achieved in most of the new democracies. Instead, as Zakaria points out, forms of limited democracy emerged as 'a growth industry' in the 1990s. The result was that

> far from being a temporary or transitional stage, it appears that many countries are settling into a form of government that mixes a substantial degree of democracy with a substantial degree of illiberalism. Just as nations across the world have become comfortable with many variations of capitalism, they could well adopt and sustain varied forms of democracy. Western liberal democracy might prove to be not the final destination on the democratic road, but just one of many possible exits. (1997: 24)

In this book, I have sought to explain the outcome Zakaria notes by analysis of the political salience of structural and contingent factors both regionally and in relation to the country case studies.

9.1   Structured contingency and democracy

I argued that structured contingency is a useful concept to help understand the array of democratic outcomes we have examined in the pages of this book. The main argument was that structural legacies – they can be broadly pro-democracy or anti-democracy – are important factors when political actors search for rules of political competition in post-authoritarian systems. In other words, there is no *tabula rasa*: no incoming regime, whatever its stated ideological proclivities or goals, democratically orientated or not, can erase historically produced societal behaviour. What structures do I have in mind? While they vary from country to country, every nation has historically established patterns of power ('structures') involving regular, systematized interaction between power-holders and the mass of ordinary people, an arrangement reflected in a country's established rules and institutions. These are not only *formal*, fixed structures of public life – laws, organizations, offices and so on – but also *informal* ones: that is, the 'dynamics of interests and identities, domination and resistance, compromise and accommodation' in every polity (Bratton and van de Walle 1997: 276). Political actors are well aware that political competition and conflict are informed by both formal and informal structures that collectively mould the range of realistic alternatives open to them. This predisposes political actors to select certain courses of action and not others.

While problems of representation can theoretically be addressed by developing strong, formal political institutions, in many countries examined in the book's case studies, for example the Philippines or Turkey, inherited structures of power were of great political significance in moulding political outcomes. As the example of the Philippines indicated, consolidating democracy was a desperately difficult and slow process, primarily because coexisting power-holders were against it as they feared the consequences for their own positions. However, as Shin remarks, democracy cannot logically 'be run by the few as in oligarchies or autocracies; nor should it be guided by intelligence or professional expertise apart from the people' (1999: 137). In sum, to understand democratic outcomes it is necessary both to focus on institutional variations in the new democracies, and also take into account *underlying political dynamics*: that is, how and with what results individuals and groups gain access to political power and what they do with it.

A potential problem for democratic progress is that if democratic *stability* depends to a considerable degree on integrating 'the military and business elites into a stable framework of efficient democratic institutions *which do not threaten their interests*', then how are such people to be persuaded that democracy is in their best interests? (Merkel 1998: 56, emphasis added). It seems plantible to suggest that the kinds of political system likely to result from prioritizing the interests of elites are forms of limited democracy. The problem is that to embed democracy – with the ramification of devolving power from elite groups to wider constituencies – to the extent that it becomes the normal and natural mode of political behaviour is likely to alienate traditional power-holders and their allies (for example, senior military figures, big capital owners, large landowners) because they are likely to see it as an unacceptable attack on their own interests. In sum, introducing democracy and ensuring regular tests of public opinion via periodic polls is normatively important – but if democracy is to be more than a simple replication of the old order in a new guise then it must seek, as Leftwich puts it, 'to correct past inequalities or new hardships' (1993: 614). And this is where the post-transition problems often begin.

While Burnell is correct to claim that 'failure to consolidate is not the same as de-consolidation' and that democratic stalling does not necessarily mean 'that democratic transition goes into reverse' (1998: 7), the important point, it seems clear, is that such a stage is not necessarily a hiccup on the way to greater democratic consolidation. Instead, as Zakaria (1997) notes, it may signify a more sustained political outcome, one characterized by limited democratic advances rather than a clear retreat to overt authoritarianism. In other words, political elites may formally comply with the dictates of democratic politics yet still behave in unhelpful ways, by showing little or no regard for democratic principles and with little interest in developing public policy to benefit most citizens. For purposes of comparison the elite may be usefully divided into political figures currently in office (or close to those in office) and the rest, including opponents who may believe that the electoral arrangements are rigged against them and that media coverage is biased in favour of the government. The point, however, is that both groups – that is, both 'ins' and 'outs' – may have a vested interest in seeking to diminish the degree to which democracy empowers ordinary people.

As Arblaster (1999) makes plain, the lack of concern that elites may have with extending democracy to the mass of ordinary people is not a recent phenomenon. In describing the ways that vested interests in Britain denied the right of the masses even to vote because of fear of the political consequences, an opposition not finally overcome until the 1920s, his account is reminiscent of the contemporary situation in many new democracies. As Arblaster puts it:

> Democracy has only become acceptable to the privileged classes because it has turned out to be less of a challenge to wealth and property than was feared, and also because democracy itself has been redefined in much narrower terms (as a method of choosing government) than it was given in the classical tradition reaching down from Pericles to John Stuart Mill and beyond. (1999: 33)

While interpretations of democratic failure or success are necessarily rather judgemental and relativistic, observers such as Huntington (1991), Kohli (1994) and Remmer (1989) all attach considerable responsibility to the elites and the degree of respect or disrespect they show for the democratic 'rules of the game'. The gravest potential political threats in the new democracies, they concur, come from among the leaders, particularly those who accumulate and concentrate power in the executive branch and weaken accountability. They posit that fraudulent practices to retain and concentrate power often seem so common as to be ubiquitous; they are a distinguishing feature not only in facade democracies (discussed in chapter 1) but also in many limited democracies.

In sum, as Burnell notes, to strike 'the right balance between demands for reform from subordinate classes, and pressures to mitigate threat perceptions on the part of the economic elites, is obviously crucial to the successful installation of democracy' (1998: 20–1). However, it also seems obvious that those with wealth and power may do all they can to resist progress towards democratic consolidation if it seems likely to undermine their privileged positions. Under such circumstances, clear democratic advances are only likely when those striving for a more equal distribution of power manage to dominate those who wish to retain the status quo.

This is where a concern with human agency comes in. A concern with structures does not mean that we should ignore the equally crucial role of what political actors *do* in helping determine democratic outcomes. When leading political actors sincerely value democracy, that is, when the *idea* of democracy as a desirable political outcome serves as an important factor informing political decision-making, then, gradually, democracy can be built – even when unpropitious conditions, such as a weak economy or a politically active military, make that outcome seem unlikely. Evidence from our case studies emphasizes the importance of the interaction of the effects of structures and human agency in determining political outcomes. Decisions taken by highly significant political figures – such as Mandela in South Africa, Ghana's Rawlings, Chavez in Venezuela or the Emir of Kuwait – were shown to be vital factors in determining political outcomes.

One of the presumptions of much of the democratic consolidation literature is that the degree to which democracy becomes consolidated is closely linked to the numbers of democrats there are in a polity. As Bratton and van de Walle note, a 'consolidated democracy requires that democratic institutions are *not only built but also valued*' by

Strenghther

political elites and ordinary citizens alike (1997: 279, emphasis added). The point is that democracy can be put in place – but to become *consolidated* it requires that political actors and the mass of ordinary people actors 'learn to love it. Until elites and citizens alike come to cherish rule by the people and exhibit a willingness to stand up for it . . . there will be no permanent defense against tyranny' (Bratton and van de Walle 1997: 279). To do this, there must be an institutionalization of democracy, that is, relevant 'organizations, procedures and norms [must] acquire value and stability' (Burnell and Calvert 1999a: 13).

In sum, structures are significant for democratic outcomes because they impose constraints and, as a consequence, are instruments in the competitive struggle for power. Political actors will be cognisant of such factors, which not only limit the range of available – that is, realistic – alternatives open to them, but also predispose them to select certain courses of action over others.

9.2   Democratic consolidation in Africa, Asia, Latin America and the Middle East

Throughout this book the examination of democratic consolidation has been undertaken under three headings:

- political culture and the legitimacy of the post-authoritarian regime;
- political participation and institutions;
- economic and international factors.

It is both consistent and convenient to sum things up in this concluding chapter by summarizing what we have discovered vis-à-vis democratic consolidation in Latin America, Asia, Africa and the Middle East under the same headings.

Political culture and the legitimacy of the post-authoritarian regime

Evidence from our regional surveys and country studies suggests that it is not necessary to have a certain set of cultural attributes present before democratic practices and institutions can emerge. But to build democracy it is necessary to forge a pro-democracy political culture among both elites and ordinary citizens and this is often difficult to achieve for various reasons. Some analysts argue that it is especially difficult in Islamic and some other cultures. Diamond noted that, of the more than 50 'not free' states in the mid-1990s, a large proportion had a 'majority Muslim population and often strong Islamic fundamentalist pressures' (1999: 261). Huntington argued that democracy was scarce not only in Muslim-majority countries, but also in those with Buddhist and Confucian cultures (1991: 73). For Fukuyama this is explained by these religions' allegedly 'hierarchical and inegalitarian' teachings that make democratic progress very difficult to achieve. For example, Buddhism, in 'confin[ing] itself to a domain of private worship centring around the family' is said to be politically passive in the face of authoritarianism, while 'Islamic fundamentalism', with its alleged 'nostalgic reassertion of an older, purer set of values', looks to Fukuyama like European-style fascism (1992: 217, 236).

To what extent were these claims borne out by the evidence of our regional surveys and case studies? We saw that India, predominantly Hindu, but with an important Muslim minority comprising some 100 million people, has been a democracy for half a century; while Algeria, Turkey, Jordan and Kuwait, with Muslim majorities, were polities with variable, in some cases increasingly plausible, claims to be developing their democratic systems. In addition, Hindu/ Buddhist Nepal, Buddhist Thailand, Confucian/Christian Taiwan and Confucian/Buddhist/Christian South Korea have all taken the democratic road in recent years. Consequently, the claims of Huntington and Fukuyama should be treated with scepticism.

Rather than a specific religious culture, it seems clear that what is necessary for democracy is an appropriate *civic* culture, characterized by high levels of mutual trust, tolerance of diversity and a propensity for accommodation and compromise. This outcome, the result of democratic institutions and structures working relatively well over time, involves processes and institutions that help generate and disseminate democratically appropriate values and beliefs among both elites and ordinary citizens.

Political participation and institutions

Because state power is always so valuable, those who have it go to very great lengths to retain it. It seems likely that in the great majority of the new democracies we have examined, public office at the apex of the political system is perceived as among the best – if not *the* best – way to achieve private profit. This is because the state is the locus of a process where 'state rulers are defined by and obtain their power and resources on the basis of their office holding' (Forrest 1988: 439). Consequently, control of the state is nearly always too appealing to be easily abandoned by incumbent power-holders. Free and fair elections on their own cannot ensure that power-holders will strive to build the conditions necessary for democratic consolidation if it means that power would, as a result, move from their hands to those of others. Under such circumstances they will do all they can *not* to facilitate democratic consolidation. Of crucial importance here are two sets of institutions: the armed forces and political and civil society.

The armed forces

The political role of the armed forces has regularly appeared in the pages of this book as an important factor in helping determine democratic outcomes. For example, given Latin America's propensity for military takeovers in the 1960s and 1970s, it would be hard to argue that Costa Rica's abolition of its armed forces in the late 1940s, and the five decades of democracy that followed, were not closely linked. As Pakistan's successful coup d'état of October 1999 highlighted, the 'political ambitions of the armed forces or senior officers have proven highly prejudicial to democracy' (Burnell and Calvert 1999a: 14).

In the past, 'waves' of military coups swamped whole regions, for example West Africa in the 1960s and Latin America in the 1960s and 1970s. This suggests that military coups have sometimes seemed contagious, bringing on a 'reverse wave' (in Huntington's terminology) away from democracy. Various countries we have examined, for example Ghana and Turkey, have seen periodic coups followed by the reinstatement of democracy seemingly *ad infinitum*. And, during the 1990s, new military coups occurred – for example, in Côte d'Ivoire and the Gambia – in countries that had apparently managed to keep the military aloof from politics for decades. In other countries, for example Turkey, military personnel remained enthusiastic, if somewhat less open, political actors. In many cases, the military's political involvement was linked to a desire to help defend members of the political and economic elite from the rigours of democracy.

Civil and political society

Democratic consolidation requires a shift from a situation where power is exercised by and for a numerically small elite to one where it is exercised for the good of the many (Doig 1999). It is facilitated by *sustained* pressure from civil society and opposition parties on incumbent elites to allow a strengthening of democracy. But, as we saw, this was often hard to achieve – not least because once democracy is won then civil society tends to fragment, while opposition parties can become more interested in their individual quests to achieve power than in helping to extend democracy *per se* (Lievesley 1999; Gill 2000).

Such a situation plays into the hands of groups of elites who might well not be notable for a sincere desire to extend and deepen democracy in ways necessary for democratic consolidation. It is important to note that power monopolies at the apex traditionally formed the political superstructure in most new democracies in Africa, Asia, Latin America and the Middle East. Organski (1965) long ago identified such power monopolies, what he called the 'syncratic alliance', as an undemocratic concord uniting traditional agrarian interests too strong to be destroyed with a modernizing urban-based elite. A bargain was struck between the two sets of interests: in exchange for obtaining the political support of agrarian interests, powerful urban-based actors agreed not to disturb significantly the often semifeudal conditions of the countryside. The question is to what extent, when a democratically elected regime gained power, was there a shift in the power balance?

Traditionally in Latin America and parts of Asia, large landowners represent the rural side of the power coalition. In India, successive post-colonial governments, despite being legitimated through the ballot box for half a century (apart from the State of Emergency, 1975–7), failed to break with powerful rural allies. Although rural-based powerful families were often formally shorn of traditional powers after independence in 1947, many still managed to maintain their long-standing position through a very successful alternative: the elected route to power. Although Organski's description may be less relevant to Africa, it seems clear that support from those with wealth and power was, and is, more crucial to political decision-makers than support from other classes. In Africa, as Clapham notes, personalist dictatorship was often the most politically salient type of authority as it 'correspond[ed] to the normal forms of social organization in [Africa's] precolonial societies' (1985: 49). In short, while precise bases of power differ, despite democratic transitions pre-existing elites often managed to maintain their control both of the bases of economic wealth and the direction of political development.

Evidence suggests that such elite coalitions were an important means of maintaining upper-class power, as in Thailand and the Philippines, even when there was a democratic system in operation (Rueschemeyer et al. 1992: 174–5; Rocamora 1993). The crucial analytical point is that while many dictatorial regimes were over-thrown during the third wave and replaced by elected alternatives, this was rarely sufficient to oust from positions of power and influence long-entrenched, narrowly based, elitist groups. While traditionally oligarchical political systems may have disappeared, *traditional power monopolies* may remain under a democratic veneer of variable thickness.

A strong civil society is theoretically a crucial step towards realiz-ing politically freer polities. It is very hard to imagine a participant political system that is capable of surviving for long without a vibrant civil society. But while the emergence of a dynamic and vigorous civil society is a necessary development, it is not on its own sufficient to consolidate democracy. When the first battle is won and the authoritarian ancien régime is gone, the struggle for democratic consolidation creates a new kind of political environment with novel challenges to both civil and political society. The rallying point of the common enemy is no longer there. Now, the challenge shifts from cooperating in the common goal of removing unwelcome rulers to institutionalizing democratic competition between the interests and aspirations of various groups in the society; so that democracy becomes, in the words of Linz and Stepan (1996), the 'only game in town'. Demands put on the skills and commitment of leading actors to meet this challenge are different from those required during the transition phase itself. Henceforward, as Karl emphasizes, political actors must show the 'ability to differentiate political forces rather than draw them into a grand coalition, the capacity to define and channel competing political projects rather than seek to keep poten-tially divisive reforms off the agenda, and the willingness to tackle incremental reforms . . . rather than defer them to some later date' (1990: 17). Thus, while popular mobilization and organization undoubtedly improve democratic prospects, it is how popular power manifests itself *after* democratic transition that is a crucial factor in consolidating democracy.

Much of the relevant literature contends that civil societies that struggled against one-party and military dictatorships had the poten-tial to weaken the cultural foundations of authoritarianism – that is, to serve as a genuine base for democracy. What was needed, it was suggested, was that a new democratic consensus be created and strengthened – and political instability reduced – by robust electoral and institutional forms enabling democratic governments to work. This would mean that democratic regimes would be less at the mercy than before of the self-interested competition of elite politicians. But for this to come to pass, there had to be a learning process, a development explicit to Linz and Stepan's (1996) conception of democratic consolidation: the destructive confrontations of the past must not be repeated by the new generation of politicians seeking power. Instead, they must seek to deepen democracy and extend it to previously excluded classes and groups.

But the momentum of the reform process was often not kept up in the post-transition phase. As Arblaster notes, 'transitions from dictatorship to democracy [in the third wave] were very often neither smooth, automatic or complete.' Further, the 'considerable obstacles to the wholesale adoption of the institutions of liberal democracy' and the ability to 'combine a quite minimal use of popular election with forms of strong, centralized government . . . amounted in some cases to presidential or prime ministerial dictatorship' (1999: 33). The failure of persistence led to 'stalled', 'flawed' or 'incomplete' democracies. In other words, there is 'transition from' authoritarianism but not 'transition to' democracy; there is 'stunted' rather than 'full' democratic consolidation, that is, when all groups of significant political actors explicitly accept that democracy is 'the only game in town'.

A combination of minimal state and minimal party institutions is apt to prove destabilizing to all kinds of socioeconomic systems. A fusion of penetrated states and elite-dominated parties may help strengthen anti-democratic trends in most structural environments, as the example of Venezuela indicated. It also showed that while a high degree of party control may well assuage the concerns of economic elites, low internal coherence helped prevent state agencies from delivering the collective goods necessary to elicit the citizenry's long-term commitment to democratic principles.

In this context, the political role of civil society is highly important. While transitions to democracy were often explained by a focus on elites, it is important not to overlook the upsurges in popular mobilization and organization which were nearly always a crucial factor in their genesis and initial development (Foweraker and Landman 1997). However, as Sørensen notes, a strong civil society 'improves the conditions for democracy and *simultaneously makes the reversal to authoritarian rule more difficult*' (1993: 60, emphasis added). Theoretically this suggests the democratic importance of an array of civil society organizations; however, the democratic salience of such organizations may be undermined when significant groups of actors, including those with religious and/or ethnic goals, are less interested in democracy *per se* than in their own aspirations. In other words, because such particularistic groups are motivated by extreme self-interest, chauvinism and animosity towards rival groups, the contribution to achieving democratic goals is likely to be limited.

In sum, to make democratic progress, it is highly important for a polity to make the 'right' institutional choices, that is, they should be (1) politically appropriate; (2) able to command society's respect; and (3) technically sound. As Burnell and Calvert point out, 'bungled attempts at constitutional engineering and ill-suited electoral rules . . . can ultimately prove near fatal if they go uncorrected' (1999a: 13). The parliamentary model is sometimes perceived as having more going for it than presidential models (characterized by the separate and independent election of the executive and legislature and fixed terms of office). But there is no definitive evidence in this regard. However, in Latin America, Mainwaring (1993) has suggested that a combination of presidentialism and extensive multipartyism – say more than three effective parties at any one time – is highly conducive to political instability.

Economic and international factors

Economic progress and a concern with welfare issues are often seen as central to chances of democratic consolidation. What is the relationship between economic changes and political changes in countries striving to build democracy? Everything else being equal, growing national wealth, relatively equitably distributed, and a concern with extending welfare mechanisms to all citizens should help reinforce democratic progress. There is also the issue of the distribution of material benefits and citizens' perceptions of the justice of the pattern of distribution. Do a privileged minority consume an inappropriate proportion of available resources? It seems plausible that popular adherence to democracy is likely to grow if government not only presides over sustained economic growth but also manages to convince the mass of people that its fruits are not too unequally shared. Przeworski et al.'s (1996) comprehensive survey of evidence – covering 1950 to 1990 – suggests that democracies' chances of survival increase when they (1) develop economically in a sustained fashion; and (2) gradually, yet consistently, reduce socioeconomic inequalities. On the other hand, some types of resource bases, notably those which convey large sums by way of rent to whoever controls national government, through for example the exploitation of oil reserves, are inherently vulnerable to inequality, corruption and a lack of democracy. This helps explain why only very few non-Western oil-exporting countries have managed to build democratic systems.

Turning to the international dimension, the concept of a 'third wave of democracy' was premised on there being something happening at the global level to encourage democratic transitions around the world. This not only included global events and developments (known as 'the diffusion effect'), but also specific encouragement from aid donors. Leftwich suggested that the pace of democratic progress, especially in poor countries in Central America and Africa, would be 'influenced, sometimes to a considerable degree, by various international . . . factors' (1997: 522; Karl 1995). However, as we have seen, linking democratic progress to such international factors was, in fact, problematic.

Democracy and how to achieve it in non-democratic countries became an urgent focus of Western attention after the Cold War. Western governments, as well as the World Bank and the IMF, began to attach 'political conditionalities' to aid and investment, and regimes which denied human and civil rights to their citizens were, it was claimed, to be refused funding. The reasoning behind political conditionality was partly economic, as it was argued that economic failures were very often linked to an absence of democracy and political accountability. Without significant political changes, economic reforms, a precondition for continued foreign aid and investment, would not produce the desired results.

However, as Diamond explains, outcomes were disappointing: 'Too many international policy makers have taken electoral democracy as an end state in itself. . . . Some observers seem to assume that democratic consolidation is bound to follow transition in much of the world. . . . These assumptions are false and counterproductive' (1999: 273). Once democratic transitions were complete – marked by the first free and fair elections – then both the ability and the desire of foreign governments and other important actors to influence democratic progress seemed to become less significant. Evidence from this book indicates that external factors were rarely if ever crucial to progress towards democratic consolidation in the post-transition phase.

Gills, Rocamora and Wilson (1993) claim that the pace and content of democratic reforms were often controlled by Western governments, in cahoots with local conservative elites, anxious to prevent 'too much' democracy that would lead to political instability. Both parties, they argue, shared a strong interest in limiting the extent of political changes. This is a theory of democracy which highlights an important role for external actors in democratic outcomes. This 'low intensity democracy' (LID) was, at best, no more than a thin democratic covering overlaying otherwise unreformed political structures. Power stayed in more or less the same hands as before, with only the illusion of greater democracy. LID was said to satisfy Western governments' allegedly insincere concerns for wider democracy. In sum, the LID argument was that external forces helped deliver strictly limited processes of political change because this suited their own aims: first, continued economic control of dependent polities; and second, the survival in power of their local allies.

There was little or no evidence for the salience of the 'low intensity democracy' argument in any of our case studies. It seems that the LID argument seriously overestimates the extent of Western influence on democracy in most Latin American, Asian, Middle Eastern and African countries. For example, despite its best efforts the government of the United States was quite unable decisively to influence the direction of political change in countries deemed of great strategic influence in the 1990s, such as Afghanistan, Somalia, Nigeria and Sudan. Our case studies suggest that Western governments have two, not necessarily congruous, aims: they may well wish to see liberal democracy as a moral and political good; on the other hand, they may also prefer non-democratic governments under some circumstances (Cumming 1999; Lawson 1999). For example, over the years successive American governments were ambivalent about the prospect of social democratic governments coming to power – even by the ballot box – in countries such as Brazil and Chile in the 1960s and 1970s (Arblaster 1999: 46–7). The main point, however, is that, generally speaking, Western governments seem reasonably satisfied if regimes in Latin America, Asia, Africa and the Middle East are stable and run benignly; if they are democratic too, it is a welcome bonus.

It is tempting to suppose that in the eyes of Western governments, a country's endorsement of Western economic growth strategies would go some way to compensate for the lack of 'conventional' democracy in countries such as Uganda. And this would seem to be the case. The national president, Yoweri Museveni, has made a successful diplomatic offensive to sell his no-party version of democracy to the West. His success in convincing the West that his all-inclusive 'movement system' democracy can work without political parties has surprised many observers. While neighbouring countries, such as Kenya, were forced by Western backers to adopt multiparty democratic systems, Museveni managed to side-step this outcome by the use both of subtle diplomacy and innovative appointments, such as that of Specioza Wandira Kazibwe who, as vice-president, was the highest-ranking female politician in Africa.

It is clear from the above that international pressure or encouragement to democracy cannot be overlooked – but at the same time it should not be seen as inevitably one-way traffic. Forms can range from deliberate subversion to well-intentioned but unhelpful interventions. Structural adjustment programmes, as Burnell notes, demanded 'radical economic reforms that [often] prove socially damaging and politically destabilising, or which encourage a greater executive concentration of power in order to make the unpalatable reforms enforceable' (1998: 11). Withdrawal of peer support from authoritarian regimes, as well as external support and encouragement of the sort extended to political reforms by donor governments and international organizations like the Commonwealth following the Harare declaration in 1991 were also important in keeping the pressure on recalcitrant regimes to allow more and better human rights (Sylvester 1999). However, overall such external factors were applied rather unevenly.

In sum, international aspects are not as important as domestic factors in shaping democratic progress. On the other hand, an adverse external environment, such as a 'global economic slump or international financial crisis can significantly increase the chances of democratic deconsolidation, or failures to consolidate' (Burnell 1998: 12). However, in general, it is widely reckoned that the external environment is of more importance in the liberalization and transition, rather than the consolidation, stage of democracy. Finally, international pressures on countries in the 1990s to adopt the neoliberal economic agenda may have helped persuade economically privileged elites that democratic transition would not seriously harm their interests, and thus have helped to limit their opposition. But 'by further entrenching such groups in the economy, these same international forces are possibly dimming the longer term prospects for greater social and political equality' (Burnell 1998: 23).

9.3   The future

We have seen that failures to consolidate democracy are probably best explained by the power of anti-democratic structural forces to prevent that outcome. But, unconducive structural factors can be overcome by the determination of individual political leaders to work towards democratic outcomes. This helps explain why, when there are apparently similar forces at work in different countries, there may be contrasting democratic outcomes. It is highly likely that the extent to which there is a theoretically significant pattern can only be known after detailed empirical research in a large number of new democracies; so far, this has not been done. What does seem clear, however, is that we should not assume that all societies are destined to arrive sooner or later at an identical political destination, or, indeed, that they should be expected to do so.

No doubt, political change will follow a variety of paths in Asia, Africa, Latin America and the Middle East. In some cases, people will be led in circles, only later to find themselves essentially back where they began. However, it is equally sure that the pressures to open up political systems will almost certainly not abate – and if civil and political society develops in ways conducive to democratic consolidation then issues of accountability and performance will remain or become of political importance in numerous countries. While many countries continue to be characterized by regular encroachments on the dignity of individuals, there is some evidence that political trajectories in many new democracies will gradually focus more clearly than before on the right of the individual to be free of arbitrary abuse at the hands of the state and to enjoy a wide array of political rights and civil liberties. The evidence is still mixed, but an optimist might conclude that there is enough in the pages of this book to suggest that the time has come when most governments – of whatever political and democratic stripe – must begin to take seriously demands for the dignity and the equality of the individual expressed collectively by the still unabated demands for more and better democracy in many new democracies.

Appendix

The Freedom House Survey and Organization

The Freedom House Survey (reproduced from http://www.freedomhouse.org/survey99/method/)

Survey Methodology

Since its inception in the 1970s, Freedom House's Freedom in the World survey has provided an annual evaluation of political rights and civil liberties throughout the world. The Survey attempts to judge all countries and territories by a single standard and to emphasize the importance of democracy and freedom. At a minimum, a democracy is a political system in which the people choose their authoritative leaders freely from among competing groups and individuals who were not designated by the government. Freedom represents the opportunity to act spontaneously in a variety of fields outside the control of the government and other centers of potential domination.

The Survey rates countries and territories based on real world situations caused by state and nongovernmental factors, rather than on governmental intentions or legislation alone. Freedom House does not rate governments per se, but rather the rights and freedoms enjoyed by individuals in each country or territory. The Survey does not base its judgment solely on the political conditions in a country or territory (i.e., war, terrorism, etc.), but by the effect which these conditions have on freedom.

Freedom House does not maintain a culture-bound view of democracy. The Survey demonstrates that, in addition to countries in Europe and the Americas, there are free states with varying forms of democracy functioning among people of all races and religions in Africa, the Pacific, and Asia. In some Pacific islands, free countries can have political systems based on competing family groups and personalities rather than on European- or American-style political parties. In recent years, there has been a proliferation of democracies in developing countries, and the Survey reflects their growing numbers. To reach its conclusions, the Survey team employs a broad range of international sources of information, including both foreign and domestic news reports, NGO publications, think tank and academic analyses, and individual professional contacts.

Definitions and Categories of the Survey

The Survey's understanding of freedom encompasses two general sets of characteristics grouped under political rights and civil liberties. Political rights enable people to participate freely in the political process, which is the system by which the polity chooses authoritative policy makers and attempts to make binding decisions affecting the national, regional, or local community. In a free society, this represents the right of all adults to vote and compete for public office, and for elected representatives to have a decisive vote on public policies. Civil liberties include the freedoms to develop views, institutions, and personal autonomy apart from the state.

The Survey employs two series of checklists, one for questions regarding political rights and one for civil liberties, and assigns each country or territory considered a numerical rating for each category. The political rights and civil liberties ratings are then averaged and used to assign each country and territory to an overall status of 'Free,' 'Partly Free,' or 'Not Free.' (See the section below, 'Rating System for Political Rights and Civil Liberties,' for a detailed description of the Survey's methodology.) Freedom House rates both independent countries and their territories. For the purposes of the Survey, countries are defined as internationally recognized independent states whose governments are resident within their officially claimed borders. In the case of Cyprus, two sets of ratings are provided, as there are two governments on that divided island. In no way does this imply that Freedom House endorses Cypriot division. We note only that neither the predominantly Greek Republic of Cyprus, nor the Turkish-occupied, predominantly Turkish territory of the Republic of Northern Cyprus, is the de facto government for the entire island.

This year [1999], Freedom House has divided the previously single related territory category into two parts: related territories and disputed territories. Related territories consist mostly of colonies, protectorates, and island dependencies of sovereign states which are in some relation of dependency to that state and whose relationship is not currently in serious legal or political dispute. Puerto Rico, Hong Kong, and French Guiana are three examples of related territories. Since most related territories have a broad range of civil liberties and some form of self-government, a higher proportion of them have the 'Free' designation than do independent countries. Disputed territories represent areas within internationally recognized sovereign states which are usually dominated by a minority ethnic group and whose status is in serious political or violent dispute. This group also includes territories whose incorporation into nation-states is not universally recognized. In some cases, the issue of dispute is the desire of the majority of the population of that territory to secede from the sovereign state and either form an independent country or become part of a neighboring state. Tibet, East Timor, and Abkhazia are examples falling within this category. Freedom House added Chechnya to its Survey this year as a disputed territory of Russia, reflecting the decline of effective Russian central authority over this secessionist region.

Freedom House assigns only designations of 'Free,' 'Partly Free,' and 'Not Free' for the eight related territories with populations under 5,000, designated as 'microterritories,' without corresponding category numbers. However, the same methodology is used to determine the status of these territories as for larger territories and independent states. The microterritories in the Survey are Cocos (Keeling) Islands, Rapanui (Easter Island), Falkland Islands, Niue, Norfolk Island, Pitcairn Islands, Svalbard, and Tokelau. The Survey excludes from its consideration uninhabited territories and such entities as the U.S.-owned Johnston Atoll, which has only a transient military population and no native inhabitants.

Political Rights Checklist

1. Is the head of state and/or head of government or other chief authority elected through free and fair elections?

2. Are the legislative representatives elected through free and fair elections?

3. Are there fair electoral laws, equal campaigning opportunities, fair polling, and honest tabulation of ballots?

4. Are the voters able to endow their freely elected representatives with real power?

5. Do the people have the right to organize in different political parties or other competitive political groupings of their choice, and is the system open to the rise and fall of these competing parties or groupings?

6. Is there a significant opposition vote, de facto opposition power, and a realistic possibility for the opposition to increase its support or gain power through elections?

7. Are the people free from domination by the military, foreign powers, totalitarian parties, religious hierarchies, economic oligarchies, or any other powerful group?

8. Do cultural, ethnic, religious, and other minority groups have reasonable self-determination, self-government, autonomy, or participation through informal consensus in the decision-making process?

Additional Discretionary Political Rights Questions

A. For traditional monarchies that have no parties or electoral process, does the system provide for consultation with the people, encourage discussion of policy, and allow the right to petition the ruler?

B. Is the government or occupying power deliberately changing the ethnic composition of a country or territory so as to destroy a culture or tip the political balance in favor of another group?

To answer the political rights questions, Freedom House considers the extent to which the system offers the voter the chance to make a free choice among candidates, and to what extent the candidates are chosen independently of the state. Freedom House recognizes that formal electoral procedures are not the only factors that determine the real distribution of power. In many Latin American countries, for example, the military retains a significant political role, and in Morocco the king maintains considerable power over the elected politicians. The more that people suffer under such domination by unelected forces, the less chance the country has of receiving credit for self-determination in our Survey.

The Civil Liberties Checklist

A. Freedom of Expression and Belief

1. Are there free and independent media and other forms of cultural expression? (Note: In cases where the media are state-controlled but offer pluralistic points of view, the Survey gives the system credit.)

2. Are there free religious institutions and is there free private and public religious expression?

B. Association and Organizational Rights

1. Is there freedom of assembly, demonstration, and open public discussion?

2. Is there freedom of political or quasi-political organization? (Note: this includes political parties, civic organizations, ad hoc issue groups, etc.)

3. Are there free trade unions and peasant organizations or equivalents, and is there effective collective bargaining? Are there free professional and other private organizations?

C. Rule of Law and Human Rights

1. Is there an independent judiciary?

2. Does the rule of law prevail in civil and criminal matters? Is the population treated equally under the law? Are police under direct civilian control?

3. Is there protection from political terror, unjustified imprisonment, exile, or torture, whether by groups that support or oppose the system? Is there freedom from war and insurgencies? (Note: Freedom from war and insurgencies enhances the liberties in a free society, but the absence of wars and insurgencies does not in and of itself make a not free society free.)

4. Is there freedom from extreme government indifference and corruption?

D. Personal Autonomy and Economic Rights

1. Is there open and free private discussion?

2. Is there personal autonomy? Does the state control travel, choice of residence, or choice of employment? Is there freedom from indoctrination and excessive dependency on the state?

3. Are property rights secure? Do citizens have the right to establish private businesses? Is private business activity unduly influenced by government officials, the security forces, or organized crime?

4. Are there personal social freedoms, including gender equality, choice of marriage partners, and size of family?

5. Is there equality of opportunity, including freedom from exploitation by or dependency on landlords, employers, union leaders, bureaucrats, or other types of obstacles to a share of legitimate economic gains?

When analyzing the civil liberties checklist, Freedom House does not mistake constitutional guarantees of human rights for those rights in practice. For states and territories with small populations, particularly tiny island nations, the absence of trade unions and other types of association is not necessarily viewed as a negative situation unless the government or other centers of domination are deliberately blocking their formation or operation. In some cases, the small size of these countries and territories may result in a lack of sufficient institutional complexity to make them fully comparable to larger countries. The question of equality of opportunity also implies a free choice of employment and education. Extreme inequality of opportunity prevents disadvantaged individuals from enjoying full exercise of civil liberties. Typically, very poor countries and territories lack both opportunities for economic advancement and other liberties on this checklist. The question on extreme government indifference and corruption is included because when governments do not care about the social and economic welfare of large sectors of the population, the human rights of those people suffer. Government corruption can pervert the political process and hamper the development of a free economy.

For this year's Survey, Freedom House reorganized the existing questions in the civil liberties checklist into four subsets. A new question on personal autonomy was added under section D, resulting in an increase in the total number of possible points that could be awarded in the civil liberties category.

Rating System for Political Rights and Civil Liberties

The Survey rates political rights and civil liberties separately on a seven-category scale, 1 representing the most free and 7 the least free. A country is assigned to a particular numerical category based on responses to the checklist and the judgments of the Survey team at Freedom House. According to the methodology, the team assigns initial ratings to countries by awarding from 0 to 4 raw points per checklist item, depending on the comparative rights or liberties present. (In the Surveys completed from 1989–90 through 1992–93, the methodology allowed for a less nuanced range of 0 to 2 raw points per question.) The only exception to the addition of 0 to 4 raw points per checklist item is additional discretionary question B in the political rights checklist, for which 1 to 4 raw points are subtracted depending on the severity of the situation. The highest possible score for political rights is 32 points, based on up to 4 points for each of eight questions. The highest possible score for civil liberties is 56 points, based on up to 4 points for each of fourteen questions.

After placing countries in initial categories based on checklist points, the Survey team makes minor adjustments to account for factors such as extreme violence, whose intensity may not be reflected in answering the checklist questions. These exceptions aside, in the overwhelming number of cases, the results of the checklist system reflect the real world situation and are adequate for placing countries and territories into the proper comparative categories.

At its discretion, Freedom House assigns up or down trend arrows to countries and territories to indicate general positive or negative trends that may not be apparent from the ratings. Such trends may or may not be reflected in raw points, depending on the circumstances in each country or territory. Only countries or territories without ratings changes since the previous year warrant trend arrows. Distinct from the trend arrows, the triangles located next to the political rights and civil liberties ratings (see accompanying tables of comparative measures of freedom for countries and related and disputed territories) indicate changes in those ratings caused by real world events since the last Survey.

Without a well-developed civil society, it is difficult, if not impossible, to have an atmosphere supportive of democracy. A society that does not have free individual and group expressions in nonpolitical matters is not likely to make an exception for political ones. There is no country in the Survey with a rating of 6 or 7 for civil liberties and, at the same time, a rating of 1 or 2 for political rights. Almost without exception in the Survey, countries and territories have ratings in political rights and civil liberties that are within two ratings numbers of each other.

Political Rights

Category Number	Raw Points
1	28–32
2	23–27
3	19–22
4	14–18
5	10–13
6	5–9
7	0–4

Civil Liberties

Category Number	Raw Points
1	50–56
2	42–49
3	34–41
4	26–33
5	17–25
6	9–16
7	0–8

Explanation of Political Rights and Civil Liberties Ratings

Political Rights

Countries and territories which receive a rating of 1 for political rights come closest to the ideals suggested by the checklist questions, beginning with free and fair elections. Those who are elected rule, there are competitive parties or other political groupings, and the opposition plays an important role and has actual power. Citizens enjoy self-determination or an extremely high degree of autonomy (in the case of territories), and minority groups have reasonable self-government or can participate in the government through informal consensus. With the exception of such entities as tiny island states, these countries and territories have decentralized political power and free subnational elections.

Countries and territories rated 2 in political rights are less free than those rated 1. Such factors as gross political corruption, violence, political discrimination against minorities, and foreign or military influence on politics may be present and weaken the quality of democracy.

The same conditions which undermine freedom in countries and territories with a rating of 2 may also weaken political rights in those with a rating of 3, 4, and 5. Other damaging elements can include civil war, heavy military involvement in politics, lingering royal power, unfair elections, and one-party dominance. However, states and territories in these categories may still enjoy some elements of political rights, including the freedom to organize quasi-political groups, reasonably free referenda, or other significant means of popular influence on government.

Countries and territories with political rights rated 6 have systems ruled by military juntas, one-party dictatorships, religious hierarchies, and autocrats. These regimes may allow only a minimal manifestation of political rights, such as competitive local elections or some degree of representation or autonomy for minorities. Some countries and territories rated 6 are in the early or aborted stages of democratic transition. A few states are traditional monarchies that mitigate their relative lack of political rights through the use of consultation with their subjects, toleration of political discussion, and acceptance of public petitions.

For countries and territories with a rating of 7, political rights are absent or virtually nonexistent due to the extremely oppressive nature of the regime or severe oppression in combination with civil war. States and territories in this group may also be marked by extreme violence or warlord rule which dominates political power in the absence of an authoritative, functioning, central government.

Civil Liberties

Countries and territories which receive a rating of 1 come closest to the ideals expressed in the civil liberties checklist, including freedom of expression, assembly, association, and religion. They are distinguished by an established and generally equitable system of rule of law and are comparatively free of extreme government indifference and corruption. Countries and territories with this rating enjoy free economic activity and tend to strive for equality of opportunity.

States and territories with a rating of 2 have deficiencies in three or four aspects of civil liberties, but are still relatively free.

Countries and territories which have received a rating of 3, 4, and 5 range from those that are in at least partial compliance with virtually all checklist standards to those with a combination of high or medium scores for some questions and low or very low scores on other questions. The level of oppression increases at each successive rating level, particularly in the areas of censorship, political terror, and the prevention of free association. There are also many cases in which groups opposed to the state engage in political terror that undermines other freedoms. Therefore, a poor rating for a country is not necessarily a comment on the intentions of the government, but may reflect real restrictions on liberty caused by nongovernmental terror.

Countries and territories rated 6 are characterized by a few partial rights, such as some religious and social freedoms, some highly restricted private business activity, and relatively free private discussion. In general, people in these states and territories experience severely restricted expression and association, and there are almost always political prisoners and other manifestations of political terror.

States and territories with a rating of 7 have virtually no freedom. An overwhelming and justified fear of repression characterizes these societies.

Free, Partly Free, Not Free

The Survey assigns each country and territory the status of 'Free,' 'Partly Free,' or 'Not Free' by averaging their political rights and civil liberties ratings. Those whose ratings average 1–2.5 are generally considered 'Free,' 3–5.5 'Partly Free,' and 5.5–7 'Not Free.' The dividing line between 'Partly Free' and 'Not Free' usually falls within the group whose ratings numbers average 5.5. For example, countries that receive a rating of 6 for political rights and 5 for civil liberties, or a 5 for political rights and a 6 for civil liberties, could be either 'Partly Free' or 'Not Free.' The total number of raw points is the definitive factor which determines the final status. Countries and territories with combined raw scores of 0–30 points are 'Not Free,' 31–59 points are 'Partly Free,' and 60–88 are 'Free.' Based on raw points, this year there are several unusual cases: Mali's and Argentina's ratings average 3.0, but they are 'Free,' and Chad, Côte d'Ivoire, and Swaziland are rated 5.0, but they are 'Not Free.'

It should be emphasized that the 'Free,' 'Partly Free,' and 'Not Free' labels are highly simplified terms that each cover a broad third of the available raw points. Therefore, countries and territories within each category, especially those at either end of each category, can have quite different human rights situations. In order to see the distinctions within each category, one should examine a country's or territory's political rights and civil liberties ratings.

The differences in raw points between countries in the three broad categories represent distinctions in the real world. There are obstacles which 'Partly Free' countries must overcome before they can be called 'Free,' just as there are impediments which prevent 'Not Free' countries from being called 'Partly Free.' Countries at the lowest rung of the 'Free' category (2 in political rights and 3 in civil liberties, or 3 in political rights and 2 in civil liberties) differ from those at the upper end of the 'Partly Free' group (e.g., 3 for both political rights and civil liberties). Typically, there is more violence and/or military influence on politics at 3, 3 than at 2, 3.

The distinction between the least bad 'Not Free' countries and the least free 'Partly Free' may be less obvious than the gap between 'Partly Free' and 'Free,' but at 'Partly Free,' there is at least one additional factor that keeps a country from being assigned to the 'Not Free' category. For example, Lebanon, which was rated 6, 5, 'Partly Free' in 1994, was rated 6, 5, but 'Not Free,' in 1995 after its legislature unilaterally extended the incumbent president's term indefinitely. Though not sufficient to drop the country's political rights rating to 7, there was enough of a drop in raw points to change its category.

Freedom House does not view democracy as a static concept, and the Survey recognizes that a democratic country does not necessarily belong in our category of 'Free' states. A democracy can lose freedom and become merely 'Partly Free.' Sri Lanka and Colombia are examples of such 'Partly Free'

Appendix

democracies. In other cases, countries that replaced military regimes with elected governments can have less than complete transitions to liberal democracy. Guatemala fits the description of this kind of 'Partly Free' democracy. Some scholars use the term 'semi-democracy' or 'formal democracy,' instead of 'Partly Free' democracy, to refer to countries that are democratic in form but less than free in substance.

The designation 'Free' does not mean that a country enjoys perfect freedom or lacks serious problems. As an institution which advocates human rights, Freedom House remains concerned about a variety of social problems and civil liberties questions in the U.S. and other countries that the Survey places in the 'Free' category. An improvement in a country's rating does not mean that human rights campaigns should cease. On the contrary, the findings of the Survey should be regarded as a means to encourage improvements in the political rights and civil liberties conditions in all countries.

The Freedom House organization (reproduced from http://www.freedomhouse.org/aboutfh/funders.htm)

Freedom House is a non-profit, nonpartisan organization that relies upon tax-deductible grants and donations under Section 501(c)(3) of the IRS code.

Major support has been provided by:

- The Lynde and Harry Bradley Foundation
- The Byrne Foundation
- The Carthage Foundation
- The Eurasia Foundation
- The Ford Foundation
- The Freedom Forum
- Grace Foundation, Inc.
- Lilly Endowment, Inc.
- The LWH Family Foundation
- Charles Stewart Mott Foundation
- National Endowment for Democracy
- The Pew Charitable Trusts
- Sarah Scaife Foundation
- The Schloss Family Foundation
- Smith Richardson Foundation, Inc.
- The Soros Foundations
- The Tinker Foundation
- Unilever United States Foundation, Inc.
- US Agency for International Development
- US Information Agency

Note: Freedom House material reproduced by permission.

Bibliography

Abukhalil, A. (1997) 'Change and democratisation in the Arab world: the role of political parties', *Third World Quarterly*, 18, 1, pp. 149–63.

Aglionby, J. and Denny, C. (2000) 'Estrada risks replay of the domino effect', *Guardian*, 31 Oct.

Ajami, F. (1993) 'The summoning', *Foreign Affairs*, 72, 4, pp. 1–12.

Ali, T. (1999) 'The panic button', *Guardian*, 14 Oct.

Arblaster, A. (1999) 'Democratic society and its enemies', in P. Burnell and P. Calvert (eds), *The Resilience of Democracy: Persistent Practice, Durable Idea*, special issue of *Democratization*, 6, 1, pp. 33–49.

Asad, T. (1986) *The Idea of an Anthropology of Islam*, Occasional Paper 15, Washington DC: Center for Contemporary Arab Studies, Georgetown University.

Ayoade, J. A. (1988) 'States without citizens: an emerging African phenomenon', in D. Rothchild and N. Chazan (eds), *The Precarious Balance: State and Society in Africa*, Boulder: Lynne Rienner, pp. 100–18.

Ayubi, N. (1991) *Political Islam: Religion and Politics in the Arab World*, London: Routledge.

Banks, A. and Muller, T. (eds) (1998) *Political Handbook of the World 1998*, Binghamton, N.Y.: CSA Publications.

Bartlett, D. and Hunter, W. (1997) 'Market structures, political institutions, and democratization: the Latin American and East European experiences', *Review of International Political Economy*, 4, 1, pp. 87–126.

Bauer, J. and Bell, D. (eds) (1999) *The East Asian Challenge for Human Rights*, Cambridge: Cambridge University Press.

Baumhogger, G. (1999) 'Botswana', in D. Nohlen, M. Krennerich and B. Thibault (eds), *Elections in Africa: A Data Handbook*, Oxford: Oxford University Press, pp. 102–21.

Bayart, J.-F. (1991) 'Finishing with the idea of the Third World: the concept of the political trajectory', in J. Manor (ed.), *Rethinking Third World Politics*, Harlow: Longman, pp. 51–71.

Bayart, J.-F. (1993) *The State in Africa*, Harlow: Longman.

Bealey, F. (1999) *The Blackwell Dictionary of Political Science*, Oxford: Blackwell.

Beeley, B. (1992) 'Islam as a global political force', in A. McGrew and P. Lewis (eds), *Global Politics: Globalization and the Nation State*, Cambridge: Polity, pp. 293–311.

Beetham, D. (1999) *Democracy and Human Rights*, Cambridge: Polity.

Bellos, A. (1999a) 'Ex-paratrooper storms political arena to drag Venezuela out of mire', *Guardian*, 7 June.

Bellos, A. (1999b) 'Venezuela's democracy faces threat at the polls', *Guardian*, 19 July.

Bellos, A. (1999c) 'Charismatic leader wins vote for change', *Guardian*, 17 Dec.

Bentsi-Enchill, N. (1998) 'Tough times ahead for Ghana', *Africa Recovery*, 11, 3, pp. 4–8.

Bertrand, J. (1998) 'Growth and democracy in Southeast Asia', *Comparative Politics*, 30, 4, pp. 355–75.

Bill, J. and Springborg, R. (1994) *Politics in the Middle East*, 4th edn, New York: HarperCollins.

Black, J. Knippers (1993) 'Elections and other trivial pursuits: Latin America and the New World Order', *Third World Quarterly*, 14, 3, pp. 545–54.

Boafo-Arthur, K. (1998) 'The international community and Ghana's transition to democracy', in K. Ninsin (ed.), *Ghana: Transition to Democracy*, Dakar: CODESRIA, pp. 167–86.

Boone, C. (1998) ' "Empirical statehood" and reconfigurations of political order', in L. Villallón and P. Huxtable (eds), *The African State at a Critical Juncture: Between Disintegration and Reconfiguration*, Boulder: Lynne Rienner, pp. 129–41.

Booth, J. and Seligson, M. (1993) 'Paths to democracy and the political culture of Costa Rica, Mexico, and Nicaragua', in L. Diamond (ed.), *Political Culture and Democracy in Developing Countries*, Boulder: Lynne Rienner, pp. 107–38.

Borger, J. (1997a) 'Peace gives no dividend to Jordan', *Guardian*, 27 Oct.

Borger, J. (1997b) 'Opposition attacks King Hussein's press clampdown', *Guardian*, 29 Oct.

Bratton, M. and van de Walle, N. (1994) 'Neopatrimonial regimes and political transitions in Africa', *World Politics*, 46, 4, pp. 453–89.

Bratton, M. and van de Walle, N. (1997) *Democratic Experiments in Africa*, Cambridge: Cambridge University Press.

Bromley, S. (1994) *Rethinking Middle East Politics*, Cambridge: Polity.

Bromley, S. (1997) 'Middle East exceptionalism – myth or reality', in D. Potter, D. Goldblatt, M. Kiloh and P. Lewis (eds), *Democratization*, Cambridge: Polity in association with the Open University, pp. 321–44.

Brynen, R., Korany, B. and Noble, P. (1995) 'Introduction: theoretical perspectives on Arab liberalization and democratization', in R. Brynen, B.

Korany and P. Noble (eds), *Political Liberalization and Democratization in the Arab World*, vol. 1: *Theoretical Perspectives*, Boulder: Lynne Rienner, pp. 3–27.

Burnell, P. (1998) 'Arrivals and departures: a preliminary classification of democratic failures and their explanation', *Journal of Commonwealth and Comparative Politics*, 36, 3, pp. 1–29.

Burnell, P. (2000) 'The significance of the December 1998 local elections in Zambia and their aftermath', *Journal of Commonwealth and Comparative Politics*, 38, 1, pp. 1–20.

Burnell, P. and Calvert, P. (1998) 'The resilience of democracy: persistent practice, durable idea', MS.

Burnell, P. and Calvert, P. (1999a) 'The resilience of democracy: an introduction', in P. Burnell and P. Calvert (eds), *The Resilience of Democracy: Persistent Practice, Durable Idea*, special issue of *Democratization*, 6, 1, pp. 1–32.

Burnell, P. and Calvert, P. (1999b) 'Democracy: persistent practice or durable idea', in P. Burnell and P. Calvert (eds), *The Resilience of Democracy: Persistent Practice, Durable Idea*, special issue of *Democratization*, 6, 1, pp. 271–84.

Buxton, J. (1999) 'Venezuela: degenerative democracy', in P. Burnell and P. Calvert (eds), *The Resilience of Democracy: Persistent Practice, Durable Idea*, special issue of *Democratization*, 6, 1, pp. 246–71.

Buxton, J. and Phillips, N. (eds) (1999) *Case Studies in Latin American Political Economy*, Manchester: Manchester University Press.

Callaghy, T. (1993) 'Vision and politics in the transformation of the global political economy: lessons from the Second and Third Worlds', in R. Slater, B. Schutz and S. Dorr (eds), *Global Transformation and the Third World*, Boulder: Lynne Rienner, pp. 161–256.

Callahan, W. (1996) 'Rescripting East/West relations, rethinking Asian democracy', *Pacific Review*, 8, 1, pp. 3–16.

Calvert, S. and Calvert, P. (1996) *Politics and Society in the Third World*, Hemel Hempstead: Prentice Hall.

Cammack, P. (1994) 'Democratization and citizenship in Latin America', in G. Parry and M. Moran (eds), *Democracy and Democratization*, London: Routledge, pp. 174–95.

Cammack, P. (1997) 'Democracy and dictatorship in Latin America, 1930–80', in D. Potter, D. Goldblatt, M. Kiloh and P. Lewis (eds), *Democratization*, Cambridge: Polity in association with the Open University, pp. 152–73.

Cammack, P., Pool, D. and Tordoff, W. (1993) *Third World Politics: A Comparative Introduction*, 2nd edn, London: Macmillan.

Carothers, T. (1997) 'Democracy without illusions', *Foreign Affairs*, 76, 1, pp. 85–99.

Carothers, T. (1999) *Aiding Democracy Abroad: The Learning Curve*, Washington, DC: Carnegie Endowment for Peace.

Case, W. (1997) 'The 1996 UMNO party election: "two for the show"', *Pacific Affairs*, 3, pp. 393–411.

Castañeda, J. (1994) *Utopia Unarmed: The Latin American Left after the Cold War*, New York: Vintage.

Chabal, P. (1998) 'A few considerations on democracy in Africa', *International Affairs*, 74, 2, pp. 289–303.

Chakravartty, N. (1997) 'Indian democracy: reflections and challenges', *World Affairs*, 2, 1, pp. 80–90.

Chan Heng Chee (1993) 'Democracy: evolution and implementation. An Asian perspective', in R. Bartley et al. (eds), *Democracy and Capitalism: Asian and American Perspectives*, Singapore: Institute of Southeast Asian Studies, pp. 1–26.

Chazan, N. (1991) 'The political transformation of Ghana under the PNDC', in D. Rothchild (ed.), *Ghana: The Political Economy of Recovery*, Boulder: Lynne Rienner, pp. 15–38.

Chiriyankandath, J. (1996) 'The 1996 Indian general election', Briefing Paper 31, London: Royal Institute of International Affairs.

Clapham, C. (1985) *Third World Politics: An Introduction*, London: Routledge.

Clapham, C. and Wiseman, J. (1995) 'Conclusion: assessing the prospects for the consolidation of democracy in Africa', in J. Wiseman (ed.), *Democracy and Political Change in Sub-Saharan Africa*, London: Routledge, pp. 220–32.

Collier, D. and Levitsky, S. (1997) 'Democracy with adjectives: conceptual innovation in comparative research', *World Politics*, 49, 3, pp. 430–51.

Cornelius, W. (2000) 'Blind spots in democratization: sub-national politics as a constraint on Mexico's transition', *Democratization*, 7, 3, pp. 117–32.

Cox, R. (1993) 'Social forces, states and world orders: beyond international relations theory', in H. Williams, M. Wright and T. Evans (eds), *International Relations and Political Theory*, Buckingham: Open University Press, pp. 274–308.

Crook, R. and Manor, J. (1998) *Democracy and Decentralisation in South Asia and West Africa*, Cambridge: Cambridge University Press.

Cumming, G. (1999) 'French and British Aid to Africa: a comparative study', Ph.D. thesis, School of European Studies, Cardiff University.

Cummings, B. (1989) 'The abortive abertura: South Korea in the light of Latin American experience', *New Left Review*, no. 173, pp. 5–32.

Cummings, B. (1995) 'The origins and development of the Northeast Asia political economy: industrial sectors, product cycles, and political consequences', *International Organization*, 38, 1, pp. 1–40.

Dahl, R. (1971) *Polyarchy*, New Haven: Yale University Press.

Dahl, R. (1989) *Democracy and its Critics*, New Haven: Yale University Press.

Daloz, J.-P. (1992) 'L'itinéraire du pionnier sur l'évolution politique beninoise', *Politique Africaine*, no. 46, pp. 132–7.

Davies, N. (1999) 'Dangers of the aid game', *Guardian*, 14 June.

Davis, P. and McGregor, A. (2000) 'Civil society, international donors and poverty in Bangladesh', *Journal of Commonwealth and Comparative Politics*, 38, 1, pp. 47–64.

Decalo, S. (1997) 'Benin: first of the new democracies', in J. Clark and D. Gardinier (eds), *Political Reform in Francophone Africa*, Boulder: Westview, pp. 51–85.

Deeb, M.-J. (1989) 'Algeria', in S. Mews (ed.), *Religion in Politics: A World Guide*, Harlow: Longman, pp. 6–8.

Deegan, H. (1996) *Third Worlds: The Politics of the Middle East and North Africa*, London: Routledge.

Degregori, C. (1993) 'The maturation of a cosmocrat and the building of a discourse community: the case of Shining Path, 1963–80', mimeo, UN Research Institute for Social Development, Geneva.

Di Palma, G. (1990) *To Craft Democracies*, Berkeley: University of California Press.

Diamond, L. (1988) 'Introduction', in L. Diamond, J. Linz and S. M. Lipset (eds), *Democracy in Developing Countries*, vol. 2: *Africa*, Boulder: Lynne Rienner, pp. 2–32.

Diamond, L. (1993) 'The globalization of democracy' in R. Slater, B. Schutz and S. Dorr (eds), *Global Transformation and the Third World*, Boulder: Lynne Rienner, pp. 31–70.

Diamond, L. (1996) 'Democracy in Latin America: degrees, illusions, and directions for consolidation', in T. Farer (ed.), *Beyond Sovereignty: Collectively Defending Democracy in the Americas*, Baltimore: Johns Hopkins University Press, pp. 53–85.

Diamond, L. (1999) *Developing Democracy: Toward Consolidation*, Baltimore: Johns Hopkins University Press.

Diamond, L., Linz, J. and Lipset, S. M. (eds) (1988) *Democracy in Developing Countries*, vol. 2: *Africa*, Boulder: Lynne Rienner.

Doig, A. (1999) 'In the state we trust? Democratisation, corruption and development', *Journal of Commonwealth and Comparative Politics*, 37, 3, pp. 13–36.

Dorr, S. (1993) 'Democratization in the Middle East', in R. Slater, B. Schutz and S. Dorr (eds), *Global Transformation and the Third World*, Boulder: Lynne Rienner, pp. 131–57.

El-Kenz, A. (1991) *Algerian Reflections on Arab Crises*, trans. R. W. Stooley, Austin: University of Texas Center for Middle Eastern Studies.

Elliot, L. and Denny, C. (1999) 'Asia tiptoes warily back to work', *Guardian*, 6 July.

Emmerson, D. K. (1995) 'Singapore and the "Asian values" debate', *Journal of Democracy*, 6, 4, pp. 95–105.

Encarnacion, T. and Tadem, E. (1993) 'Ethnicity and separatist movements in South-East Asia', in P. Wignaraja (ed.), *New Social Movements in the South*, London: Zed Books, pp. 153–73.

Engberg, J. and Ersson, S. (1999) 'Illiberal democracy in the Third World – an empirical enquiry', paper presented at the workshop on Democratic Consolidation in the Third World: What Should be done?, ECPR Joint Sessions of Workshops, University of Mannheim, March.

Esposito, J. (2000) 'Political Islam and global order', in J. Esposito and M. Watson (eds), *Religion and Global Order*, Cardiff: University of Wales Press, pp. 119–30.

Esposito, J. and Piscatori, J. (1991) 'Democratization and Islam', *Middle East Journal*, 45, 3, pp. 427–40.

Ethier, D. (1990) 'Processes of transition and democratic consolidation: theoretical indicators', in D. Ethier (ed.), *Democratic Transition and Consolidation in Southern Europe, Latin America and Southeast Asia*, Basingstoke: Macmillan, pp. 3–21.

Fawcett, L. and Sayigh, Y. (eds) (1999) *The Third World Beyond the Cold War: Continuity and Change*, Oxford: Oxford University Press.

Forrest, J. (1988) 'The quest for state "hardness" in Africa', *Comparative Politics*, 20, 4, pp. 423–42.

Foweraker, J. (1998) 'Institutional design, party systems and governability: differentiating the presidential regimes of Latin America', *British Journal of Political Science*, 28, pp. 651–78.

Foweraker, J. and Landman, T. (1997) *Citizenship Rights and Social Movements: A Comparative and Statistical Analysis*, Oxford: Oxford University Press.

Friedman, E. (1994) 'Generalizing the East Asian experience', in E. Friedman (ed.), *The Politics Of Democratization*, Boulder: Westview, pp. 19–57.

Fukuyama, F. (1992) *The End of History and the Last Man*, London: Penguin.

Fukuyama, F. (1995) 'Confucianism and democracy', *Journal of Democracy*, 6, 2, pp. 20–33.

Fukuyama, F. (1997) 'The illusion of exceptionalism', *Journal of Democracy*, 8, 3, pp. 145–9.

Gallardo, E. (1999) 'Argentina's new leader vows to fight corruption', *Guardian*, 26 Oct.

Galpin, R. (1999) 'Pakistan tightens screw on opposition', *Guardian*, 15 May.

Gastil, R. (1988) *Freedom in the World. Political Rights and Civil Liberties 1987–1988*, New York: Freedom House.

Gastil, R. (1992) *Freedom in the World: Political Rights and Civil Liberties 1991–1992*, New York: Freedom House.

Gill, G. (2000) *The Dynamics of Democratization: Elites, Civil Society and the Transition Process*, Basingstoke: Macmillan.

Gills, B. (1993) 'Korean capitalism and democracy', in B. Gills, J. Rocamora and R. Wilson (eds), *Low Intensity Democracy*, London: Pluto Press, pp. 226–57.

Gills, B. and Rocamora, J. (1992) 'Low intensity democracy', *Third World Quarterly*, 13, 3, pp. 501–24.

Gills, B., Rocamora, J. and Wilson, R. (eds) (1993) *Low Intensity Democracy*, London: Pluto Press.

Ginsburg, D. (1996) 'The democratisation of South Africa: transition theory tested', *Transformation*, 29, pp. 74–102.

Gittings, J. (1998) 'Cool young cats held the key in Taipei', *Guardian*, 7 Dec.

Goldberg, E., Kasaba, R. and Migdal, J. (eds) (1993) *Rules and Rights in the Middle East: Democracy, Law and Society*, Seattle: University of Washington Press.

Goldenberg, S. (1998) 'Sharif wades deep into controversy', *Guardian*, 16 Nov.

Goldenberg, S. (1999a) 'Third poll in three years signifies erosion of big-party rule in India', *Guardian*, 28 Apr.

Goldenberg, S. (1999b) 'Court orders Bhutto to return for hearing', *Guardian*, 14 May.

Grayson, J. (1989) 'Korea', in S. Mews (ed.), *Religion in Politics*, Harlow: Longman, p. 153.

Green, D. (1999) 'The lingering moment: an historical perspective on the global durability of democracy after 1989', *Democratization*, 6, 2, pp. 1–41.

Guelke, A. (1999) *South Africa in Transition: The Misunderstood Miracle*, London: I. B. Tauris.

Günes-Ayata, A. (1994) 'Roots and trends in clientelism in Turkey', in L. Roniger and A. Günes-Ayata (eds), *Democracy, Clientelism, and Civil Society*, Boulder: Lynne Rienner, pp. 49–64.

Gunther, R. P., Diamandouros, N. and Puhle, H.-J. (eds) (1995) *The Politics of Democratic Consolidation: Southern Europe in Comparative Perspective*, Cambridge: Cambridge University Press.

Habib, A., Pillay, D. and Ashwin, D. (1998) 'South Africa and the global order: the structural conditioning of a transition to democracy', *Journal of Contemporary African Studies*, 16, 1, pp. 95–115.

Hadjor, K. (1993) *Dictionary of Third World Terms*, London: Penguin.

Hagopian, F. (1993) 'After regime change: authoritarian legacies, political representation, and the democratic future of Latin America', *World Politics*, 45, 4, pp. 464–500.

Hall, J. (1993) 'Consolidations of democracy', in D. Held (ed.), *Prospects for Democracy*, Cambridge: Polity, pp. 271–90.

Hansen, H. B. and Twaddle, M. (1995) 'Uganda: the advent of no-party democracy', in J. Wiseman (ed.), *Democracy and Political Change in Africa*, London: Routledge, pp. 137–51.

Harsch, E. (1996) 'Global coalition debates Africa's future', *Africa Recovery*, 10, 1, pp. 24–31.

Hawthorn, G. (1996) 'Constitutional democracy in the South', in R. Luckham and G. White (eds), *Democratization in the South: The Jagged Wave*, Manchester: Manchester University Press, pp. 11–36.

Haynes, J. (1995a) 'From personalistic to democratic rule in Ghana', in J. Wiseman (ed.), *Democracy and Political Change in Africa*, London: Routledge, pp. 92–115.

Haynes, J. (1995b) 'Religion, fundamentalism and identity: a global perspective', Discussion Paper 65, UN Research Institute for Social Development, Geneva.

Haynes, J. (1996a) *Religion and Politics in Africa*, London: Zed Books.

Haynes, J. (1996b) 'Politics of the natural environment in the Third World', *Journal of Contemporary Politics*, 2, 2, pp. 19–42.

Haynes, J. (1996c) *Third World Politics: A Concise Introduction*, Oxford: Blackwell.

Haynes, J. (1997) *Democracy and Civil Society in the Third World: Politics and New Political Movements*, Cambridge: Polity.

Haynes, J. (1998) *Religion in Global Politics*, Harlow: Longman.

Haynes, J. (1999a) 'The possibility of democratic consolidation in Ghana', in P. Burnell and P. Calvert (eds), *The Resilience of Democracy: Persistent Practice, Durable Idea*, special issue of *Democratization*, 6, 1, pp. 108–21.

Haynes, J. (1999b) 'Power, politics and environmental movements in the Third World', *Environmental Politics*, 8, 1, pp. 222–42.

Haynes, J. (2001) '"Limited" democracy in Ghana and Uganda. What is most important to international actors: stability or political freedom?' *Journal of Contemporary African Studies*, 19, 2, pp. 1–22.

Held, D. (1993) 'Democracy: from city-states to a cosmopolitan order?' in D. Held (ed.), *Prospects for Democracy*, Cambridge: Polity, pp. 13–52.

Herring, R. (1999) 'Embedded particularism: India's failed developmental state', in M. Woo-Cumings (ed.), *The Developmental State*, Ithaca: Cornell University Press, pp. 306–34.

Hewison, K. (1999) 'Political space in Southeast Asia: "Asian-style" and other democracies', in P. Burnell and P. Calvert (eds), *The Resilience of Democracy: Persistent Practice, Durable Idea*, special issue of *Democratization*, 6, 1, pp. 224–45.

Hirst, D. (1999) 'Where tyranny spells peace', *Guardian*, 10 Mar.

Hoag, C. (1998) 'Venezuela celebrates poll victory for Chávez', *Guardian*, 8 Dec.

Horowitz, D. (1992) 'Comparing democratic systems', in A. Liphart (ed.), *Parliamentary versus Presidential Democracy*, Oxford: Oxford University Press, pp. 78–109.

Huber, E., Rueschemeyer, D. and Stephens, J. (1997) 'The paradoxes of contemporary democracy: formal, participatory, and social dimensions', *Comparative Politics*, 29, 3, pp. 323–42.

Huntington, S. (1968) *Political Order in Changing Societies*, New Haven: Yale University Press.

Huntington, S. (1984) 'Will more countries become democratic?' *Political Science Quarterly*, 99, 2, pp. 193–218.

Huntington, S. (1991) *The Third Wave: Democratization in the Late Twentieth Century*, Norman: University of Oklahoma Press.

Ibrahim, S. E. (1995) 'Liberalization and democratization in the Arab world: an overview', in R. Brynen, B. Korany and P. Noble (eds), *Political Liberalization and Democratization in the Arab World*, vol. 1: *Theoretical Perspectives*, Boulder: Lynne Rienner, pp. 29–57.

IDEA (International Institute for Democracy and Electoral Assistance) (1998) *Voter Turnout from 1945 to 1997: A Global Report on Political Participation*, Stockholm: IDEA.

International Forum for Democratic Studies (1996) *Democracy in East Asia: Conference Report*, Washington DC: International Forum for Democratic Studies.

Izaguirre, I. (1998) 'Recapturing the memory of politics', *North American Congress on Latin America (NACLA) Report on the Americas*, 31, 6, pp. 28–34.

Jacques, M. (1999) 'Maverick Mahathir cashes in', *Observer*, 12 Sep.

Jeffries, R. (1998) 'The Ghanaian elections of 1996: towards the consolidation of democracy?' *African Affairs*, 97, 387, pp. 189–208.

Jesudason, J. (1995) 'Statist democracy and the limits to civil society in Malaysia', *Journal of Commonwealth and Comparative Politics*, 33, 3, pp. 335–56.

Jesudason, J. (1996) 'The syncretic state and the structuring of opposition politics in Malaysia', in G. Rodan (ed.), *Political Oppositions in Industrialising Asia*, London: Routledge, pp. 128–66.

Joll, J. (1977) *Gramsci*, London: Fontana/Collins.

Joseph, R. (1997) 'Democratization in Africa after 1989: comparative and theoretical perspectives', *Comparative Politics*, 23, 2, pp. 363–82.

Joseph, R. (1998) 'Africa, 1990–97: from abertura to closure', *Journal of Democracy*, 9, 2, pp. 3–17.

Kamrava, M. (1998) 'Non-democratic states and liberalisation in the Middle East: a structural analysis', *Third World Quarterly*, 19, 1, pp. 63–85.

Kaplan, R. (1997) 'Was democracy just a moment?' *Atlantic Monthly*, Dec., pp. 55–80.

Karatnycky, A. (1999) 'The decline of illiberal democracy', *Journal of Democracy*, 10, 1, pp. 112–25.

Karl, T. (1990) 'Dilemmas of democratization in Latin America', *Comparative Politics*, 23, 1, pp. 1–21.

Karl, T. (1991) 'El Salvador's negotiated revolution', *Foreign Affairs*, 70, 2, pp. 147–64.

Karl, T. (1995) 'The hybrid regimes of Central America', *Journal of Democracy*, 6, 3, pp. 72–86.

Karl, T. and Schmitter, P. (1991) 'Modes of transition in Latin America, Southern and Eastern Europe', *International Social Science Journal*, no. 138, pp. 269–84.

Kasfir, N. (1998a) 'Civil society, the state and democracy in Africa', *Journal of Commonwealth and Comparative Politics*, 36, 2, pp. 123–49.

Kasfir, N. (1998b) ' "No-party democracy" in Uganda', *Journal of Democracy*, 9, 2, pp. 49–63.

Katsouris, C. (1997) 'Debtors queue up after Uganda's deal', *Africa Recovery*, 11, 1, pp. 14–15.

Kaviraj, S. (1991) 'On state, society and discourse in India', in J. Manor (ed.), *Rethinking Third World Politics*, Harlow: Longman, pp. 72–99.

Kelly, D. and Reid, A. (eds) (1998) *Asian Freedoms: The Idea of Freedom in East and Southeast Asia*, Cambridge: Cambridge University Press.

Kepel, G. (1994) *The Revenge of God*, Cambridge: Polity.

Kiloh, M. (1997a) 'South Africa: democracy delayed', in D. Potter, D. Goldblatt, M. Kiloh and P. Lewis (eds) *Democratization*, Cambridge: Polity in association with the Open University, pp. 294–320.

Kiloh, M. (1997b) 'Afterword', in D. Potter, D. Goldblatt, M. Kiloh and P. Lewis (eds), *Democratization*, Cambridge: Polity in association with the Open University, pp. 387–92.

King, A. Y. C. (1993) 'A nonparadigmatic search for democracy in a post-Confucian culture: the case of Taiwan, R.O.C.', in L. Diamond (ed.), *Political Culture and Democracy in Developing Countries*, Boulder: Lynne Rienner, pp. 139–62.

Kirya, G. (1998) ' "No-party democracy" ', *West Africa*, 16–22 Feb., pp. 170–1.

Kjaer, M. (1999) 'Fundamental change or no change? Institutionalizing politics in Uganda', paper presented at the workshop on Democratic Consolidation in the Third World: What Should be done?, ECPR Joint Sessions of Workshops, University of Mannheim, March.

Kjaer, M. (2000) "Fundamental change or no change? The process of constitutionalizing Uganda', *Democratization*, 6, 4, pp. 93–111.

Kohli, A. (1994) 'Centralization and powerlessness: India's democracy in a comparative perspective', in J. Migdal, A. Kohli and V. Shue (eds), *State Power and Social Forces: Domination and Transformation in the Third World*, Cambridge: Cambridge University Press, pp. 89–107.

Kohli, A. (1999) 'Where do high-growth political economies come from? The Japanese lineage of Korea's "developmental state"', in M. Woo-Cumings (ed.), *The Developmental State*, Ithaca: Cornell University Press, pp. 93–136.

Kramer, G. (1992) 'Liberalization and democracy in the Arab world', *Middle East Report*, 22, Feb.–Mar., pp. 12–28.

Kumaraswamy, P. R. (1999) 'South Asia after the cold war', in L. Fawcett and Y. Sayigh (eds), *The Third World Beyond the Cold War: Continuity and Change*, Oxford: Oxford University Press, pp. 170–99.

Lane, J.-E., and Ersson, S. (1994) *Comparative Politics: An Introduction and New Approach*, Cambridge: Polity.

Lane, J.-E. and Ersson, S. (1997) 'The possibility of democratic success in South Africa', *Democratization*, 4, 4, pp. 1–15.

Lapidus, I. (1988) *A History of Islamic Societies*, Cambridge: Cambridge University Press.

Lawson, L. (1999) 'External democracy promotion in Africa: another false start?' *Journal of Commonwealth and Comparative Politics*, 37, 1, pp. 1–30.

Leftwich, A. (1993) 'Governance, democracy and development in the Third World', *Third World Quarterly*, 14, 3, pp. 605–24.

Leftwich, A. (1997) 'Conclusion', in D. Potter, D. Goldblatt, M. Kiloh and P. Lewis (eds), *Democratization*, Cambridge: Polity in association with the Open University, pp. 517–36.

Leftwich, A. (1998) 'Forms of the democratic developmental state: democratic practices and development capacity', in M. Robinson and G. White (eds), *The Democratic Developmental State: Political and Institutional Design*, Oxford: Oxford University Press, pp. 52–83.

Liddle, W. (1999) 'The Islamic turn in Indonesia: a political explanation', in J. Haynes (ed.), *Religion, Globalization and Political Culture in the Third World*, Basingstoke: Macmillan, pp. 112–38.

Lievesley, G. (1999) *Democracy in Latin America: Mobilization, Power and the Search for a New Politics*, Manchester: Manchester University Press.

Lijphart, A. and Waisman, C. (1996) 'Conclusion', in A. Lijphart and C. Waisman (eds), *Institutional Design in New Democracies*, Boulder: Westview, pp. 240–64.

Linz, J. (1990) 'Transitions to democracy', *Washington Quarterly*, 13, 3, pp. 143–64.

Linz, J. and Stepan, A. (1978) *The Breakdown of Democratic Regimes*, Baltimore: Johns Hopkins University Press.

Linz, J. and Stepan, A. (1996) *Problems of Democratic Transition and Consolidation: Southern Europe, South America, and Post-Communist Europe*, Baltimore: Johns Hopkins University Press.

Lipset, S. M. (1963) 'Economic development and democracy', in S. M. Lipset (ed.), *Political Man*, Garden City, N.Y.: Anchor, pp. 27–63.

Lipset, S. M. (1992) 'The centrality of political culture', in A. Liphart (ed.), *Parliamentary versus Presidential Democracy*, Oxford: Oxford University Press, pp. 23–46.

Lipset, S. M. (1994) 'The social requisites of democracy revisited', *American Sociological Review*, 59, 1, pp. 1–22.

Little, W. (1997) 'Democratization in Latin America, 1980–95', in D. Potter, D. Goldblatt, M. Kiloh and P. Lewis (eds), *Democratization*, Cambridge: Polity in association with the Open University, pp. 174–94.

Luckham, R. (1998) 'Are there alternatives to liberal democracy', in M. Robinson and G. White (eds), *The Democratic Developmental State: Political and Institutional Design*, Oxford: Oxford University Press, pp. 306–42.

Luckham, R. and White, G. (1996) 'Conclusion', in R. Luckham and G. White (eds), *Democratization in the South: The Jagged Wave*, Manchester: Manchester University Press, pp. 274–89.

McCargo, D. (1992) 'The political ramifications of the 1989 "Santi Asoke" case in Thailand', paper presented at the annual conference of the Association of South-East Asian Studies, School of Oriental and African Studies, University of London, 8–10 Apr.

McCargo, D. (1999) 'Media and democratic transitions in Southeast Asia', paper presented at the workshop on Democratic Consolidation in the Third World: What Should be Done?, ECPR Joint Sessions of Workshops, University of Mannheim, March.

McCarthy, R. (2000) 'One man's mission to bring Pakistan's corrupt to account', *Guardian*, 17 Mar.

McCoy, J. (1988) 'The state and democratic compromise in Venezuela', *Journal of Developing Societies*, 4, 1, pp. 85–104.

McGarry, J. (1998) 'Political settlements in Northern Ireland and South Africa', *Political Studies*, 46, 5, pp. 853–70.

McGreal, C. (2000) 'Clinton's visit shows US fears for Nigeria', *Guardian*, 26 Aug.

McMahon, R. (1999) *The Limits of Empire: The United States and Southeast Asia since World War II*, New York: Columbia University Press.

Mainwaring, S. (1988) 'Political parties and democratization in Brazil and the Southern Cone', *Comparative Politics*, Oct., pp. 91–120.

Mainwaring, ·S. (1993) 'Presidentialism, mutlipartyism, and democracy', *Comparative Political Studies*, 26, 2, pp. 199–228.

Mainwaring, S. (1999) *Rethinking Party Systems in the Third Wave of Democratization: The Case of Brazil*, Stanford: Stanford University Press.

Mainwaring, S., O'Donnell, G. and Valenzuela, J. (1992) 'Introduction', in S. Mainwaring, G. O'Donnell, and J. Samuel Valenzuela (eds), *Issues in Democratic Consolidation: The New South American Democracies in Comparative Perspective*, Notre Dame, Ind.: University of Notre Dame Press, pp. 3–28.

Manning, P. (1998) *Francophone Sub-Saharan Africa 1880–1995*, Cambridge: Cambridge University Press.

Manor, J. (1991) 'Introduction', in J. Manor (ed.), *Rethinking Third World Politics*, Harlow: Longman, pp. 1–11.

Manor, J. (1998) 'Democratization and the developmental state: the search for institutional design', in M. Robinson and G. White (eds), *The Democratic Developmental State: Political and Institutional Design*, Oxford: Oxford University Press, pp. 125–49.

Marais, H. (1998) *South Africa: Limits to Change: The Political Economy of Transformation*, London and Cape Town: Zed Books and University of Cape Town Press.

Maravall, J. M. (1995) 'The myth of the authoritarian advantage', in L. Diamond and M. Plattner (eds), *Economic Reform and Democracy*, Baltimore: Johns Hopkins University Press, pp. 13–27.

March, J. and Olsen, J. (1995) *Democratic Governance*, New York: Free Press.

Means, G. P. (1996) 'Soft authoritarianism in Malaysia and Singapore', *Journal of Democracy*, 7, 4, pp. 103–17.

Merkel, W. (1998) 'The consolidation of post-autocratic democracies: a multi-level model, *Democratization*, 5, 3, pp. 33–67.

Mews, S. (ed.) (1989) *Religion in Politics: A World Guide*, Harlow: Longman.

Mitra, S. (ed.) (1990) *The Post-Colonial State in Asia*, Hemel Hempstead: Wheatsheaf.

Mitra, S. (1992) 'Democracy and political change in India', *Journal of Commonwealth and Comparative Politics*, 30, 1, pp. 9–38.

Mitra, S. and Enskat, M. (1999) 'Parties and the people: India's changing party system and the resilience of democracy', in P. Burnell and P. Calvert (eds), *The Resilience of Democracy: Persistent Practice, Durable Idea*, special issue of *Democratization*, 6, 1, pp. 123–54.

Mitra, S. and Rothermund, D. (eds) (1998) *Legitimacy and Conflict in South Asia*, New Delhi: Manohar.

Molomo, M. (2000) 'Understanding government and opposition parties in Botswana', *Journal of Commonwealth and Comparative Politics*, 38, 1, pp. 65–92.

Moody, P. (1988) *Political Opposition in Post-Confucian Society*, New York: Praeger.

Moore, B. (1966) *Social Origins of Dictatorship and Democracy: Lord and Peasant in the Making of the Modern World*, Harmondsworth: Penguin.

Moore, M. (1998) 'Death without taxes', in M. Robinson and G. White (eds), *The Democratic Developmental State: Political and Institutional Design*, Oxford: Oxford University Press, pp. 84–121.

Morlino, L. (1998) *Democracy between Consolidation and Crisis: Parties, Groups, and Citizens in Southern Europe*, New York: Oxford University Press.

Morris, C. (1999a) 'Scarf triggers attack on Virtue', *Guardian*, 8 May.

Morris, C. (1999b) 'Ankara faces tough reform battle', *Guardian*, 26 July.

Morris, S. (1995) *Political Reform in Mexico*, Boulder: Lynne Rienner.

Munck, G. and Leff, C. (1997) 'Modes of transition and democratization: South America and Eastern Europe in comparative perspective', *Comparative Politics*, Apr., pp. 342–62.

Munck, R. (1997) 'Democratic discourses and paradoxes', *Bulletin of Latin American Research*, 16, 2, pp. 219–24.

Nagle, J. and Mahr, A. (1999) *Democracy and Democratization: Post-Communist Europe in Comparative Perspective*, London: Sage.

National Endowment for Democracy (1996) 'Constructing democracy and markets: East Asia and Latin America', report of international conference, 26–27 Jan. 1996, at http://www.ned.org/publications/publications.html

Neher, C. (1994) 'Asian style democracy', *Asian Survey*, 34, 11, pp. 949–61.

Nohlen, D. (1992) 'Prasidentialismus versus Parlamentarismus in Lateinamerika', in *Lateinamerikanische Jahrbuch*, pp. 86–99.

O'Donnell, G. (1992) 'Transitions, continuities, and paradoxes', in S. Mainwaring, G. O'Donnell and J. Samuel Valenzuela (eds), *Issues in Democratic Consolidation: The New South American Democracies in Comparative Perspective*, Notre Dame, Ind.: University of Notre Dame Press, pp. 24–52.

O'Donnell, G. (1993) 'On the state, democratization and some conceptual problems: a Latin American view with glances at some post-communist countries', *World Development*, 21, 8, pp. 1355–69.

O'Donnell, G. (1994) 'Delegative democracy', *Journal of Democracy*, 5, 1, pp. 55–69.

O'Donnell, G. (1996) 'Illusions about consolidation', *Journal of Democracy*, 7, 1, pp. 34–51.

O'Donnell, G., Schmitter, P. and Whitehead, L. (eds) (1986) *Transitions from Authoritarian Rule: Prospects for Democracy*, vol. 4: *Tentative Conclusions about Uncertain Democracies*, Baltimore: Johns Hopkins University Press.

Odgaard, L. (1997) 'International society and liberal democracy in East Asia', paper presented at the 25th ECPR Joint Sessions of Workshops, University of Bern, Feb.–Mar.

Oh, I. and Park, I. (1999) 'Political democratization and persistent cold-war confrontations: the cases of South Korea and Taiwan', paper presented at the workshop on Democratic Consolidation in the Third World: What Should be Done? ECPR Joint Sessions of Workshops, University of Mannheim, March.

Organski, A. (1965) *The Stages of Political Development*, New York: Knopf.

Ortíz, R. (2000) 'Comparing types of transitions: Spain and Mexico', *Democratization*, 7, 3, pp. 65–92.

Osaghae, E. (1995) 'The study of political transitions in Africa', *Review of African Political Economy*, 64, pp. 183–97.

Ottaway, M. (1999) *Africa's New Leaders: Democracy or State Reconstruction?* Washington, DC: Carnegie Endowment for International Peace.

Ottemoeller, D. (1998) 'Popular perceptions of democracy: elections and attitudes in Uganda', *Comparative Political Studies*, 33, 1, pp. 98–124.

Owen, R. (1992) *State, Power and Politics in the Making of the Modern Middle East*, London: Routledge.

Ozbudun, E. (1996) 'Turkey: how far from consolidation?', *Journal of Democracy*, 7, 3, pp. 123–38.

Payne, T. (1988) 'Multi-party politics in Jamaica', in V. Randall (ed.), *Political Parties in the Third World*, London: Sage, pp. 135–54.

Pei, M. (1995) 'The puzzle of East Asian exceptionalism', in L. Diamond and M. Plattner (eds), *Economic Reform and Democracy*, Baltimore: Johns Hopkins University Press, pp. 112–25.

Pempel, T. J. (1999) 'The developmental regime in a changing world economy', in M. Woo-Cumings (ed.), *The Developmental State*, Ithaca: Cornell University Press, pp. 137–81.

Pendle, G. (1976) *A History of Latin America*, Harmondsworth: Penguin.

Pettiford, L. (1999) 'Simply a matter of luck? Why Costa Rica remains a democracy', in P. Burnell and P. Calvert (eds), *The Resilience of Democracy: Persistent Practice, Durable Idea*, special issue of *Democratization*, 6, 1, pp. 87–104.

Philip, G. (1999) 'Washington consensus politics in Latin American context: some lessons from Mexico, Peru and Venezuela', paper presented at the workshop on Democratic Consolidation in the Third World: What Should be Done?, ECPR Joint Sessions of Workshops, University of Mannheim, March.

Picard, E. (1990) 'Arab military in politics', in G. Luciani (ed.), *The Arab State*, London: Routledge, pp. 175–201.

Pinkney, R. (1993) *Democracy in the Third World*, Buckingham: Open University Press.

Piscatori, J. (1986) *Islam in a World of Nation-States*, Cambridge: Cambridge University Press.

Potter, D. (1997a) 'Democratization at the same time in South Korea and Taiwan', in D. Potter, D. Goldblatt, M. Kiloh and P. Lewis (eds), *Democratization*, Cambridge: Polity in association with the Open University, pp. 219–39.

Potter, D. (1997b) 'Afterword', in D. Potter, D. Goldblatt, M. Kiloh and P. Lewis (eds), *Democratization*, Cambridge: Polity in association with the Open University, pp. 264–8.

Potter, D., Goldblatt, D., Kiloh, M. and Lewis, P. (eds) (1997) *Democratization*, Cambridge: Polity in association with the Open University.

Premdas, R. and Ragoonath, B. (1998) 'Ethnicity, elections and democracy in Trinidad and Tobago: analysing the 1995 and 1996 elections', *Journal of Commonwealth and Comparative Politics*, 36, 3, pp. 30–53.

Pridham, G. (ed.) (1991) *Encouraging Democracy: The International Dimension of Democratization in Southern Europe*, London: Leicester University Press.

Pridham, G. and Vanhanen, T. (eds) (1994) *Democratization in Eastern Europe: Domestic and International Perspectives*, London: Routledge.

Przeworski, A. (1986) 'Some problems in the study of the transition to democracy', in G. O'Donnell, P. Schmitter and L. Whitehead (eds), *Transitions from Authoritarian Rule: Southern Europe*, Baltimore: Johns Hopkins University Press, pp. 47–63.

Przeworski, A. (1991) *Democracy and the Market: Political and Economic Reform in Eastern Europe and Latin America*, Cambridge: Cambridge University Press.

Przeworski, A., Alvarez, M., Cheibib, J. A. and Limongi, F. (1996) 'What makes democracies endure?' *Journal of Democracy*, 7, 1, pp. 39–55.

Putnam, R. (1993) *Making Democracy Work: Civic Traditions in Modern Italy*, Princeton: Princeton University Press.

Putzel, J. (1997) 'Why has democratization been a weaker impulse in Indonesia and Malaysia than in the Philippines?', in D. Potter, D. Goldblatt, M. Kiloh and P. Lewis (eds), *Democratization*, Cambridge: Polity in association with the Open University, pp. 240–63.

Putzel, J. (1999) 'Survival of an imperfect democracy in the Philippines', in P. Burnell and P. Calvert (eds), *The Resilience of Democracy: Persistent Practice, Durable Idea*, special issue of *Democratization*, 6, 1, pp. 198–223.

Quigley, K. (1996) 'Towards consolidating democracy: the paradoxical role of democracy groups in Thailand', *Democratization*, 3, 3, pp. 264–86.

Randall, V. (1988) 'The Congress Party of India: dominance and competition', in V. Randall (ed.), *Political Parties in the Third World*, London: Sage, pp. 75–98.

Randall, V. (1997) 'Why have the political trajectories of India and China been different?', in D. Potter, D. Goldblatt, M. Kiloh and P. Lewis (eds), *Democratization*, Cambridge: Polity in association with the Open University, pp. 195–218.

Remmer, K. (1989) *Military Rule in Latin America*, Boston: Unwin Hyman.
Remmer, K. (1993) 'Democratization in Latin America', in R. O. Slater,
  B. M. Schutz and S. R. Dorr (eds), *Global Transformation and the Third
  World*, Boulder: Lynne Rienner, pp. 91–112.
Riggs, F. (1992) 'Presidentialism: a problematic regime type', in A. Liphart
  (ed.), *Parliamentary versus Presidential Democracy*, New York: Oxford
  University Press, pp. 187–201.
Risse, T., Ropp, S. and Sikkink, K. (eds) (1999) *The Power of Human
  Rights: International Norms and Domestic Change*, Cambridge: Cam-
  bridge University Press.
Risse-Kappen, T. (1995) 'What have we learnt?', in T. Risse-Kappen (ed.),
  Bringing Transnational Relations Back In, Cambridge: Cambridge
  University Press, pp. 280–313.
Rizvi, G. (1995) 'South Asia and the New World Order', in H.-H. Holm
  and G. Sørensen (eds), *Whose World Order?* Boulder: Westview, pp.
  69–88.
Roberts, H. (1991) 'A trial of strength: Algerian Islamism', in J. Piscatori
  (ed.), *Islamic Fundamentalisms and the Gulf Crisis*, Cambridge: Cam-
  bridge University Press, pp. 131–54.
Roberts, H. (1992) 'The Algerian state and the challenge of democracy',
  Government and Opposition, 27, 4, pp. 433–54.
Robinson, M. (1998) 'Democracy, participation and public policy: the
  politics of institutional design', in M. Robinson and G. White (eds), *The
  Democratic Developmental State: Political and Institutional Design*,
  Oxford: Oxford University Press, pp. 150–86.
Robinson, M. (1999a) 'Corruption and development: an introduction', in
  M. Robinson (ed.), *Corruption and Development*, London: Frank Cass,
  pp. 1–14.
Robinson, M. (ed.) (1999b) *Corruption and Development*, London: Frank
  Cass.
Robinson, P. (1994) 'Understanding regime change and the culture of poli-
  tics', *African Studies Review*, 37, pp. 39–67.
Rocamora, J. (1993) 'The Philippines under Cory Aquino', in B. Gills, J.
  Rocamora and R. Wilson (eds), *Low Intensity Democracy*, London: Pluto
  Press, pp. 195–225.
Rodan, G. and Hewison, K. (1996) 'A "clash of cultures" or the conver-
  gence of political ideology', in R. Robinson (ed.), *Pathways to Asia*, St
  Leonards: Allen and Unwin, pp. 118–34.
Roniger, L. and Günes-Ayata, A. (eds) (1994) *Democracy, Clientelism, and
  Civil Society*, Boulder: Lynne Rienner.
Rueschemeyer, D., Stephens, E. and Stephens, J. (1992) *Capitalist Develop-
  ment and Democracy*, Cambridge: Polity.
Rustow, D. (1970) 'Transitions to democracy: toward a dynamic model',
  Comparative Politics, 2, 3, pp. 330–56.
Sadiki, L. (1997) 'Towards Arab liberal governance: from the democracy of
  bread to the democracy of the vote', *Third World Quarterly*, 18, 1, pp.
  127–48.

Said, E. (1996) 'War babies', *Observer*, 14 Jan.

Samudavanija, C.-A. (1993) 'The new military and democracy in Thailand', in L. Diamond (ed.), *Political Culture and Democracy in Developing Countries*, Boulder: Lynne Rienner, pp. 269–94.

Sandbrook, R. (1993) *The Politics of Africa's Economic Recovery*, Cambridge: Cambridge University Press.

Sartori, G. (1991) 'Rethinking democracy: bad policy and bad politics', *International Social Science Journal*, no. 129, pp. 437–50.

Sayeed, K. (1995) *Western Dominance and Political Islam: Challenge and Response*, Albany: State University of New York Press.

Schmidt, S. (1999) 'Uganda', in D. Nohlen, M. Krennerich and B. Thibault (eds), *Elections in Africa: A Data Handbook*, Oxford: Oxford University Press, pp. 925–38.

Schmitter, P. (1986) 'An introduction to the Southern European transitions from authoritarian rule', in G. O'Donnell, P. Schmitter and L. Whitehead (eds), *Transitions from Authoritarian Rule in Latin America*, Baltimore: Johns Hopkins University Press, pp. 3–16.

Schmitter, P. (1994) 'Dangers and dilemmas of democracy', *Journal of Democracy*, 5, 2, pp. 57–74.

Scott, J. (1977) 'Hegemony and the peasant', *Politics and Society*, 7, 3, pp. 267–96.

Scott, J. (1985) *Weapons of the Weak: Everyday Forms of Peasant Resistance*, New Haven: Yale University Press.

Scott, J. (1990) *Domination and the Arts of Resistance: Hidden Transcripts*, New Haven: Yale University Press.

Sharrock, D. (1999) 'King bequeaths hunger for reform', *Guardian*, 26 July.

Shin, D. C. (1994) 'On the third wave of democratization: a synthesis and evaluation of recent theory and research', *World Politics*, 47, pp. 135–70.

Shin, D. C. (1999) *Mass Politics and Culture in Democratizing Korea*, Cambridge: Cambridge University Press.

Showstack Sassoon, A. (1982) 'Passive revolution and the politics of reform', in A. Showstack Sassoon (ed.), *Approaches to Gramsci*, London: Writers and Readers Publishing Cooperative, pp. 127–48.

Sisk, T. (1995) *Democratization in South Africa*, Princeton: Princeton University Press.

Sisson, R. (1993) 'Culture and democratization in India', in L. Diamond (ed.), *Political Culture and Democracy in Developing Countries*, Boulder: Lynne Rienner, pp. 37–66.

Sørensen, G. (1993) *Democracy and Democratization*, Boulder: Westview.

Southall, R. (2000) 'The state of democracy in South Africa', *Journal of Commonwealth and Comparative Politics*, 38, 3, pp. 147–70.

Stepan, A. (1988) *Rethinking Military Politics: Brazil and the Southern Cone*, Princeton: Princeton University Press.

Stepan, A. and Skach, C. (1993) 'Constitutional frameworks and democratic consolidation: parliamentarianism versus presidentialism', *World Politics*, 46, Oct., pp. 1–22.

Stiefel, M. and Wolfe, M. (1994) *A Voice for the Excluded: Popular Participation in Development, Utopia or Necessity?* London and Geneva: Zed and UN Research Institute for Social Development.

Sylvester, R. (1999) 'Four nations "fail the freedom test"', *The Times*, 15 Oct.

Tahi, M. S. (1992) 'The arduous democratisation process in Algeria', *Journal of Modern African Studies*, 30, 3, pp. 400–20.

Taylor, I. (n.d.) 'South Africa's "democratic transition" in a globalised world: the "change industry" and the promotion of polyarchy', MS, Department of Political Science, University of Stellenbosch.

Taylor, R. (1994) 'A consociational path to peace in Northern Ireland and South Africa', in A. Guelke (ed.), *New Perspectives on the Northern Ireland Conflict*, Aldershot: Avebury, pp. 161–74.

Thomas, A. (1994) *Third World Atlas*, 2nd edn, Buckingham: Open University Press.

Thompson, M. (1993) 'The limits of democratisation in ASEAN', *Third World Quarterly*, 14, 3, pp. 469–84.

Tornquist, O. (1999) 'On the dynamics of the Indonesian democratisation', paper presented at the workshop on Democratic Consolidation in the Third World: What Should be Done?, ECPR Joint Sessions of Workshops, University of Mannheim, March.

Tremewan, C. (1994) *The Political Economy of Social Control in Singapore*, New York: St Martin's Press.

Tripp, A. (1999) 'Political reform in Tanzania: the struggle for associational autonomy', paper presented at the workshop on Democratic Consolidation in the Third World: What Should be Done?, ECPR Joint Sessions of Workshops, University of Mannheim, March.

Turner, F. and Martz, J. (1997) 'Institutional confidence and democratic consolidation in Latin America', *Studies in Comparative International Development*, 32, 3, pp. 65–84.

Turner, M. and Hulme, D. (1997) *Governance, Administration and Development: Making the State Work*, Basingstoke: Macmillan.

UNDP (United Nations Development Programme) (1996) *Human Development Report 1996*, Oxford, Oxford University Press for the UNDP.

Van Ness, P. (ed.) (1999) *Debating Human Rights: Critical Essays from the United States and Asia*, London: Routledge.

Vanhanen, T. (1998) *Prospects for Democracy in Asia*, New Delhi: Sterling Private Ltd.

Vidal, J. (1996) 'Harmed and dangerous', *Guardian*, 8 May.

Villalón, L. (1995) *Islamic Society and State Power in Senegal: Disciples and Citizens in Fatick*, Cambridge: Cambridge University Press.

Villalón, L. (1998) 'The African state at the end of the twentieth century: parameters of the critical juncture', in L. Villalón and P. Huxtable (eds), *The African State at a Critical Juncture: Between Disintegration and Reconfiguration*, Boulder: Lynne Rienner, pp. 3–26.

Villalón, L. and Kane, O. (1998) 'Senegal: the crisis of democracy and the emergence of an Islamic opposition', in L. Villalón and P. Huxtable (eds), *The African State at a Critical Juncture: Between Disintegration and Reconfiguration*, Boulder: Lynne Rienner, pp. 143–66.

Vincent, R. J. (1986) *Human Rights and International Relations*, Cambridge: Cambridge University Press.

Wallis, D. (1999) 'Democratic transition and consolidation in Mexico', paper presented at the workshop on Democratic Consolidation in the Third World: What Should be Done?', ECPR Joint Sessions of Workshops, University of Mannheim, March.

Waterbury, J. (1994) 'Democracy without democrats? The potential for political liberalization in the Middle East', in G. Salamé (ed.), *Democracy without Democrats? The Renewal of Politics in the Muslim World*, London: I. B. Tauris, pp. 3–26.

Weber, M. (1969) 'Major features of world religions', in R. Robertson (ed.), *The Sociology of Religion*, Baltimore: Penguin, pp. 19–41.

Weldon, J. (1997) 'The political sources of presidencialismo in Mexico', in S. Mainwaring and M. Shugart (eds), *Presidentialism and Democracy in Latin America*, Cambridge: Cambridge University Press, pp. 220–42.

White, G. (1998) 'Constructing a developmental democratic state', in M. Robinson and G. White (eds), *The Democratic Developmental State: Political and Institutional Design*, Oxford: Oxford University Press, pp. 17–51.

Whitehead, L. (1993) 'The alternatives to "liberal democracy": a Latin American perspective', in D. Held (ed.), *Prospects for Democracy*, Cambridge: Polity, pp. 312–29.

Wiarda, H. and Kline, F. (eds) (1996) *Latin American Politics and Development*, 4th edn, Boulder: Westview.

Wiseman, J. A. (1997) 'The rise and fall and rise (and fall?) of democracy in sub-Saharan Africa', in D. Potter, D. Goldblatt, M. Kiloh and P. Lewis (eds), *Democratization*, Cambridge: Polity Press in association with the Open University, pp. 272–93.

Wiseman, J. A. (1999) 'The continuing case for demo-optimism in Africa', *Democratization*, 6, 2, pp. 128–55.

Woo-Cumings, M. (ed.) (1999) *The Developmental State*, Ithaca: Cornell University Press.

Woollacott, M. (1999) 'The democratic tendency lingers on in troubled Asia', *Guardian*, 22 Oct.

World Bank (1997) *World Development Report 1997: The State in a Changing World*, New York: Oxford University Press.

World Bank (1999) *World Development Report: Knowledge for Development*, New York: Oxford University Press.

World Bank (2000) *World Development Report: Entering the 21st Century 1999/2000*, New York: Oxford University Press.

Wurfel, D. (1988) *Filipino Politics: Development and Decay*, Ithaca: Cornell University Press.

Young, C. (1982) *Ideology and Development in Africa*, New Haven: Yale University Press.

Young, C. (1990) 'Sub-Saharan Africa', in N. X. Rizopoulos (ed.), *Sea Changes: American Foreign Policy in a World Transformed*, New York: Council on Foreign Relations, pp. 84–103.

Zakaria, F. (1997) 'The rise of illiberal democracy', *Foreign Affairs*, Nov.–Dec., pp. 22–42.

Index